University of Cambridge Oriental Publications No. 35

God's conflict with the dragon and the sea

God's conflict with the dragon and the sea

Echoes of a Canaanite myth in the Old Testament

JOHN DAY

Fellow and Tutor of Lady Margaret Hall and Lecturer in Old Testament in the University of Oxford

The right of the University of Cambridge to print and sell all manner of books was granted by Henry VIII in 1534. The University has printed and published continuously since 1584.

CAMBRIDGE UNIVERSITY PRESS

CAMBRIDGE

LONDON NEW YORK NEW ROCHELLE

MELBOURNE SYDNEY

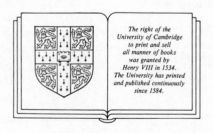

University of Cambridge Oriental Publications
published for the
Faculty of Oriental Studies
See page 232 for the complete list

Published by the Press Syndicate of the University of Cambridge
The Pitt Building, Trumpington Street, Cambridge CB2 1RP
32 East 57th Street, New York, NY 10022, USA
296 Beaconsfield Parade, Middle Park, Melbourne 3206, Australia

First published 1985

Printed in Great Britain at the University Press, Cambridge

Library of Congress catalogue card number: 83-21045

British Library Cataloguing in Publication Data
Day, John, *1948–*
God's conflict with the dragon and the
sea: echoes of a Canaanite myth in the
Old Testament. – (University of Cambridge
oriental publications; no. 35)
1. Myth in the Old Testament
2. Mythology, Canaanite
I. Title II. Series
221.6′8 BS1183

ISBN 0 521 25600 3

S T

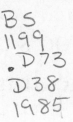

CONTENTS

PREFACE

The present monograph represents a thorough revision of part of a dissertation accepted for the degree of Ph.D by the University of Cambridge in 1977. The research was supervised by Prof. J. A. Emerton and the examiners were Dr (now Prof.) K. J. Cathcart and Dr (now Prof.) B. Lindars.

It is impossible to acknowledge fully the debt which I owe to Prof. Emerton. I am most grateful to him for all the help and encouragement he has given me both when I was a research student and subsequently. In addition to Prof. Emerton I am also indebted to Prof. D. Pardee and the Rev. B. A. Mastin for reading earlier drafts of this work, all of whom have made suggestions which considerably improved it.

I must also acknowledge my indebtedness to the Kennicott Hebrew Fund at Oxford and the Bethune-Baker Fund at Cambridge, both of which made generous grants towards the cost of publishing this work. Finally, I am grateful to Dr Gordon Johnson for accepting it for publication in the Oriental Publications Series.

Lady Margaret Hall, Oxford JOHN DAY
January, 1984

ABBREVIATIONS

AfO	*Archiv für Orientforschung*
AJSL	*American Journal of Semitic Languages and Literatures*
ANEP	J.B. Pritchard (ed.), *The Ancient Near East in Pictures Relating to the Old Testament* (2nd ed. with suppl., Princeton, N.J., 1969)
ANET	J.B. Pritchard, *Ancient Near Eastern Texts Relating to the Old Testament* (3rd ed. with suppl., Princeton, N.J., 1969)
AOAT	*Alter Orient und Altes Testament*
ASTI	*Annual of the Swedish Theological Institute*
BA	*The Biblical Archaeologist*
BASOR	*Bulletin of the American Schools of Oriental Research*
BDB	F. Brown, S.R. Driver and C.A. Briggs, *A Hebrew and English Lexicon of the Old Testament* (Oxford, 1907)
BH3	R. Kittel (ed.), *Biblia Hebraica* (3rd ed.)
BHS	R. Kittel (ed.) *Biblia Hebraica Stuttgartensia*
BJRL	*Bulletin of the John Rylands Library*
BZ	*Biblische Zeitschrift*
BZAW	*Beihefte zur Zeitschrift für die alttestamentliche Wissenschaft*
CBQ	*Catholic Biblical Quarterly*
CTA	A. Herdner, *Corpus des tablettes en cunéiformes alphabétiques* (2 vols., Paris, 1963)
ed.	edition, editor
edd.	editors, editions
Eph. Theol. Lovan.	*Ephemerides Theologicae Lovanienses*
ET	English translation
EQ	*Evangelical Quarterly*
Exp. Times	*Expository Times*
GK	A.E. Cowley, *Gesenius' Hebrew Grammar as edited and enlarged by the late E. Kautzsch* (2nd ed., Oxford, 1910)
HUCA	*Hebrew Union College Annual*
IDB	*The Interpreter's Dictionary of the Bible* (4 vols., Nashville, Ten. and New York, 1962)

IDBS	*The Interpreter's Dictionary of the Bible Supplementary Volume* (Nashville, Ten., 1976)
IEJ	*Israel Exploration Journal*
JAOS	*Journal of the American Oriental Society*
JBL	*Journal of Biblical Literature*
JCS	*Journal of Cuneiform Studies*
JEA	*Journal of Egyptian Archaeology*
JJS	*Journal of Jewish Studies*
JNES	*Journal of Near Eastern Studies*
JPOS	*Journal of the Palestine Oriental Society*
JQR	*Jewish Quarterly Review*
JRAS	*Journal of the Royal Asiatic Society*
JSOT	*Journal for the Study of the Old Testament*
JSS	*Journal of Semitic Studies*
JTS	*Journal of Theological Studies*
JThC	*Journal of Theology and the Church*
KAI	H. Donner and W. Röllig, *Kanaanäische und aramäische Inschriften* (3 vols., Wiesbaden, 1962–4)
KB	L. Koehler and W. Baumgartner (edd.), *Lexicon in Veteris Testamenti Libros* (Leiden, 1958)
Ken	B. Kennicott
KTU	M. Dietrich, O. Loretz, J. Sanmartín, *Die keilalphabetischen Texte aus Ugarit. Teil 1: Transkription* (*AOAT* 24, Neukirchen, 1976)
LXX	The Septuagint
LXX^B	The Septuagint, codex Vaticanus
MS(S)	Manuscript(s)
MT	Massoretic text
NAB	*New American Bible*
NEB	*New English Bible*
nF	neue Folge
n.s.	New series
NTS	*New Testament Studies*
NTT	*Norsk Teologisk Tidsskrift*
Old $Latin^G$	Old Latin version, Codex Parisinus Latinus, bibliothecae nationalis 11947
OT	Old Testament
PEQ	*Palestine Exploration Quarterly*
PG	J.P. Migne's *Patrologia*, Series Graeca
PL	J.P. Migne's *Patrologia*, Series Latina
Praep. Ev.	Eusebius' *Praeparatio Evangelica*
PRU	*Le Palais Royal d'Ugarit*
1QH	Qumran Thanksgiving Hymns
$1QIs^a$	Qumran Isaiah Scroll a
RB	*Revue Biblique*

RHPR	*Revue d'Histoire et de Philosophie Religieuses*
RS	*Ras Shamra*
RSV	*Revised Standard Version*
RV	*Revised Version*
SJT	*Scottish Journal of Theology*
SVT	*Supplements to Vetus Testamentum*
TGUOS	*Transactions of the Glasgow University Oriental Society*
UF	*Ugarit-Forschungen*
UT	C.H. Gordon, *Ugaritic Textbook* (Rome, 1965)
VT	*Vetus Testamentum*
WZKM	*Wiener Zeitschrift für die Kunde des Morgenlandes*
ZA	*Zeitschrift für Assyriologie*
ZAW	*Zeitschrift für die alttestamentliche Wissenschaft*
ZDMG	*Zeitschrift der deutschen morgenländischen Gesellschaft*
ZThK	*Zeitschrift für Theologie und Kirche*

1

Creation and the divine conflict with the dragon and the sea

The subject of this monograph is the divine conflict with the dragon and the sea in the Old Testament. It first received a thorough consideration in 1895 with the publication of H. Gunkel's book *Schöpfung und Chaos in Urzeit und Endzeit.* However, in spite of the fact that a fair amount has been written on this topic over the years, there are still many disputed points of interpretation, so that a reconsideration of the material is clearly desirable.

In this first chapter I shall consider the question of the divine conflict with the dragon and the sea in relation to the creation of the world. It will first be established that there are passages in which a causal relation exists between this divine conflict and the creation, and that the imagery of the conflict is Canaanite and not Babylonian in origin. Then I shall discuss the problem why there is this connection between the conflict and creation, when this seems not to be the case in the Ugaritic Baal–Yam conflict, which is generally thought to underlie the Old Testament allusions. I shall also deal with the question of the *Sitz im Leben* of the motif in the Autumn Festival. The largest part of the chapter, however, will be given over to a detailed consideration of the individual passages: first in the Psalms (Ps. 74:12–17, 89:10–15, ET 9–14, 104:1–9, 65:7–8, ET 6–7, 93, and, in addition, 24), then in Job (26:5–14, 9:5–14, 38:8–11, 7:12, 3:8), and finally, those passages in which God's control of the waters has been demythologized so that it is simply a job of work (Gen. 1:2, 6–10, with an excursus on 1:26; Ps. 33:7–8; Prov. 8:24, 27–9; Jer. 5:22b, 31:35). At the very end there is a discussion of Ps. 29 and Nah. 1:4, where Yahweh's victory over the sea is a feature of his present lordship over the Creation.

As was indicated above, the effective beginning of the study of the theme which is the subject of this monograph came about with the publication of the book by H. Gunkel entitled *Schöpfung und*

Chaos in Urzeit und Endzeit (Göttingen, 1895). The American scholar G.A. Barton[1] had written much more briefly two years earlier on the subject and it has even been suggested that he may possibly have been plagiarized by Gunkel,[2] although it is perhaps more probable that this is yet a further example of the common experience of two scholars independently coming to similar conclusions at the same time. In any case it was Gunkel who first subjected the material to a really exhaustive examination. He recognized the mythical character of the various passages in the Old Testament which speak of a conflict between Yahweh and the sea and a dragon or dragons, variously called Leviathan, Rahab, etc., and saw these as being an Israelite appropriation of the Babylonian myth of Marduk's victory over Tiamat at the time of creation recounted in Enuma elish, a work sometimes called 'the Babylonian creation epic', but which is not primarily concerned with the creation but with the glorification of Marduk. Early on J. Wellhausen is said to have referred to Gunkel's work as 'mehr Chaos als Schöpfung',[3] and subsequently a number of scholars chose to reject Gunkel's thesis. In general, however, Gunkel ultimately won the day, though, as will be seen below, the mythology in question has now proved to be specifically Canaanite rather than Babylonian in origin.

Even today, however, the occasional scholar refuses to accept that there occurs in the Old Testament a specific causal connection between the conflict with chaos and creation. This is the case with H.W.F. Saggs in his book on *The Encounter with the Divine in Mesopotamia and Israel* (London, 1978).[4] He argues that, although there are a few passages in which the creation and conflict with sea monsters are mentioned together (Ps. 74:12–17, 89:10–15, ET 9–14; Job 26), it does not necessarily or indeed probably follow

1 G.A. Barton, 'Tiamat', *JAOS* 15 (1893), pp. 1–27. Cf. too T.K. Cheyne, review of Gunkel, *Critical Review* 5 (1895), pp. 256–66.

2 W.G. Lambert, 'A new look at the Babylonian background of Genesis', *JTS* 16 n.s. (1965), p. 288. Gunkel cites Barton on p. 4, n. 4 and p. 25, n. 2, but does not admit his indebtedness to Barton for the general thesis of the work.

3 Although this quip cannot be found in any of Wellhausen's writings, it is apparently based on an authentic oral tradition. Cf. W. Klatt, *Hermann Gunkel. Zu seiner Theologie der Religionsgeschichte und zur Entstehung der formgeschichtlichen Methode* (Göttingen, 1969), p. 70, n. 2. At any rate, it clearly reflects accurately Wellhausen's earlier opinion, although he later modified it somewhat. Cf. W. Klatt, *op. cit.*, pp. 70–4.

4 Pp. 54–6. Cf. L. Vosberg, *Studien zum Reden vom Schöpfer in den Psalmen* (Munich, 1975), pp. 46–50 (inaccessible to me).

that the two were causally connected. That Saggs' position is not the most natural, however, is supported by the fact that we do have other passages in which the creation is associated and causally connected with Yahweh's conflict with or control of the primordial sea, e.g. Ps. 104:6–9, Job 38:8–11, Prov. 8:29, and since elsewhere the sea is mentioned parallel with the dragon, with which it is closely associated (e.g. Is. 51:9–10), we can only conclude that passages which refer to a conflict with the dragon in the context of creation similarly allude to a struggle at that time. Ps. 74:12–17 and 89:10–15 (ET 9–14), for example, certainly fall into this category.[5]

At this point mention should also be made of D.J. McCarthy, whose article on '"Creation" motifs in ancient Hebrew poetry'[6] also tended to play down the association of *Chaoskampf* with creation in the Old Testament. He examines examples of what he claims is the earliest Hebrew poetry (Gen. 49; Ex. 15:2–18; Deut. 32:1–43, Deut. 33; Judg. 5; 2 Sam. 22 = Ps. 18; Ps. 29, 68) and argues that when 'creation' language is there used, it is historicized, since Israel was interested in historical, not cosmic origins. He thereby cautions us to refrain from thinking of *Chaoskampf* as creation myth. However, a number of points may be made about McCarthy's study. To begin with, it should be noted that only three of the passages selected by McCarthy contain the *Chaoskampf* motif, *viz.* Ex. 15:2–18, 2 Sam. 22 = Ps. 18, and Ps. 29, and of these it is true that historicization has taken place in the first two, but the third, whilst not concerned with ultimate origins, seems to locate the *Chaoskampf* in nature rather than history (cf. vv. 3, 10). It would surely be wrong to draw large conclusions from this limited body of material. Secondly, it should be noted that McCarthy is rather selective in the texts which he includes for discussion under the heading of early Hebrew poetry, since Ps. 93 may well be just as early as Ps. 29 and 68, but here the conflict with chaos *is* associated with creation (cf. vv. 1–4). Finally, of course, there are plenty of other passages in the Old Testament, to be considered later in this chapter, where the conflict with chaos is associated with creation. Although most (though not necessarily

5 Cf. too below, p. 23, for further criticisms of Saggs in connection with Ps. 74. Saggs has also been criticized by H. Ringgren, 'Yahvé et Rahab–Léviatan', in A. Caquot and M. Delcor (edd.), *Mélanges bibliques et orientaux en l'honneur de M. Henri Cazelles* (*AOAT* 212, Neukirchen, 1981), pp. 387–93.

6 *CBQ* 29 (1967), pp. 393–406.

all) of these passages may be later in date, they reflect ancient mythological ideas. Quite often, it should be noted, the most striking parallels with Ugaritic come in relatively late texts. In any case, the number of passages associating the conflict with chaos with the creation is sufficiently large to justify our seeing it as one of the major uses of *Chaoskampf* imagery in the Old Testament.

All those passages in the Old Testament which speak about God's control of the sea at the time of creation naturally presuppose the archaic world view shared by the ancient Israelites along with other peoples of the ancient near east that both above the domed firmament of heaven and below the earth there is a cosmic sea. Rain was regarded as having its origin in the cosmic sea above the firmament and coming down through the windows of heaven, while the world's seas and lakes were thought of as being connected with the subterranean part of the cosmic sea (cf. Gen. 7:11). References to Leviathan or Rahab etc. relate to a dragon associated with this cosmic sea.

Granted that there are passages in the Old Teatament which associate the creation of the world with a divine conflict with a dragon or the sea, what is the origin of this mythological motif? As was noted above, Gunkel argued that the Old Testament references were an Israelite version of the conflict between Marduk and Tiamat contained in Enuma elish. In this myth the god Marduk, armed with the powers of the storm, defeated the terrible monster Tiamat, representing the salt-water ocean, together with her helpers, and proceeded to make heaven and earth out of the two halves of her body. Since the discovery of the Ugaritic texts from 1929 onwards, however, it has become clear that the immediate background of the Old Testament allusions to the sea monster is not Babylonian but Canaanite. The Ugaritic texts contain not only an account of Baal's defeat of the rebellious sea-god Yam, as a result of which he was acclaimed king (*CTA* 2 = *KTU* 1.2), but also allusions to a defeat of Leviathan (*ltn* = Lītān, lit. 'twisting one', from *lwh* 'to twist'),[7] whom we learn had seven heads (*CTA* 3.IIID.37–9, 5.I.1–3 = *KTU* 1.3.40–2, 1.5.I.1–3; Ps. 74:14 refers to 'heads' but does not specify how many) and who is called not only

7 There is no reason to follow S.I.L. Norin, *Er spaltete das Meer* (Lund, 1977), p. 69 in supposing that the name Leviathan is a translation of Egyptian *mḥn* (a name of Apophis), taken over when Baal was identified with Seth. Since 'twisting/coiling one' is such a natural term to describe a serpent, this is hardly necessary.

'the twisting[8] serpent' (*bṯn. brḥ*, *CTA* 5.I.1 = *KTU* 1.5.I.1, cf. *nāḥāš bārīaḥ* in Job 26:13; Is. 27:1) but also 'the crooked serpent' (*bṯn. ʿqltn*, *CTA* 3.IIID.38, 5.I.2 = *KTU* 1.3.III.41, 1.5.I.2, cf. Is. 27:1). We also find Leviathan called *tnn* 'dragon', a term identical with the *tannīn* mentioned in various Old Testament passages (cf. Is. 27:1, 51:9; Job 7:12; Ezek. 29:3, 32:2; Jer. 51:34). Ugaritic *tnn* was vocalized *tu-un-na-nu*, as we now know from *Ugaritica V*. 137.8. The name *ltn* has generally been vocalized *Lōtān* since Albright proposed this in 1932.[9] However, as J.A. Emerton[10] has noted, this raises problems when we come to relate it to the Hebrew form Leviathan (*liwyāṯān*). The latter seems to be related to the Hebrew word *liwyāh* 'wreath' and bears the meaning 'twisting one,' which is wholly appropriate for a snake. If so, Ugaritic *ltn* ought similarly to be cognate with the verb *lwy*, but then we are left wondering what has happened to the *y*. Alternatively one might claim that some other root lies behind the name and that the *y* in the Hebrew is a secondary development, but no satisfactory root has been suggested. Accordingly, Emerton suggests that the Ugaritic name should be vocalized Lītān(u), and proposes the wholly explicable development *liwyaṯān*(*u*) > *liwyiṯān*(*u*) > *līyiṯān*(*u*) > *līṯān*(*u*).

8 *Nāḥāš bārīaḥ* 'twisting serpent' appears not only in Job 26:13 but also in Is. 27:1 (in the latter without the vowel letter *yodh*), where it is parallel to *nāḥāš ʿ^a^qallāṯōn* 'crooked serpent', and similarly in the Ugaritic texts Leviathan is called *bṯn. brḥ* in parallelism with *bṯn. ʿqltn* (*CTA* 5.I.1–2 = *KTU* 1.5.I.1–2). The verb *brḥ* in the Old Testament means 'to flee' and the translation 'fleeing serpent' has been held by some (e.g. M.H. Pope, T.H. Gaster, *RSV*), but some such translation as 'twisting', 'convulsive' or 'tortuous' (C. Rabin), 'coiled' (H. Gunkel) or 'slippery' (G.R. Driver) is to be preferred. 'To twist' is one of the basic meanings of *brḥ* in Semitic languages, and this meaning fits the parallelism with *ʿqltn* 'crooked' in Ugaritic and Hebrew better than 'to flee', and in fact both the Targum and the Vulgate respectively read *ṭārīq* and *tortuosus* in Job 26:13, which gives added support to this rendering. W.F. Albright, 'Are the Ephod and the Teraphim mentioned in Ugaritic literature?', *BASOR* 83 (1941), p. 39, n. 5, suggests that *brḥ* means 'primaeval', on the basis of Arabic *bāriḥ* 'past (of time)', and he also compared Egyptian *ḏr b;ḥ* 'from of old'. However, he has been opposed by T.H. Gaster, 'Folklore motifs in Canaanite myth', *JRAS* (1944), p. 47 and C. Rabin, 'Bāriªḥ', *JTS* 47 (1946), p. 38. Gaster claims that Egyptian *ḏr b'ḥ* means 'before, previously', not 'from of old', and Rabin rightly points out that a 'past serpent' is hardly the same as a 'primaeval serpent'. In general, see C. Rabin, *op. cit*., pp. 38–41 on the subject of *brḥ*.

9 W.F. Albright, 'New light on early Canaanite language and literature', *BASOR* 46 (1932), p. 19.

10 J.A. Emerton, 'Leviathan and *ltn*: the vocalization of the Ugaritic word for the dragon', *VT* 32 (1982), pp. 327–31.

As for the name Rahab (cf. Ps. 87:4, 89:11, ET 10; Job 9:13, 26:12; Is. 30:7, 51:9)[11] however, this has not hitherto been found mentioned in any extra-biblical text, Canaanite or otherwise.[12] The name apparently means 'boisterous one,' an apt term for the personified raging sea.[13] The fact that Rahab and 'the crooked serpent' (*nāḥāš bārīaḥ*) are mentioned in parallel verses in Job 26:12–13, and that Rahab is mentioned parallel to 'the dragon' (*tannīn*) in Is. 51:9, suggests that Rahab may simply be an alternative name for Leviathan, who is likewise called 'the crooked serpent' and 'the dragon' in Is. 27:1 (cf. *CTA* 5.I.1 = *KTU* 1.5.I.1). Even though Rahab and Leviathan may be equated in the Old Testament (but even this is not certain), it is still possible that the two different names betoken that in origin they were separate (though similar) monsters. The presence of the *h* indicates that it is not an Akkadian loan word,[14] whilst the evidence of the other dragon-expressions used suggests that it is not an independent Israelite creation. Presumably it too is of Canaanite origin, though

11 H. Gunkel, *Schöpfung und Chaos in Urzeit und Endzeit* (Göttingen, 1895), p. 40, proposed that in addition Rahab is mentioned in the plural in Ps. 40:5 (ET 4), 'Heil dem Mann, der macht Jahve zu seiner Zuversicht und nicht den R^{e}habim sich ergiebt, zur Lüge abfällt.' He has been followed by a number of other scholars, e.g. M.J. Dahood, *Psalms* 1 (New York, 1965), p. 245, who renders *r^{e}hāḇīm* as 'pagan idols'. It is argued in favour of this view that *r^{e}hāḇīm* thereby provides a good parallel to *ḵāzāḇ* at the end of the verse, a term sometimes used of pagan deities, as well as being appropriate after *pānāh 'el*, sometimes used in connection with other gods. However, this view is probably to be rejected in favour of the view that *r^{e}hāḇīm* simply refers to proud or arrogant men. There are two main reasons which incline one to this view. First, the name Rahab nowhere else occurs in the plural, so that some other meaning is likely. Secondly, *r^{e}hāḇīm* occurs alongside *śāṭē ḵāzāḇ* 'those who fall away to lies'. The latter are clearly human beings, so that it is more natural to expect the parallel *r^{e}hāḇīm* to be so likewise. It may be added that *pānāh* can be used in connection with any false object of confidence, not only gods, and that *kāzāḇ* may denote falsehood in general, not necessarily gods. Accordingly this verse may be rendered, 'Blessed is the man who has made the Lord his trust, and has not turned to the proud and those who fall away to lies.'

12 B. Margalit, *A matter of 'Life' and 'Death'* (*AOAT* 206, Neukirchen, 1980), p. 178, sees some connection between Rahab and *rbm* in *CTA* 6.V.2 (= *KTU* 1.6.V.2) *rbm. ymḫṣ. bktp*, which he renders 'The Arrogant he did smite with a bludgeon (?).' However, *rbm* lacks the *h*, so that it is more natural to render it as 'the mighty'.

13 The general view that the name Rahab means 'boisterous one' may be accepted (Heb. root *rhb*): there is no reason to follow Norin in seeking an etymology in Egyptian *rꜣ* 'snake' + *ḫꜣb* 'crooked, bent' (S.I.L. Norin, *op. cit.*, p. 74f).

14 On the principle involved here, cf. A Heidel, *The Babylonian Genesis* (2nd ed., Chicago and London, 1951), p. 100, n. 58.

deriving from a place or time different from the Ugaritic texts, in view of its absence there. Occasionally it is supposed that Rahab was a female monster,[15] but there is no supporting evidence for this.

Turning now from the dragon to the sea, we find that in addition to 'the waters' (*mayim*, cf. Ps. 29:3, 77:17 (ET 16), 93:4; Is. 51:10, etc.), we find allusions not only to 'the sea' (*yām*, cf. Ps. 74:13, 89:10, ET 9; Job 7:12, 9:8, 26:12, 38:8; Nah. 1:4; Hab. 3:8, 15, etc.) but also, interestingly, to 'rivers' or 'floods' (*n*ᵉ*hārōṯ*, *n*ᵉ*hārīm*) (cf. Ps. 93:3; Nah. 1:4; Hab. 3:8, 9). This recalls Baal's opponent in *CTA* 2 (= *KTU* 1.2.) called not only *zbl ym* 'Prince Yam' but also *ṯpṭ nhr* 'Judge River'.

All the expressions considered so far prove to be Canaanite in origin. There is one more term to be mentioned, *t*ᵉ*hōm* 'the deep' (Ps. 77:17, ET 16, 104:6; Is. 51:10; Hab. 3:10; cf. Gen. 1:2; Ps. 33:7). This has often been compared with the name of Tiamat, the chaos monster defeated by Marduk in connection with the creation of the world in Enuma elish. However, although *t*ᵉ*hōm* and Tiamat are certainly etymologically related, there is no reason to think that the Hebrew term is directly derived from the Babylonian: if it were a Babylonian loan word, we should expect it to have the feminine ending in *-āh* and to have ', not *h*, as the middle radical. The form *thm*, comparable to Hebrew *t*ᵉ*hōm* is, however, attested in Ugaritic (cf. *Ugaritica V*.7.1, *RS* 24.244, 1 = *KTU* 1.100.1) thus supporting the view that the Old Testament term is Canaanite.

It may be concluded, therefore, that the dragon and sea mythology of the Old Testament is of Canaanite and not Babylonian origin as Gunkel thought, and it is a matter of regret that there are still scholars who have not fully recognized this fact.

The problem of the connection of the creation with the sea and dragon conflict in the light of its non-mention in the Ugaritic texts

Although it is now generally conceded that the allusions to God's conflict with the dragon in the Old Testament are Canaanite and not Babylonian in origin, the fact remains that the Ugaritic text containing the myth of Baal's defeat of the sea-god Yam (*CTA*

15 E.g., F.F. Bruce, *This is That. The New Testament Development of Some Old Testament Themes* (Exeter, 1968), p. 41. Presumably this is a hangover from the view of Gunkel that Rahab is to be equated with the Babylonian female monster Tiamat, rather than due to unconscious assimilation to Rahab the harlot!

2 = *KTU* 1.2), which is generally thought to underlie the Old Testament allusions, makes no reference to the creation of the world. Why is this? It is to the attempt to solve this problem that this section is directed. However, before we do this, we must first summarize the contents of *CTA* 2 (= *KTU* 1.2).

Generally placed first is *CTA* 2.III (= *KTU* 1.2.III). Although it is fragmentary, its main ideas can be made out. Kothar-and-Ḫasis, the craftsman god, went to El at the source of the rivers, who instructed him to build a palace for Yam. The god Athtar who is described as possessing kingship, was rebuked by the sun-goddess Shapash, who told him that El would deprive him of his kingship. Then Athtar complained that he had no house (i.e. palace) like the gods, whereas Yam was to have one. Athtar's lack of a wife next seems to have been proffered as a reason, but then the text breaks off.

However, the texts that really concern us in connection with Baal and Yam are *CTA* 2.I and 2.IV (= *KTU* 1.2.I and IV). *CTA* 2.I (= *KTU* 1.2.I) opens in fragmentary form but we can make it out sufficiently to see that Yam is being threatened (by Kothar-and-Ḫasis) that he will be defeated with magic weapons. Then Yam sent envoys to El and the assembly of the gods on Mount Ll in order that they demand the surrender of Baal, so that Yam might possess his gold. The envoys arrived while the gods were sitting at banquet and Baal was standing beside El. The gods, afraid, lowered their heads on to their knees but Baal rebuked them for this. Then the envoys delivered Yam's message, as instructed. El was prepared to deliver up Baal to them, but Baal was furious at this and made to attack the envoys. He had to be restrained by the goddesses Anat and Astarte. The end of the tablet is fragmentary and then breaks off altogether. *CTA* 2.II (= *KTU* 1.2.II) presumably followed here, but it is so fragmentary that nothing at all can be deduced from it. Certainly what is required here is the beginning of the conflict between Baal and Yam himself.

With the opening of *CTA* 2.IV (= *KTU* 1.2.IV) we find the battle between Baal and Yam in full flight, and Yam is clearly in the ascendant, for we read that Baal sank under the throne of Prince Yam. Kothar-and-Ḫasis then intervened, however, and encouraged Baal:

lrgmt (8) lk.lzbl.bʿl.	Truly I say to you, O Prince Baal,
ṯnt. lrkb. ʿrpt.	I repeat (to you), O Rider of the Clouds:

ht. ʾibk (9) bʿlm.	Now your enemy, Baal,
ht. ʾibk. tmḫṣ.	now your enemy you will smite,
ht. tṣmt. ṣrtk	now you will smite your foe.
(10) tqḫ. mlk. ʿlmk.	You will take your everlasting kingdom,
drkt. dt. drdrk	your dominion for ever and ever.

In order to achieve this Kothar-and-Ḫasis then fetched two clubs and called them Yagrush (Expeller) and Ayyamur (Driver), uttering incantations over them to aid their effectiveness. Although the first club was not successful in defeating Yam, the second one was.

wyrtqṣ. ṣmd. bd bʿl	The club swooped from Baal's hand,
24 [km.] nšr. bʾuṣbʿth.	[like] an eagle from his fingers.
ylm. qdqd. zbl (25) [ym.]	It struck the crown of Prince Yam,
bn. cnm. ṯpṭ. nhr.	between the eyes of Judge River.
yprsḫ. ym. yql (26) lʾarṣ	Yam collapsed, he fell to the earth;
tnǵṣn. pnth.	his joints quivered
wydlp. tmnh	and his form crumpled.
(27) yqṯ bʿl. wyšt. ym.	Baal dragged out Yam and put him down,
ykly. ṯpṭ. nhr	he made an end of Judge Nahar

The goddess Astarte then instructed Baal to scatter Yam, which he did. Finally, it is declared,

32 ym. lmt. bʿlm yml[k]	Yam is indeed dead! Baal shall be king!

After this there are a few very fragmentary lines and then the text breaks off. This is the end of the account of Baal's conflict with Yam, but *CTA* 3 and 4 (= *KTU* 1. 3 and 4), which follow,[16] tell of the building of Baal's palace, and this seems to be the natural consequence of his having defeated Yam and acquired the kingship. How exactly we are to interpret the meaning of Baal's victory over Yam is uncertain. Clearly we have to do with a battle between a storm god and the sea. Often[17] it is seen as reflecting the winter

16 J.C. de Moor, *The Seasonal Pattern in the Ugaritic Myth of Baʿlu* (*AOAT* 16, Neukirchen, 1971), pp. 40–3, proposes that *CTA* 3 (*KTU* 1.3), relating to autumn, precedes *CTA* 1 and 2 (*KTU* 1.1 and 2) (winter), whereas *CTA* 4 (*KTU* 1.4) (spring) follows them. However, as J.C.L. Gibson notes, *Canaanite Myths and Legends* (Edinburgh, 1978, p. 7, n. 5), it seems forced that Baal's palace should be started, abandoned and only later completed.

17 O. Kaiser, *Die mythische Bedeutung des Meeres* (*BZAW* 78, 1959), p. 65f.; J. Gray, *The Legacy of Canaan* (*SVT* 5, 2nd ed., 1965), p. 21; J.C. de Moor, *Seasonal Pattern*, pp. 141–2. De Moor, p. 142, n. 23 points out that the view sometimes put forward, that the text refers to equinoctial gales in September, cannot be correct, since the meteorological evidence does not support their existence in the vicinity of Ugarit.

storms at sea around Ugarit, and this may be correct. Others see it as more cosmic. However, the fact remains, as was noted at the beginning of this section, that nothing is said in *CTA* 2 (= *KTU* 1.2) of the creation of the world. How are we to account for the fact that Baal's conflict with Yam appears in no way to be connected with the creation of the world, whereas the Old Testament contains passages supposedly deriving from this Canaanite myth in which the conflict with the sea or dragon is associated with the creation?

Sometimes it seems to be assumed without further discussion that Baal's conflict with Yam was associated with the creation.[18] But nothing in the text we have (*CTA* 2 = *KTU* 1.2) is said about this. It has therefore been proposed, e.g. by Kapelrud,[19] that an account of the creation was originally preserved in the lacuna at the end of the text. But as Kapelrud himself has more recently noted,[20] the number of lines left for such an account is a bit small (seven or so); moreover, there is not a hint anywhere else in the myth that an account of the creation stood at this point. Another approach is taken by L.R. Fisher,[21] who holds that the Baal–Yam text is concerned with creation, not in the sense of ultimate origins, which he associates with El, but rather in the sense of bringing order to the world, which he claims was far more important to the Canaanites. Whilst the latter doubtless was of greater importance to the Canaanites, it seems a misuse of language to refer to it as creation. In any case, such a view does not solve the problem with which we are concerned here, since, as a matter of fact, the Old Testament does associate the conflict with chaos with ultimate origins.

Yet another line of approach is to claim that the Old Testament passages associating the creation of the world with God's conflict with the dragon and sea contain a conflation of both Babylonian and Canaanite traditions, since the former, in Enuma elish, do

18 L.R. Fisher, 'Creation at Ugarit and in the Old Testament', *VT* 15 (1965), p. 313 writes, 'Many times, in a lecture or in a conversation, I have heard it said that the battle between Baal and Yamm in Ugaritic literature is a creation myth.' This view seems to be present in N.K. Gottwald, *A Light to the Nations* (New York, 1959), p. 149.

19 A.S. Kapelrud, 'Baʿals kamp med havets fyrste i Ras Sjamra-tekstene', *NTT* 61 (1960), p. 249f.

20 A.S. Kapelrud, 'Creation in the Ras Shamra texts', *Studia Theologica* 34 (1980), p. 1. Cf. too his article 'Baʿal, Schöpfung und Chaos', *UF* 11 (1979), pp. 407–12.

21 L.R. Fisher, *op. cit.*, pp. 313–24.

associate creation with the defeat of the chaos monster Tiamat. Such a view is taken by B.S. Childs,[22] Jörg Jeremias[23] and perhaps W. Schmidt.[24] The difficulty with this view is that the monster terminology used is so definitely Canaanite, as has been noted above, that the assumption that we have here a conflation with Babylonian ideas should be accepted only if no more satisfactory explanation is forthcoming. As we have seen, not even the use of the word *t^e^hōm* for the chaos waters indicates Babylonian influence.

The claim has, indeed, been made by T. Jacobsen[25] that the Marduk–Tiamat conflict is itself West Semitic in origin. If this were the case, one could argue (though Jacobsen does not do this) that this lends support to the view that the West Semitic original, the conflict between Baal and Yam, was likewise associated with the creation. Jacobsen's case for a West Semitic origin for the Marduk–Tiamat conflict rests on the fact that, as in the Baal–Yam text, so in Enuma elish, a god uses the forces of the storm to overcome the rebellious sea (Tiamat, like Yam, means 'sea'), and he thinks it more likely that the theme originated in Syria, which is adjacent to the Mediterranean Sea, than in Mesopotamia, where the sea is a long way to the south behind extensive sweetwater marshes and reed-thickets. Jacobsen thinks we should probably think in terms of the motif having been brought into Mesopotamia by the Amorites, who founded the 1st dynasty of Babylon. However, Jacobsen's view should probably be rejected. It should be noted that W.G. Lambert, the world's leading authority on Mesopotamian creation mythology, who himself once maintained the possibility of the Amorite origin of the conflict between Marduk and Tiamat,[26] has

22 B.S. Childs, *A Study of Myth in Genesis I–XI* (PhD dissertation, Basel University, Plymouth, Wisconsin, 1955), p. 25.

23 Jörg Jeremias, *Theophanie* (Neukirchen, 1965), pp. 92–4.

24 W. Schmidt, *Königtum Gottes in Ugarit und Israel* (*BZAW* 80, 1961), p. 41. Schmidt writes, 'Dabei mag babylonischer Einfluss mitgespielt haben.' He continues, however, 'Vielleicht gab es auch kanaanäische Mythen, die beide Gottestaten verbanden.' In the 2nd ed., 1966, p. 49, the first sentence remains the same but the second is put in the form of a question, 'Oder gab es gar – nicht erhaltene – kanaanäische Mythen, die beide Gottestaten verbanden?'

25 T. Jacobsen, 'The battle between Marduk and Tiamat', *JAOS* 88 (1968), pp. 104–8.

26 W.G. Lambert, 'A new look at the Bablyonian background of Genesis', *JTS* 16 n.s. (1965), pp. 295–6. It may be noted that the Amorite origin of the Marduk–Tiamat conflict was originally suggested by A.T. Clay, *Amurru, the home of the Northern Semites* (Philadelphia, Pa., 1909), pp. 53–4, and *The Origin of Biblical Traditions* (New Haven, Conn., 1923), pp. 87–93.

now rejected it.[27] It is now clear that Enuma elish does not go back to the Amorite 1st dynasty of Babylon as Jacobsen thought but was written only about 1100 B.C. in the time of Nebuchadrezzar I.[28] It was in his reign that Marduk's plundered statue was restored to Babylon and it was in his reign Marduk is first referred to as king of the gods; accordingly, Enuma elish was written as a theological explanation of how Marduk had become king. An origin at this time makes an Amorite origin much less likely. Furthermore, it is now clear, according to Lambert, that certain themes relating to the conflict have their origin in the victories of the god Ninurta and these have been applied to Marduk. Ninurta himself is known to have defeated Tiamat and aspects of Ninurta's victory (using the force of the storm) over Anzu have been appropriated too,[29] including the idea that it is the third god who attempts to overcome the power endangering the gods of the pantheon who is successful, and who is then rewarded. Such common themes as exist between Enuma elish and the Baal–Yam conflict cannot be attributed to direct influence but must rather be attributed to a common intellectual background. The upshot of all this is that one cannot postulate a West Semitic background to Enuma elish, and consequently the latter is not capable of supplying support to the view that the Canaanite mythology of the conflict between Baal and the sea/dragon was associated with the creation.

A possible solution to our problem lies in distinguishing between

27 I am grateful to Prof. Lambert for discussing with me his revised views. A brief outline of some of them may be found in his article 'Zum Forschungsstand der sumerisch-babylonischen Literatur-Geschichte', *ZDMG* Suppl. 3, 1 (1977), pp. 69–71.

28 W.G. Lambert, 'The reign of Nebuchadnezzar I: a turning point in the history of ancient Mesopotamian religion', in W.S. McCullough (ed.), *The Seed of Wisdom. Essays in Honour of T.J. Meek* (Toronto, 1964), pp. 3–13.

29 See Sm 1875 in Landsberger, 'Einige unerkannt gebliebene oder verkannte Nomina des Akkadischen', *WZKM* 57 (1961), p. 10, n. 46, line 5: *tam-tum ṣer-ra-at be-lu-tú* x[] 'As for Tiamat, the reins of lordship .[. . .]' Presumably it went on to say that Ninurta snatched these reins for himself from her. The previous line mentions 'Asakku, his kingship [. . .', and it is well-known that Ninurta had a struggle with the Asakku demon. The following lines, 6–7, refer to his battle with the Anzu bird. Although it is not possible to give a precise date to the text, it is Late Assyrian so far as the known copy goes, but obviously a library text, and so unlikely to be the first copy ever. But no one would suspect that Ninurta mythology was based on Marduk's, since in general it is exactly the opposite way round. Cf. Marduk's appropriation of motifs from the Anzu myth. On the Anzu myth, see B. Hruška, *Der Mythenadler Anzu in Literatur und Vorstellung des alten Mesopotamien* (Budapest, 1975).

the conflict of Baal and Yam, of which we possess a detailed account, and the conflict of Baal and Anat with Leviathan, Yam, Arš ('El's calf Atik') and others of which the Ugaritic texts also make mention but give us no detailed account, and arguing that the latter was a primordial battle associated with the creation of the world.[30]

That Baal also defeated a dragon Leviathan is indicated by the following text (*CTA* 5.I.1–3 = *KTU* 1.5.I.1–3), where Mot addresses Baal as follows:[31]

1 ktmḫṣ. ltn. bṯn. brḥ	Because you smote Leviathan the twisting serpent,
2 tkly. bṯn. ʿqltn	(and) made an end of the crooked serpent,
3 šlyṭ. d.šbʿt. rʾašm	the tyrant with seven heads,
4 tṯkḥ. ttrp. šmm.	the skies will become hot (and) will shine

The fact that Leviathan is here alluded to as 'the crooked serpent, the tyrant with seven heads' makes it clear that it is Leviathan that Anat also claims to have overcome in lines 37–9 of the following passage (*CTA* 3.IIID. 34–IV.47 = *KTU* 1.3.III.37–IV.3), in which her victories over Baal's enemies are cited.

34 mn. ʾib. ypʿ. lbʿl. ṣrt	What foe has risen up against Baal,
35 lrkb. ʿrpt. lmḫšt. mdd	(What) enemy has risen against the Rider of the clouds? Surely I smote
36 ʾil ym. lklt. nhr. ʾil. rbm	Yam, beloved of El, surely I made an end of River, the mighty god.

30 This possibility was briefly suggested by J.C. de Moor, *Seasonal Pattern*, p. 41 and n. 31, although he does not treat the problem in detail. S.E. Loewenstamm, **מיתוס הים בכתבי אלגרית וזיקתו אל מיתוס הים במקרא**, *Eretz-Israel* 9 (1969), pp. 96–101, suggests that originally the conflict between Baal and the god of the sea was associated with creation, and the god of the sea would have had monstrous form. This he finds reflected in the Old Testament and Midrashic allusions to the dragon conflict and also in the Marduk–Tiamat conflict. Later the connection with creation and the monstrous form of the god would have disappeared and this he finds reflected in the Baal–Yam text from Ugarit.

31 On the problems of translation in these and the following verses, see J.A. Emerton, 'A difficult part of Mot's message to Baal in the Ugaritic texts', *Austrialian Journal of Biblical Archaeology* 2, no. 1 (1972), pp. 50–71, and again 'A further note on *CTA* 5,I,4–6', *UF* 10 (1978), pp. 73–7. In the latter article he modifies some of his conclusions in the light of A. van Selms, 'A systematic approach to *CTA* 5,I,1–8', *UF* 7 (1975), pp. 477–82.

37 l'ištbm.[32] tnn. 'ištm[ ][33]	Surely I lifted up the dragon, I . . .
38 mḫšt. bṯn. ʿqltn	(and) smote the crooked serpent,
39 šlyṭ. d.šbʿt. r'ašm	the tyrant with the seven heads.
40 mḫšt. mdd 'ilm. 'ar[š]	I smote Ar[š] beloved of El,
41 ṣmt. ʿgl. 'il. ʿtk	I put an end to El's calf Atik
42 mḫšt. klbt. 'ilm 'išt	I smote El's bitch the Fire,
43 klt. bt. 'il. ḏbb. 'imtḫṣ. ksp	made an end of El's daughter the Flame. I will conquer the silver,
44 'itrṯ. ḫrṣ. ṭrd. bʿl	I will take possession of the gold of him who has driven Baal
45 bmrym. ṣpn.mšṣṣ.k.ʿṣr	from the heights of Zaphon, causing (him) like a bird to flee
46 'udnh. gršh. lks'i. mlkh	his lordship,[34] expelling him from his royal throne,
47 lnḫt. lkḫṭ. drkth	from the resting place, the seat of his dominion.

It has sometimes been supposed that Leviathan is simply to be equated with Yam.[35] However, against this stands the fact that the names Yam and Leviathan never appear together in parallelism in such a way as to suggest that they are identical (contrast Yam and Judge River, which frequently occur in parallelism). Nor is there anything to suggest that Yam, like Leviathan, had the form of a dragon. On the one occasion in which Yam and Leviathan are mentioned together, in the above text, it is clear that they are two of a series of four creatures overcome by Anat (cf. lines 36, 37–9, 40–1, 42–3), the verb *mḫš* 'smite' being employed once in connection with each of them.

32 *šbm* has generally been rendered as 'muzzle'. However, J. Barr, 'Ugaritic and Hebrew "*šbm*"?', *JSS* 18 (1973), pp. 17–39, has shown that the Arabic evidence on which this view was based does not substantiate such a meaning. Barr tentatively suggests that the meaning is something like 'lift up, remove, get rid of' in *CTA* 3.IIID.37 (= *KTU* 1.3.III.40), a meaning developing from a basic meaning 'be high' attested in South Arabian. In *KTU* 1.83.8–9 (*UT* 1003.8–9), a passage reminiscent of *CTA* 3.IIID.37 (= *KTU* 1.3.III.40), we read in connection with Anat, *t'an* (*tnn*). *lšbm tšt*. If we follow Barr, this means 'She put the dragon on high', which then forms an excellent parallel to the following words in lines 9–10, *trks lmrym* 'she bound it to the heights'.

33 Prof. D. Pardee has examined the text at first hand and states that *'ištm*[ ] is to be read here. Accordingly, this form is not a repetition of the first word in the line as is often supposed. The second-last letter is probably *l* or *d*, and the last letter certainly *h*, *p* or *'i*.

34 See J. Sanmartín, 'Die ug. Basis NṢṢ und das "Nest" des Bʿl (*KTU* 1.3 IV 1f.)', *UF* 10 (1978), pp. 449–50 for this rendering of *mšṣṣ. k.ʿṣr 'udnh*. It has the advantage of putting a verb of expulsion in this line, 'cause to flee' (Š-participle of *nṣṣ*), paralleling *ṭrd* 'drive out' in the preceding line and *grš* 'expel' in the following line.

35 A.S. Kapelrud, *Baal in the Ras Shamra texts* (Copenhagen, 1952), pp. 101–2.

It is important to note that neither Leviathan nor any of the other monsters alluded to in the above text, is mentioned in the account of Baal's defeat of Yam in *CTA* 2 (= *KTU* 1.2). One might care to argue, of course, that their defeat was described in part of the broken section of *CTA* 2 (= *KTU* 1.2). Although this cannot be ruled out entirely, it is striking that the preserved fragments of *CTA* 2 (= *KTU* 1.2) strongly give the impression that Yam stands alone against Baal and it seems surprising that the text as we have it has not the slightest allusion to any accomplices, if such there were. The virtually decisive argument in support of the view that *CTA* 3.IIID.34–IV.47 (= *KTU* 1.3.III.37–IV.3) refers to some other occasion than the events of *CTA* 2 (= *KTU* 1.2), however, lies in the role ascribed to Anat in the former passage. There she herself lays claim to have smitten Yam, thus making an end of him. It seems impossible to reconcile this with the account in *CTA* 2 (= *KTU* 1.2), for there it is clear that Baal alone slew Yam. By the time the text breaks off Yam is already dead (cf. *CTA* 2.IV.32, 34 = *KTU* 1.2.IV.32, 34) so that there is no role for Anat to play in killing Yam in the few broken lines that remain. At the same time, the story of Baal's defeat of Yam is sufficiently well preserved to make it clear that Anat did not assist in killing Yam, whatever other role she might conceivably have had in any earlier broken part of *CTA* 2 (= *KTU* 1.2). The only conclusion that it seems possible to draw is that Anat, together with Baal (cf. *CTA* 5.I.1–3 = *KTU* 1.5.I.1–3) defeated Yam, Leviathan, and the other monsters on some occasion other than the events of *CTA* 2 (= *KTU* 1.2.). This conclusion is reinforced by the fact that we do possess brief, though fragmentary, allusions to the defeat of the dragon (i.e. Leviathan) by both Baal and Anat, in Ugaritic texts which clearly come from a different scribe from Elimelek, the one who transcribed *CTA* 1–6 (= *KTU* 1.1–6). The occurrence of the rare root *šbm* in connection with Anat's defeat of the dragon in the first of these passages, in *KTU* 1.83.8, as in *CTA* 3.IIID.37 (= *KTU* 1.3.III.40) above, puts it beyond doubt that this is the event to which the latter passage is referring.

KTU 1.83.3–10 (*UT* 1003.3–10)

3 b'arṣ	In the land of
4 mḫnm. ṯrp[36] ym.	Mḫnm it swirled (?) the sea,

36 *KTU* has ʿ(*?*)*rp* or *t*(*?*)ʿ(*?*)*rp* for this word and *tʿrp* in line 6 but Prof. Pardee, who has examined the tablet at first hand, informs me that *ṯrp* and *tṯrp* are virtually certain (with *UT*).

5 lšnm. tlḫk.	its tongues licked
6 šmm. ṯṯrp	the heaven, its tails
7 ym. ḏnbtm.	swirled (?) the sea.
8 t'an (tnn). lšbm	She put the dragon
9 tšt. trks	on high,[37] she bound it
10 lmrym. lbnn[38]	to the heights of Lebanon.

KTU 1.82.1–3 (*UT* 1001.1–3)

1 [ ] mḫṣ. bʿl [ ]y. tnn. wygl. wynsk. ʿ[ ]
2 [ ]y. l'arṣ. [.i]dy. 'alt. l'aḫš. 'idy. 'alt. 'in ly
3 [ ]t. bʿl. ḫẓ ršp. bn. km. yr. klyth. wlbh

1 Baal smote . . . the dragon and rejoiced and poured out . . .
2 . . . on the earth . . . support . . . I have no support
3 . . . the archer Resheph, son of *Km*, shot his kidneys and his heart.

The fact that both Baal and Anat are said to have overcome the dragon need involve no contradiction, since in the Baal–Mot cycle both Baal and Anat are similarly represented as attacking Mot (cf. *CTA* 6.II.30–7, 6.VI.17–22 = *KTU* 1.6.II.30–7, 1.6.VI.17–22).

When did the conflict with the dragon take place? An indication is provided by the Ugaritic text *CTA* 6.VI.50–2 (= *KTU* 1.6.VI.51–3), where at the very end of the Baal cycle contained in *CTA* 1–6 (= *KTU* 1.1–6) we find a reference to the threat posed by the sea monsters Arš and the dragon (*tnn* = Leviathan).

50 bym. 'arš. wtnn	In the sea are Arš and the dragon,
51 kṯr. wḫss. yd	May Kothar-and-Ḫasis drive (them) away,
52 ytr. kṯr. wḫss	May Kothar-and-Ḫasis cut (them) off.

Since the Baal myth clearly contains seasonal elements[39] (e.g. Anat's treatment of Mot like corn[40] in *CTA* 6.II.30–35 = *KTU*

37 Cf. above, n. 32.

38 *KTU* has *lbn*t* but *lbnn* is certain (Prof. D. Pardee).

39 Cf. especially, J.C. de Moor, *op. cit.*, *passim*, who sees a seasonal pattern underlying the whole Baal cycle. We need not follow all de Moor's examples in order to accept that there are clear seasonal elements in the work.

40 We read there, 'She seized divine Mot, with a blade she split him, with a sieve she winnowed him, with fire she burnt him, with mill-stones she ground him, in a field she sowed him.' The piling up of agricultural terms here is unmistakable. See J.C. de Moor, *op. cit.*, pp. 208–15 for the detailed interpretation of this passage and a refutation of S.E. Loewenstamm, 'The Ugaritic fertility myth – the result of a mistranslation', *IEJ* 12 (1962), pp. 87–8, and 'The Ugaritic fertility myth – a reply', in *IEJ* 13 (1963), pp. 130–2, who thought that nothing more than the simple destruction of Mot was in mind. In 'The making and destruction of the golden calf', *Biblica* 48 (1967), pp. 481–90, Loewenstamm

1.6.II.30–35), it is possible that this passage, coming as it does at the very end of the Baal cycle, refers to the time of the very end of the year and the approach of the New Year when the battle with the dragon was in people's minds.[41] This is significant for the point at issue here, since the creation of the world would naturally have been regarded as occurring at the time of the very first New Year, so that this provides evidence that the Canaanites may have associated the creation with the conflict with the dragon.[42] In any case, quite apart from this line of argument it must be strongly emphasized that the fact that the Old Testament so frequently uses the imagery of the divine conflict with the dragon and the sea in association with creation, when this imagery is Canaanite, leads one to expect that the Canaanites likewise connected the two themes.

There are grounds for believing, therefore, that the Canaanites may have associated the creation of the world with Baal's victory over the dragon and the sea, even though the Ugaritic Baal–Yam text (*CTA* 2 = *KTU* 1.2) is not concerned with the creation. This does not imply that we should regard Baal as the creator, however. Rather this function amongst the Canaanites seems to have been appropriated by El,[43] as is attested by various inscriptions referring

compared the description of the destruction of the golden calf in Ex. 32:20. See my critical comments in Ch. 2, n. 62.

41 Cf. J.C. de Moor, *op. cit.*, p. 244, and *New Year with Canaanites and Israelites 1* (Kampen, 1972), pp. 5–6. M.J. Mulder, 'Hat man in Ugarit die Sonnenwende begangen?', *UF* 4 (1972), pp. 79–96, relates this passage to the time of the winter solstice. However, this is surely too late. The passage follows immediately after Baal's victory over Mot, corresponding to the time of the first rain in the autumn, which is usually in September (cf. de Moor, *Seasonal Pattern*, pp. 98, 238.)

42 If *KTU* 1.83 (*UT* 1003) and *KTU* 1.82 (*UT* 1001) are explicitly concerned with the creation of the world, the references to the heavens and Lebanon (*KTU* 1.83.6, 10) and the earth (*KTU* 1.82.2) as already existing would have to be taken as referring to them in their primordial chaotic state, comparable to Gen. 1:1–2 and Ps. 74:12. On the other hand, if they presuppose the world in its present state and simply relate to the time of the New Year, one may still argue that creation, the time of the first New Year, presupposed similar events.

43 B. Margalit, 'The Ugaritic Creation Myth: fact or fiction?', *UF* 13 (1981), pp. 137–45, has recently queried the view that El was regarded as creator of the cosmos at Ugarit. However, his argument is based on silence and no alternative deity is proposed for this role. Indeed, there is no more likely candidate, in view of the fact that El is clearly alluded to as creator of the earth outside the Ugaritic texts, including one from the time of their composition (Elkunirša), and El certainly is the creator of mankind (as well as the gods) at Ugarit. The fact that El, on present evidence, seems unlikely to have engaged in theomachic conflict (unlike Baal), is not an argument against his having been creator of the cosmos.

to *'l qn 'rṣ* 'El creator of the earth'[44] (cf. Gen. 14:19, 22) which appears as Elkuniršа in a Canaanite–Hittite myth of the 2nd millennium B.C.[45] and the Ugaritic epithets of El *bny bnwt* 'creator of created things' (*CTA* 4.II.11, 6.III.5, etc. = *KTU* 1.4.II.11, 1.6.III.5, etc) and *'ab 'adm* 'Father of mankind' (*CTA* 14.I.37, 43, etc. = *KTU* 1.14.I.37, 43, etc.).[46]

We shall now turn to the Old Testament material bearing on the theme of the divine conflict with the dragon and the sea, but before considering individual passages we shall deal with the question of the *Sitz im Leben* of the motif in ancient Israel.

The Psalms

Sitz im Leben of the Chaoskampf motif

A number of passages in the Psalter allude to the *Chaoskampf* motif. Those which relate it specifically to the creation include Ps.

44 The expression *'l qn 'rṣ* occurs in the Phoenician inscription of Azitawadda from Karatepe (*KAI* 26 A.III.18) and in a neo-Punic inscription from Leptis Magna, Tripolitania (*KAI* 129. 1). In addition, the form *'lqwnr'* occurs in a bilingual text from Palmyra, where he is equated with Poseidon (J. Cantineau, 'Tadmorea. No. 31: Un Poséidon palmyrénien', *Syria* 19, 1938, pp. 78–9, cf. G. Levi della Vida, 'El 'Elyon in Genesis 14 18–20', *JBL* 63, 1944, p. 8). N. Avigad, 'Excavations in the Jewish quarter of the old city of Jerusalem, 1971', *IEJ* 22 (1972), pp. 195–6, refers to a seventh century B.C. inscription which he restores as ['l] *qn 'rṣ*, but there can be no certainty that this reconstruction is correct.

45 The Hittite text containing the form Elkuniršа clearly refers to El, as his wife is Ašertu (Asherah) (*ANET*, p. 519, cf. H. Otten, 'Ein kanaanäischer Mythus aus Boğazköy', *Mitteilungen des Instituts für Orientforschung* 1, 1953, pp. 125–50).

46 J.C. de Moor, 'El, the Creator', in G. Rendsburg, R. Adler, M. Arfa, N.H. Winter (edd.), *The Bible World. Essays in Honor of Cyrus H. Gordon* (New York, 1980), pp. 171–87, attempts to go beyond this and show that El was creator of the cosmos on the basis of two lists from Ugarit, *KTU* 1.148.23–5 and *Ugaritica V*. 170:13–15 (*RS* 26.142, lines 13–15). In the former, part of a list of offerings to various gods, we find a list of sacrifices to *'il'ib*, then *'arṣ w šmm* and finally *'il* (El). The latter, part of a list of Ugaritic deities written in Akkadian, has in succession ^{d}?[ ], ^{d}*erṣetu* [(?) *u šamû*(??)] and *ilum* [(?)]. De Moor thinks that the first name in the latter list was DINGIR.AD, i.e. *'il'ib*, 'on the analogy of the almost identical list' in *Ugaritica V*. 170 (so J.C. de Moor, 'The Semitic Pantheon of Ugarit', *UF* 2, 1970, p. 199). However, a comparison of the two lists shows that the similarity is in reality not very great, so that the reconstruction DINGIR.AD in the *Ugaritica V* is uncertain. Anyway, the fact that *'il'ib* is mentioned before *'arṣ w šmm* is held to justify the conclusion that *'il'ib*, regarded as a form of El, was creator of heaven and earth, De Moor goes on, in fact, to correlate the series of three deities with those in Philo of Byblos, Elioun called the Most High, Heaven and Earth, and Elos who is Kronos. However, de Moor draws larger conclusions from the evidence than are justified, since, whilst *'il'ib* is very likely a form of El (cf. *Ugaritica V*,

74, 89, 104, 65, and 93, (cf. Ps. 29 and the implications of Ps. 24). What was the specific *Sitz im Leben* of this important motif in the Jerusalem cult? There are many factors which strongly suggest that it was an aspect of the Feast of Tabernacles, and here it would have been one of the motifs associated with Yahweh's kingship.

Ps. 74, 93 and 29 explicitly associate the *Chaoskampf* with Yahweh's kingship, just as the Ugaritic Baal myth connects Baal's victory over Yam with his enthronement and Enuma elish links Marduk's kingship with his overcoming of Tiamat. We know that the latter was celebrated in the Babylonian New Year (Akitu) festival,[47] and the thesis was first suggested by P. Volz,[48] and greatly elaborated by S. Mowinckel,[49] that Yahweh's kingship, more specifically his enthronement, was similarly associated with the Feast of Tabernacles, which took place around the time of the Autumnal New Year in pre-exilic Israel (cf. Ex. 23:16, 34:22).[50] Probably we should regard it as taking place on the eve of the New Year, rather than at the beginning of the New Year, since, of the expressions

18.1 [*RS* 1929, no. 17, 1], where *'il'ib* appears to be mentioned alongside *'il ṣpn* and *'il*), the fact that *'arṣ w šmm* are mentioned after him in no way guarantees that they are his children.

47 The festival was celebrated under the Late Babylonian kings (625–539 B.C.) and was essentially the same as far back as 750 B.C. in Babylon. How much farther it went back is not known. It is clear that Enuma elish was recited on 4th Nisan and that later, either on the 8th, 10th or 11th Nisan Marduk's victory over Tiamat was ritually enacted, his statue (or cult symbol) being placed on a dais representing the sea in the Akitu house. On all this see W.G. Lambert, 'The great battle of the Mesopotamian religious year. The conflict in the Akītu house', *Iraq* 25 (1963), pp. 189–90, and 'Myth and ritual as conceived by the Babylonians', *JSS* 13 (1968), pp. 104–12. See too S.A. Pallis, *The Babylonian Akîtu Festival* (Copenhagen, 1926) for material relating to the festival, though note that it is now recognized that neither Marduk's resurrection nor a ritual marriage formed part of the celebrations as Pallis supposed. Cf. W. von Soden, 'Gibt es ein Zeugnis dafür, dass die Babylonier an die Wiederauferstehung Marduks geglaubt haben?', *ZA* 51, n.F. 17 (1955), pp. 130–66, and W.G. Lambert, *JSS* 13 (1968), pp. 106–7.

48 P. Volz, *Das Neujahrsfest Jahwes* (Tübingen, 1912).

49 S. Mowinckel, *Psalmenstudien* 2 (Kristiania, 1922). Cf. too his work *The Psalms in Israel's Worship* 1 (ET, Oxford, 1962), pp. 106–92 and 2, pp. 222–50.

50 It is generally accepted that Ex. 23:16 and 34:22 testify to the existence of an autumnal New Year in pre-exilic Israel and that the spring New Year was adopted from the Babylonians just prior to or during the exile, as indicated by the use of Babylonian month names. D. Clines, however, in 'The evidence for an autumnal new year in pre-exilic Israel reconsidered', *JBL* 93 (1974), pp. 22–40, doubts the existence of an autumnal New Year in pre-exilic Israel and claims that Ex. 23:16 and 34:22 simply refer to the agricultural cycle and not the calendar year. This is unlikely, however. *Inter alia* later Judaism's celebration of the New Year in the Autumn is rendered inexplicable.

used to define the time of the festival, *b^e^ṣē'ṯ haššānāh* 'at the going out of the year' (Ex. 23:16) and *t^e^qūpaṯ haššānāh* 'at the circuit of the year' (Ex. 34:22), the former almost certainly refers to the end of the year.[51] In any case, the *Chaoskampf* motif, intimately related to that of Yahweh's kingship, would have had its setting there also. Clearly so significant a theme as that of Yahweh's kingship or enthronement must have had its setting in a feast of great importance – one of the three great feasts – and numerous other pieces of evidence support the view that this was Tabernacles. There is a wide measure of support for this, even amongst scholars who are otherwise sceptical of Mowinckel's theories.

First it may be noted that Zech. 14:16f. specifically refers to the celebration of Yahweh's kingship in connection with the Feast of Tabernacles: 'Then everyone that survives of all the nations that have come against Jerusalem shall go up year after year to worship the king, the Lord of hosts, and to keep the Feast of Tabernacles. And if any of the families of the earth do not go up to Jerusalem to worship the king, the Lord of hosts, there will be no rain upon them.' The mention of rain here fits in well with the motif of Yahweh's control of the cosmic waters (cf. the Tabernacles Psalm, Ps. 65:8ff. ET 7ff., which combines these two motifs), and it is also interesting that Zech. 14 contains the motif of the conflict with the nations, which derives from the conflict with chaos (cf. below, chapter 3). Although the evidence of Zech. 14:16f. is sometimes dismissed as late, it should be noted that (a) this passage may well not be quite as late as is sometimes supposed,[52] (b) the cult tends to be very conservative so that Zech. 14:16f. probably reflects much older ideas, and (c) the testimony of Zech. 14:16f. is reinforced by other evidence to be considered below.

Secondly, the LXX heading of Ps. 29 specifically associates it with the Feast of Tabernacles and, similarly, Jewish tradition connected the Enthronement Psalm, Ps., 47 with the New Year Festival. Indeed, the kingship of Yahweh was at the centre of the Jewish New Year.[53]

51 See E. Kutsch, '"... am Ende des Jahres"', *ZAW* 83 (1971), pp. 15–21. He shows that when the root *yṣ'* is used of day, night, month or year in post-Biblical Hebrew and Akkadian it refers to its end. I would also note that this fits the fact that Tabernacles is the last mentioned of the three major festivals in both Ex. 23 and 34.

52 Thus, P.D. Hanson, *The Dawn of Apocalyptic* (Philadelphia, Pa., 1975), p. 400, sets Zech. 14 between 475 and 425 B.C.

53 Cf. I. Elbogen, *Der jüdische Gottesdienst in seiner geschichtlichen Entwicklung* (Frankfurt a. Main, 1931), pp. 140–9.

Thirdly, it appears that the Ark was carried in procession at the festival of Yahweh's enthronement/kingship – cf. Ps. 24:7ff., 47:6 (ET 5), 68:2 (ET 1; cf. Num. 10:35). This is also referred to in Ps. 132 (cf. 2 Sam. 6–7), and it is probably significant that 1 Kings 8:1f specifically links the bringing up of the Ark into the Temple with the Feast of Tabernacles.

Fourthly, the theme of Yahweh's kingship was closely associated with the creation of the world – cf. Ps. 74:12ff., 93:1f., 24:1f., 7ff., etc. Also, it should be noted that other psalms dealing with the *Chaoskampf*, to be dealt with below, associate it with the creation – cf. Ps. 89:10ff. (ET 9ff.), 104:5ff., 65:7f. (ET 6f.). What would be more appropriate than for the creation (and with it the *Chaoskampf*) to be celebrated about the time of New Year, when we recall that for the ancient Israelites creation would naturally have been regarded as taking place at the time of the first New Year?

Finally, there is evidence suggesting a link between the festival of Yahweh's enthronement and the Covenant. Thus, the reference to the sin at Massah and Meribah in the Enthronement Psalm, Ps. 95:8 is referred to in the Covenant renewal Psalm, Ps. 81:8 (ET 7). Jewish tradition actually associated Ps. 81 with the New Year, and similarly we find that the Covenant book Deutronomy was to be read out every seven years at the Feast of Tabernacles (Deut. 31:9ff.), and in Neh. 8:2 we read that Ezra read the book of the law at the time of the New Year.

Taking all these points into consideration, it may be argued that a strong case can be made in support of the argument that the motif of Yahweh's kingship, and with it the *Chaoskampf* with which we are primarily concerned here, had its *Sitz im Leben* in the Feast of Tabernacles at New Year's eve. Since both the Feast of Tabernacles (cf. Judg. 9:27) and the festal theme of the king-god in conflict with the chaos waters were appropriated from the Canaanites, it is reasonable to suppose that this motif was also a feature of the Canaanite Autumn Festival.[54]

Psalm 74:12–17

V. 12 But you O God,[55] are my king from of old,
doing victorious things in the earth.

54 For an interesting but admittedly speculative attempt at a reconstruction of the Canaanite Autumn Festival, cf. J.C. de Moor, *New Year with Canaanites and Israelites* (2 vols., Kampen, 1972).

55 Reading *w*^{e}*'attāh '*^{e}*lōhīm* for MT *w'ēlōhīm*, since comparison with the surrounding verses suggests the metre is one beat too short.

V. 13 You divided[56] the sea by your might,
you broke the heads of the dragons on the waters.
V. 14 You shattered the heads of Leviathan,
you gave him to the people of the wild beasts[57] as food.
V. 15 You cleaved open spring and torrent,
you dried up ever-flowing streams.
V. 16 Yours is the day, yours also the night,
you have established the moon[58] and the sun.
V. 17 You have fixed all the boundaries of the earth,
you did create summer and winter.

These words form part of a psalm of lament for the destruction of the Temple in 586 B.C.[59] As in Ps. 89:10–11 (ET 9–10) and Is. 51:9–11 (cf. too Ps. 77:17–21, ET 16–20), Yahweh's defeat of the chaos monster(s) in the past is appealed to as a ground of confidence for him to act to deliver his people in the present when the powers of chaos seem to have triumphed, the Deutero-Isaianic passage likewise dating from the exile. That the defeat of the chaos monster is appealed to in this way clearly indicates that the mythology was already well established in pre-exilic Israel. We shall in fact be considering in a moment psalms from pre-exilic times which contain this mythology.

56 Alternatively, the translation may be 'you set in commotion', cf. Arabic *farfara*, *KB* (1958), p. 782. However, it may be alleged in favour of the traditional translation 'divide' that it provides a somewhat better parallel to the *breaking* of the dragon's heads in the second half of the verse.

57 *lᵉʿām lᵉṣīyyīm* is a noteworthy *crux*. Perhaps the simplest way of dealing with it is to make the slight emendation to *lᵉʿam ṣīyyīm*. Animals are referred to as a 'people' elsewhere in the Old Testament. Cf. Prov. 30:25–6 and Joel 2:2. The popular view that one should read *lᵉʿamlᵉṣē yām* 'to the sharks', first suggested by I. Löw, is to be rejected, since it is unlikely that a root whose basic meaning is 'smooth' would have given rise to a word meaning 'shark'.

58 The word translated 'moon' is *mā'ōr*, lit. 'luminary'. The fact that it is mentioned alongside the sun would suggest the meaning 'moon'. Alternatively, it could be taken collectively as 'luminaries'.

59 The main alternative view that has been held, namely that the psalm refers to Antiochus IV Epiphanes' desecration of the Temple in 168 B.C., is untenable in the light of the fact that he did not destroy the Temple (cf. v. 7) but only burned the doors of the Temple (cf. 1 Macc. 4:38; 2 Macc. 1:8) and desecrated the sanctuary (1 Macc. 1:23, 39; 2 Macc. 6:5). J. Morgenstern, 'Jerusalem – 485 B.C.', *HUCA* 27 (1956), pp. 101–79, esp. p. 130f., relates this psalm to an alleged defilement and devastation of the Temple by the Edomites in ca. 485 B.C., whilst others have connected it with a hypothetical pollution of the Temple in the reign of Artaxerxes III Ochus (359–38 B.C.), but both these views are very dubious. Similarly implausible is the view of F. Willesen, 'The cultic situation of Psalm lxxiv', *VT* 2 (1952), pp. 289–306, that the psalm has no relation to any specific historical event but merely to a cultic one.

Scholars have argued whether the reference to the defeat of the chaos monster alludes to the time of the creation, a view first propounded by Gunkel,[60] or to the deliverance of the Hebrews at the Reed Sea at the time of the Exodus, a view going back to the Targum,[61] or perhaps, as in Is. 51:9–11, to both.[62] Against the view that the Exodus is referred to and in favour of seeing here a reference to the creation is the fact that the context clearly alludes to the creation of the world (cf. vv. 16–17), so that vv. 13–14 must allude to a mythological battle at this time. Saggs' argument[63] that the close conjunction of the divine conflict with the chaos monster and the creation of the world does not necessarily or indeed probably imply that the two are causally connected is improbable, since we have other passages in which the creation is associated with a conflict between Yahweh and the primordial sea or with Yahweh's control of the sea, e.g. Ps. 104:6–9, Job 38:8–11, Prov. 8:29. Since this sea could be personified by the dragon (e.g. Is. 51:9–10), it is only natural to suppose that we similarly have a conflict with the dragon at the time of creation here. The reference to the earth in v. 12 does not constitute a valid objection to this, since the earth in its primaeval chaotic state is similarly alluded to in Gen. 1:2 before God's effective creative work began. Again, the obscure and uncertain reference in v. 14 to the giving of Leviathan to the people of the wild beasts as food need not imply that the battle occurred after Yahweh's effective work of creation had taken place. There is therefore no need to see an allusion to any event other than the creation here. If it were the case that the reference is simultaneously to the creation and the Exodus, the creation would certainly be the dominant allusion, but there is in fact no need to see any reference to the Exodus here.

The fact that Yahweh is addressed as king in v. 12 relates to the notion that Yahweh's victory over the chaotic sea was associated

60 Originally proposed by H. Gunkel, *Schöpfung und Chaos*, pp. 42–5; cf. J.A. Emerton, '"Spring and torrent" in Psalm LXXIV 15', *SVT* 15 (1966), pp. 122–3, 130–3, and A. Lelièvre, 'YHWH et la mer dans les psaumes', *RHPR* 56 (1976), pp. 256–63.

61 Cf. E. König, *Die Psalmen* (Gütersloh, 1927), pp. 485 n. 4, 670–1; A. Heidel, *The Babylonian Genesis* (2nd ed., Chicago and London, 1951), pp. 106, 109, 112–13; S.I.L. Norin, *Er spaltete das Meer* (Lund, 1977), pp. 112–14. (V. 15 would then refer to the provision of water in the wilderness wanderings.) See the criticisms of this view in Lelièvre, *loc. cit.*

62 Cf. A. Weiser, *Die Psalmen* (5th ed., Göttingen, 1959), p. 354, (ET *The Psalms*, London, 1962, p. 520); H.-J. Kraus, *Psalmen* 2 (Neukirchen, 1978), p. 681.

63 H.W.F. Saggs, *op. cit.*, pp. 24–6.

with his assumption of effective kingship (cf. Ps. 93), just as was the case with Baal in the Ugaritic Baal–Yam myth and Marduk in the Babylonian Enuma elish. In this connection it is interesting to note, following Lelièvre,[64] that the assumption of kingship by Baal and Marduk resulted, after the victory over the sea, in a temple being built in their honour. Similarly Yahweh's receiving of a temple could be portrayed as following on his manifestation of kingship in his victory at the sea as we know from Ex. 15:17. This fact enables us to see the special relevance of vv. 12–17 in the present psalm, motivated as it is by the destruction of the temple, since if Yahweh's temple has been destroyed, it is fitting to remind him of his victory over the sea and his accompanying kingship which provided the basis on which he received his temple.

It is interesting that v. 14 refers to the *heads* of Leviathan. It has been established from the Ugaritic texts that Leviathan in fact possessed seven heads (cf. *CTA* 3.IIID.39 and 5.I.3 = *KTU* 1.3.III.42 and 1.5.I.3) and this tradition is independently reflected in the seven heads of the 'dragon' in the Odes of Solomon 22, 5, Pistis Sophia 66 and Ḳiddushin 29b, and is taken up into apocalyptic in the New Testament in the seven heads of the 'dragon' in Rev. 12:3 and the seven heads of the 'beast' in Rev. 13:1 and 17:3. There is no evidence that Tiamat had seven heads, as is sometimes still claimed.[65] M.J. Dahood[66] maintains that Leviathan's seven heads explain why there are seven *'attāh*'s in Ps. 74:13–17, which he thereby supposes contains a subtle artistry. This view is to be rejected, however, since it is quite likely that a further *'attāh* is to be read in the text in v. 12, making eight altogether, and it is a further disadvantage for Dahood's view that not all the *'attah*'s occur in those verses relating specifically to the conflict with Leviathan or even the sea (cf. vv. 16–17).

V. 13 refers to dragons (*tannīnīm*) whose heads are broken. These are probably to be seen as helpers of Leviathan: one may compare the reference to 'the helpers of Rahab (probably = Leviathan)' in Job 9:13 (cf. Tiamat's 'helpers' in Enuma elish tablet IV, line 107), one of whom, it will later be argued, was Behemoth (Job 40:15–24), and the list of dragons associated with Leviathan in *CTA*

64 A. Lelièvre, *op. cit.*, pp. 266–8.

65 *Contra* F.M. Cross, *Canaanite Myth and Hebrew Epic* (Cambridge, Mass., 1973), p. 119; G.R. Beasley-Murray, *The Book of Revelation* (London, 1974), pp. 192, 198.

66 M.J. Dahood, *Psalms* 2 (New York, 1968), p. 205.

3.IIID.34ff. (= *KTU* 1.3.III.37ff.) which Anat claims to have defeated. Ps. 89:11 (ET 10) similarly speaks of a plurality of enemies in Yahweh's conflict with Rahab. It thus seems unnecessary to follow O. Eissfeldt,[67] who emends the MT of Ps. 74:13 from plural *tannīnīm* 'dragons' to singular *tannīn* 'dragon', presumably equating him with Leviathan.

V. 15 has traditionally been understood as referring to the creation of springs and streams. J.A. Emerton,[68] however, has noted against this that the second half of the verse alludes to the drying up of 'ever-flowing streams', referring back to the chaos waters of vv. 13–14, so that a reference to the creation of ordinary springs and streams would be premature. Furthermore, he notes, a friendly reference to the waters at the beginning of v. 15 would be strange when the second half of the verse and the preceding verses depict them as hostile. He also rejects the view that v. 15 speaks generally of God's power over the waters to make them flow or stop, since this does not fit the context which speaks of specific primaeval events. He argues convincingly that we have here rather a reference to springs cleft open so that the primaeval waters might be removed from the earth, comparable to the removal of the waters of the flood in this way in 1 Enoch 89:7f., Jubilees 6:26 and Lucian of Samosata, *De Dea Syria* 13. Some other of the water would have flowed off the land by rivers into the sea, and this is probably the reason for the allusion to *naḥal* 'torrent, stream, wadi'.

Psalm 89:10–15 (ET 9–14)

V. 10 You rule the surging of the sea,
when its waves rise, you still them.
V. 11 You did crush Rahab with a mortal blow,
you did scatter your enemies with your mighty arm.
V. 12 Yours are the heavens, yours also is the earth,
you have founded the world and all that is in it.
V. 13 You have created the north and the south,
Tabor and Hermon joyously praise your name.
V. 14 You have a mighty arm;
Strong is your hand, exalted your right hand.
V. 15 Righteousness and justice are the foundation of your throne,
Steadfast love and faithfulness go before you.

67 O. Eissfeldt, 'Gott und das Meer', *Kleine Schriften* 3 (Tübingen, 1966), p. 259, n. 2. Originally published in *Studia Orientalia Ioanni Pedersen septuagenario dicata* (Copenhagen, 1953), p. 79, n. 11.

68 J.A. Emerton, *op. cit.*, pp. 122–33.

In this Lament Psalm too, Yahweh's defeat of the chaotic sea at the time of creation is presented as a ground of confidence in Yahweh's power to deliver Israel from present distress, here a situation in which the Davidic covenant seems abrogated. Unlike the comparable Ps. 74 an exilic date appears to be ruled out, since following the reference to the king's humiliation we find him alive and still speaking in vv. 51–2 (ET 50–1). The psalm must therefore be pre-exilic. Whether we have here a reference to a specific historical calamity or a cultic event is disputed. In my view such scholars as A.R. Johnson[69] are correct who think the latter, since no known historical event adequately fits the description. In its reference to the king's humiliation it is similar to Ps. 18, and in the latter the king is spoken of as being in the grip of the chaotic power of the waters (cf. Ps. 18:5ff., ET 4ff.). If this were implicit also in Ps. 89, it would give added meaning to the reference to Yahweh's primaeval victory over the sea in vv. 10f.: just as Yahweh defeated chaos in the past, so he would be implored to renew his victory over chaos.[70]

The majority of scholars since Gunkel[71] have held that the defeat of the chaos monster is here associated with the creation of the world (cf. Ps. 74) and this is strongly supported by the reference to the creation in vv. 12–13 (ET 11–12). A minority of scholars,[72] however, hold that the reference is to the Exodus and the deliverance at the Reed Sea, but this ignores the context, whilst others think that there is simultaneous allusion to both the creation and the Exodus.[73] S.I.L. Norin,[74] who recently defended the Exodus

69 A.R. Johnson, *Sacral Kingship in Ancient Israel* (2nd ed., Cardiff, 1967), pp. 106ff.

70 It has been suggested to me that Ps. 89 cannot be equating the enemy with the chaos powers, since elsewhere in the psalm it is Yahweh himself who is said to bring the disaster on Israel (cf. vv. 39ff., ET 38ff.) However, one should consider the possibility of double agency: Yahweh allows the powers of chaos temporarily to be dominant. Cf. Deutero-Isaiah, who seems to regard the coming deliverance from Babylon as a new deliverance from the powers of chaos (Is. 51:9–11; cf. 44:27, 50:2), even though elsewhere the Babylonians are regarded as God's instrument of judgement on Israel.

71 Cf. H. Gunkel, *Schöpfung und Chaos*, pp. 34–5, and *Die Psalmen* (4th ed., Göttingen, 1926), p. 387; H.-J. Kraus, *Psalmen* 2 (Neukirchen, 1978), pp. 787–8; A. Weiser, *Die Psalmen* 2 (5th ed., Göttingen, 1959), p. 403 (ET *The Psalms*, London, 1962, p. 592).

72 Cf. E. König, *Die Psalmen* (Gütersloh, 1927), p. 485; E.J. Kissane, *The Book of Psalms* 2 (Dublin, 1954), p. 89; S.I.L. Norin, *op. cit.*, p. 115.

73 Cf. G.W. Ahlström, *Psalm 89: eine Liturgie aus dem Ritual des leidenden Königs* (Lund, 1959), p. 71.

74 See n. 72.

view, points to the similarities in expression between Ps. 89 and part of the Song of the Sea in Ex. 15:11, a verse extolling the incomparability of Yahweh amongst the gods,[75] but this motif appears to be related to the sea-conflict itself rather than specifically to the Exodus. One may compare the Baal myth from Ugarit, where the council of the gods is afraid of Yam and his messengers (cf. *CTA* 2.I.22ff. = *KTU* 1.2.I.22ff.) and it is left to Baal to overcome him; Baal may therefore be said to be incomparable among the gods.

The motif of Yahweh's victory over the dragon and the sea here alluded to is, of course, an appropriation to Yahweh of a theme originally associated with the Canaanite god Baal. There may therefore be, as has been suggested, a polemical element here and in other comparable passages against Baalism.[76] Beginning with Eissfeldt,[77] a number of scholars have held that in v. 13 (ET 12) we have a polemical reference to Baal's Syrian sacred mountain Zaphon (as well as other sacred mountains). They would translate this verse as follows: 'You have created *Zaphon and Amanus* (*or Amana*), Tabor and Hermon joyously praise your name' in place of the more traditional rendering 'You have created *the north and the south*, Tabor and Hermon joyously praise your name', understanding *ṣāp̱ōn wᵉyāmīn* as referring to the names of mountains, though in order to achieve this *yāmīn* has to be emended to *'amn*, *ḥmn* or *'amnh*, or in the case of Dahood,[78] understood as an umparalleled alternate spelling of *'amn*. It is thought that this then provides a better parallel to the second half of the verse with its allusions to Tabor and Hermon than the traditional rendering 'the north and the south'. The most detailed study of this question has been made by O. Mowan,[79] who argues in support of the view that there are two mountain names in the first half of the verse, maintaining that *yāmīn* with the meaning 'south' is nowhere else in the Old Testa-

75 On this motif, cf. C.J. Labuschagne, *The Incomparability of Yahweh in the Old Testament* (Leiden, 1966).

76 Cf. A.H.W. Curtis, 'The "subjugation of the waters" motif in the psalms; imagery of polemic?', *JSS* 23 (1978), pp. 245–56.

77 O. Eissfeldt, *Baal Zaphon*, pp. 12–13; M.H. Pope, in H.W. Haussig (ed.), *Wörterbuch der Mythologie* 1 (Stuttgart, 1965), p. 258; O. Mowan, 'Quatuor montes sacri in Ps. 89, 13?', *Verbum Domini* 41 (1963), pp. 11–20; R. de Vaux, 'Jérusalem et les prophètes', *RB* 73 (1966), p. 506; M.J. Dahood, *Psalms* 2 (New York, 1968), pp. 308, 314; *NEB*; F.M. Cross, *Canaanite Myth and Hebrew Epic* (Cambridge, Mass., 1973), p. 135, n. 79.

78 M.J. Dahood, *op. cit.*, p. 314.

79 O. Mowan, *loc. cit.*

ment attested parallel to *ṣāpōn* 'north' and that this indicates that the word *yāmīn* is corrupt. This, however, is to ignore the evidence of Ps. 107:3, where the MT reads as follows: *ūmē'ᵃrāṣōṯ qibbᵉṣām mimmizrāḥ ūmaʿᵃraḇ miṣṣāp̄ōn ūmiyyām.* As it stands this declares 'and (he) gathered in from the lands, from the east and from the west, from the north and from the west (lit. sea)', but since the parallelism clearly requires that the last word should mean 'south' and not 'west', one should follow the generally accepted emendation of the MT from *yām* to *yāmīn.* Accordingly, there is no reason why Ps. 89:13 (ET 12) should not similarly refer to the north and the south. Since the extremities of the earth were themselves thought to be mountainous, being known as the 'pillars of heaven' (cf. Job 26:11), the translation 'the north and the south' is quite satisfactory as a parallel to Tabor and Hermon. It is also worthy of note that Deutero-Isaiah, whose prophecy contains a remarkably high number of parallels to Ps. 89, has a reference in Is. 40:28 to Yahweh as *bōrē' qᵉṣōṯ hā'āreṣ* 'the Creator of the ends of the earth', thus paralleling Ps. 89:13a (ET 12a) 'You have created the north and the south.' Finally, it should be noted that those who see a reference to Mt Zaphon in Ps. 89:13 (ET 12) are forced to emend *yāmīn* so as to gain an allusion to Mt Amanus or Amana, or in the case of Dahood to regard it as an unparalleled alternate spelling and this is clearly a disadvantage to the view in question when the text makes good sense as it stands. Consequently, I conclude that the superficially attractive view which finds a polemical reference to Mt Zaphon in Ps. 89:13 (ET 12) – the Syrian mountain where Baal was believed to have defeated the dragon – is to be rejected.

Psalm 104:1–9

V. 1 Bless the Lord, O my soul!
O Lord my God, you are very great!
You are clothed with honour and majesty,
V. 2 you cover yourself with light as with a garment,
you have stretched out the heavens like a tent,
V. 3 you have laid the beams of your chambers on the waters,
you make the cloud your chariot,
you ride on the wings of the wind,
V. 4 you make the wind your messengers,
fire and flame[80] your ministers.

80 Reading *'ēš wālāhaṭ* for MT *'ēš lōhēṭ.*

V. 5 You set the earth on its foundations,
so that it should never be shaken.
V. 6 The deep covered it[81] like a garment,
the waters stood above the mountains.
V. 7. At your roar[82] they fled,
at the sound of your thunder they hurried away.
V. 8 They went up the mountains, down the valleys,[83]
to the place which you appointed for them.
V. 9 You set a boundary which they should not pass,
that they might not return to cover the earth.

Ps. 104 is perhaps best understood as a wisdom psalm. This would account for its Egyptian background – as is well known, it is dependent in some way on Akhenaten's hymn to the sun god (Aton)[84] – for the wise men were in close touch with Egypt, and it would also explain the concentration on the theme of creation, which was central to wisdom theology, and the reference to Yahweh's wisdom in v. 24.

However, besides Egyptian influence this psalm also shows an ultimate dependence on Canaanite mythology, as is attested by the

81 Since both the subject *t^{e}hōm* and the object *'ereṣ* are feminine, we should read *kissattāh* for MT *kissīṯō*.

82 The word here rendered 'roar' is *g^{e}ʿārāh*, which is used elsewhere in connection with God's conflict with the sea in Ps. 18:16 (ET 15) = 2 Sam. 22:16, Job 26:11 and Is. 50:2, whilst the verb *gʿr* is associated with the conflict in Is. 17:13 and Nah. 1:4. Usually the noun and verb are rendered 'rebuke' by modern scholars, but as P. Joüon, 'Notes de lexicographie hébraïque', *Biblica* 6 (1925), pp. 318–21 has pointed out, this is often inadequate. There is evidence that the root often includes in its meaning the notion of the emission of a sound, cf. amongst cognate Semitic languages Ugaritic *gʿr* 'to neigh' (or possibly 'to cry out', 'to cough', or 'to moan'), Arabic *jaʿara* 'to moo, low', Ethiopic *gaʿara* 'to scream, cry', and Syriac *g^{e}ʿārtā* 'bellow'. It is clear that this was also sometimes the case in Biblical Hebrew, cf. Is. 30:17, where LXX renders *gaʿ^{a}raṯ* by *φωνὴν* (twice), and in connection with passages concerned with the conflict with the sea, it is significant that in Ps. 104:7 *gaʿ^{a}rāṯ^{e}ḵā* is parallel with *qōl raʿam^{e}ḵā* 'the sound of your thunder' and in Ps. 18:16 (ET 15) = 2 Sam. 22:16, *gaʿ^{a}rāṯ^{e}ḵā* is parallel with *nišmaṯ rûaḥ 'appeḵā* 'the blast of the breath of your nostrils'. I have accordingly rendered *gʿr* and *g^{e}ʿārāh* as 'roar' throughout this monograph in passages concerned with Yahweh's conflict with the sea, by which we are to understand an allusion to the deity's manifestation of anger in the thunder. On the meaning of *gʿr*, see also A.A. Macintosh, 'A consideration of Hebrew גער', *VT* 19 (1969), pp. 471–9, who also regards the traditional translation of the root as 'rebuke' as inadequate, and contends that it denotes both God's anger and the effective working out of his anger. Cf. too, S.C. Reif, 'A note on גער', *VT* 21 (1971), pp. 241–4.

83 The context clearly requires that it is the waters and not the mountains and valleys, as the *RSV* holds, which are the subject here.

84 Cf. the parallels noted in *ANET*, pp. 370–1.

allusion to the *Chaoskampf* and accompanying storm theophany in the above passage and also by the reference to Leviathan in v. 26. The above passage is valuable because it unambiguously makes it clear that the Old Testament can depict the creation as having been associated with a primordial conflict with chaos (cf. *gʿr* in v. 7), something which is attested elsewhere of course, but which some scholars have found it easier there to deny. Yahweh's onslaught against the chaos waters was in the thunder (cf. v. 7), a motif ultimately deriving from the Canaanite god Baal who manifested himself in the storm against the waters. Vv. 3–4 also apply storm theophany language to Yahweh, the parallel in Ps. 18.11 (ET 10) confirming that it too is to be understood as being directed against the chaos waters.

In v. 3 Yahweh rides a cloud-chariot. This imagery ultimately derives from Baal, whose stock epithet *rkb ʿrpt* (*CTA* 2.IV.8, 29, etc. = *KTU* 1.2.IV.8, 29) may be accepted with the majority of scholars to mean 'Rider of the clouds'. Ullendorff, followed by Brock,[85] however, comparing the epithet of Zeus νεφεληγερέτης or νεφεληγερέτα holds that Baal's epithet should rather be translated 'Gatherer of the clouds', but against this the following points may be made. First, as de Moor has pointed out,[86] the name Be-'-li-ra-kab-bi, 'Baal of the Chariot' is known from Sam'al, and the Egyptian king Rameses III compared himself with Baal when he drove out in his chariot. Secondly, the rare occasions when *rkb* is found in Ugaritic apart from the expression *rkb ʿrpt* show that 'ride' or 'mount' is the meaning, not 'gather'. Thus, in *CTA* 14.IV.165–7 (= *KTU* 1.14.IV.2–4) we read *wʿly lẓr. mgdl. rkb ṯkmn. ḥmt.* 'he went up to the top of the tower, mounted the shoulder of the wall', and we find almost the identical words in *CTA* 14.II.74–5 (= *KTU* 1.14.II.21–2). Thirdly, it is significant that in various Old Testament texts, including the one currently under consideration, the verb *rkb* 'to ride' or related nouns meaning 'chariot' are associated with the clouds, whether explicitly or implicitly (Deut. 33:26; Ps. 18:11,

85 E. Ullendorff, 'Ugaritic studies within their Semitic and Eastern Mediterranean setting', *BJRL* 46 (1963–4), pp. 243–4; S.P. Brock, '*Νεφεληγερέτα = rkb ʿrpt*', *VT* 18 (1968), pp. 395–7. For a study of both the expressions 'Rider of the clouds' and 'Gatherer of the clouds', see M. Weinfeld, 'Rider of the clouds' and 'Gatherer of the clouds"', *Journal of the Ancient Near Eastern Society of Columbia University* 5 (Gaster Festschrift, 1973), pp. 421–6. Weinfeld shows that both concepts are found in Greek mythology and Near Eastern mythology, in which latter, he claims, they both had their origin.

86 J.C. de Moor, *Seasonal Pattern*, p. 98.

ET 10 = 2 Sam. 22:11 [emended], 68:34, ET 33, 104:3; Is. 19:11, 66:15). Since the Israelites were far more intimately related to the Canaanites than the Greeks, the Old Testament parallels involving *rkb* are far more relevant in elucidating the meaning of Ugaritic *rkb ʿrpt* than an epithet of the Greek god Zeus. (Interestingly, where Canaanite and other near eastern traditions are appropriated to Zeus, in the conflict with the dragon Typhon, he is represented as *mounting* a winged horse, as we shall see presently.)

However, I do not think that the Ugaritic *rkb ʿrpt* 'Rider of the clouds' has its exact equivalent in the expression *rōḵēḇ bāʿᵃrāḇōṯ* used of Yahweh in Ps. 68:5 (ET 4), contrary to what is now a widely held opinion.[87] It is a sound principle that if a Hebrew word makes good sense in its normally attested meaning, it should be accepted, rather than creating an unnecessary *hapax legomenon*. Therefore, since *ʿᵃrāḇāh* in Hebrew means desert, it would seem wiser to translate *rōḵēḇ bāʿᵃrāḇōṯ* as 'Rider through the deserts' rather than 'Rider on the clouds'. Moreover, as A.R. Johnson rightly points out,[88] this rendering makes excellent sense in the context, which clearly reflects the Hebrew traditions of the Wandering and the Settlement. Thus, e.g., vv. 8–9 (ET 7–8), like Judges 5:4–5, recall Yahweh's marching through the wilderness from Sinai, and v. 7 (ET 6) refers to 'the wilderness' (*ṣᵉḥīḥāh*). The full phrase in Ps. 68:5 (ET 4) is *sōllū lārōḵēḇ bāʿᵃrāḇōṯ*, the verb *sll* which is used here being found elsewhere in the Old Testament with the

87 Earliest of all in perceiving a reference to the clouds in this expression, even before the discovery of the Ugaritic texts, was apparently Bishop J.W. Colenso. *The Pentateuch and Book of Joshua Critically Examined*, Part 7 (London, 1879), appendix 150, pp. 114–15, who compared Ps. 68:34 (ET 33) and wondered whether *bāʿᵃrāḇōṯ* should be emended to *bāʿāḇōṯ*. Similarly, S. Mowinckel, *Det Gamle Testamentes Salmebok. Første del: Salmene i oversettelse* (Kristiania, 1923), p. 94 rendered 'clouds', 'vielleicht in Anlehnung an Grätz's Vorschlag 'rabot' (S. Mowinckel, *Der achtundsechzigste Psalm*, Oslo, 1953, p. 27, n. 1). Since the discovery of the Ugaritic texts it has become very common to equate *rōḵēḇ bāʿᵃrāḇōṯ* with *rkb ʿrpt*. Some even emend the Hebrew text to *rōḵēḇ (bā)ʿᵃrāp̄ōṯ* in order to bring it even closer to the Ugaritic, e.g. H.L. Ginsberg. 'The Ugaritic texts and textual criticism', *JBL* 62 (1943), pp. 112–13, W.F. Albright, 'A catalogue of early Hebrew lyric poems (Psalm LXVIII)', *HUCA* 23, Part 1 (1950–1), pp. 12, 18, whilst others, e.g. G.R. Driver, *Canaanite Myths and Legends* (Edinburgh, 1956), p. 128, noting the interchange of Ugaritic *p* and Hebrew *b*, maintain that no emendation is necessary. The emendation of *ʿᵃrāḇōṯ* to *ʿᵃrāp̄ōṯ* was made even before the discovery of the Ugaritic texts by F.X. Wutz, *Die Psalmen, textkritisch untersucht* (Munich, 1925), p. 171, referring to Akkadian *eriptu, urpatu* 'clouds', with the secondary form *irbitu*.

88 A.R. Johnson, *Sacral Kingship in Ancient Israel* (2nd ed., Cardiff, 1967), p. 78, n. 6.

meaning 'to cast up a way (or highway)', and never with the meaning 'lift up a song', which is sometimes understood here. Now in Is. 40:3 we read of *bāʿᵃrāḇāh mᵉsillāh* 'a highway in the desert'. The fact that we here have *ʿᵃrāḇāh* 'desert' used in connection with a noun from the root *sll* adds support to the view that *rōḵēḇ baʿᵃrāḇōṯ* should be rendered 'Rider through the deserts'.[89] Deutero-Isaiah may have been dependent on this very psalm for the expression; if so, this would be in keeping with his dependence on other psalms concerned with Yahweh's kingship, which is generally conceded. Nevertheless, in spite of all that has been said, it is still likely that Yahweh is here conceived as riding on a cloud (cf. Ps. 68:34, ET 33), i.e. it is thinking of him as riding *on* a cloud *through* the deserts. It is also possible, perhaps even probable, that the expression *rōḵēḇ bāʿᵃrāḇōṯ* is a deliberate distortion of the epithet *rkb ʿrpt*.[90]

Returning to Ps. 104:3, we read that Yahweh 'rides on the wings of the wind' which implies that his cloud-chariot is drawn by winged horses symbolizing the wind. This concept is found in the context of the *Chaoskampf* not only in the almost identical phrase in Ps. 18:11 (ET 10) alluded to above, but also in Hab. 3:8,[91] where we read 'Was your wrath against the rivers, O Lord? Was your anger against the rivers, or your indignation against the sea, when you rode your horses, upon your chariot of victory?' (Admittedly no wings are mentioned here.) Very striking also is the fact that Zeus is represented as mounting a winged horse in his conflict with the dragon Typhon (Apollodorus, *The Library*, I.6.3), a conflict which certainly reflects Baal's struggle with the dragon, since part of it takes place at Mt Casius, i.e. Mt Zaphon, the mountain where Baal was in conflict with the dragon (Apollodorus, *The Library*, I.6.3; cf. *CTA* 3.IIID.44–IV.45 = *KTU* 1.3.III.47–IV.1). It may therefore be plausibly argued that this motif is ultimately derived from Baal mythology.[92] The very fact that Baal had

89 This point has also been made by A. Ohler, *Mythologische Elemente im Alten Testament* (Düsseldorf, 1969), p. 63.

90 This is noted as a possibility by J.C. de Moor, in *IDBS*, p. 169, but the same idea occurred to me independently.

91 Cf. below ch. 3, p. 107f.

92 That Mt Casius (Zaphon) was the location of the struggle between Zeus and Typhon is also supported by the evidence of Strabo (16.2.7) who reports the local tradition that the struggle between Zeus and Typhon took place near the river Orontes – a river, it should be noted, which flows into the Mediterranean just a little north of Mt Casius – and that this was carved out by Typhon, who

a cloud-chariot implies that it was drawn by horses, and I have elsewhere argued the Ugaritic texts may actually allude to them (in the word *mdl*).[93] Thus, in *CTA* 5.V.6b–11 (= *KTU* 1.5.V.6b–11) we read that the god Mot commanded Baal to descend into the underworld with his meteorological phenomena: *w'at. qḥ ʿrptk. rḥk. mdlk mṭrk. ʿmk. šbʿt ǵlmk. ṯmn. ḫnzrk ʿmk. pdry. bt. 'ar ʿmk. {t}ṭly. bt. rb*, 'And you, (take) your clouds, your wind, your chariot team, your rain, take with you your seven servitors (and) your eight boars, (take) Pidriya daughter of dew with you, and Ṭaliya daughter of showers with you.'

A further theophanic reference of ultimately Baalistic origin is to be found in v. 4, where Yahweh is addressed, 'you make . . . fire and flame your messengers'. From the context this can be inter-

disappeared in the earth at its source, whence the Orontes was originally called Typhon. Also, it may be noted that Herodotus (III.5) reports that Typhon was buried by the Sirbonian Sea, which in its turn was adjacent to the Egyptian Mt Casius (Baal Zaphon). Although the location of the struggle between Zeus and Typhon at Mt Casius clearly goes back ultimately to the Canaanite myth of Baal and the dragon, it seems that this motif was mediated not directly from Canaan but through the Hurrian–Hittite myth of Ullikummi, as this is now generally held to lie behind the Typhon myth. Cf. H.G. Güterbock, *Kumarbi* (Zurich and New York, 1946), pp. 100–15, and in S.N. Kramer (ed.), *Mythologies of the Ancient World* (New York, 1961), p. 172. In the Ullikummi myth it is at Mt Ḫazzi (i.e. Cassius) that the monster Ullikummi is seen rising out of the sea. For the text of Ullikummi, see H.G. Güterbock, 'The song of Ullikummi. Revised text of the Hittite version of a Hurrian myth', *JCS* 5 (1951), pp. 135–61, and *JCS* 6 (1952), pp. 8–42. There is also a translation by A. Goetze in *ANET*, pp. 121–5.

93 J. Day, 'Echoes of Baal's seven thunders and lightnings in Psalm xxix and Habakkuk iii 9 and the identity of the seraphim in Isaiah vi', *VT* 29 (1979), p. 147, n. 18. The meaning of *mdl* is, however, disputed. J.C. de Moor, 'Der *mdl* Baals in Ugaritischen', *ZAW* 78 (1966), pp. 69–71, suggests the translation 'thunderbolt', comparing Akkadian *mudulu* 'pole', but the fact that the Hebrew and Aramaic cognates have *ṭ* rather than *d* renders this improbable. G.R. Driver, *Canaanite myths and legends* (Edinburgh, 1956), p. 161, holds the word to mean 'bucket' (cf. Heb. *dᵉlī, Akk. madlū*). The translation 'chariot team' is admittedly uncertain, but rests on a comparison with the Ugaritic verb *mdl* meaning 'to harness' (cf. *CTA* 4.IV.9 and 19.II.52, 57 = *KTU* 1.4.IV.9 and 1.19.II.3, 8). Baal's *mdl* would then be 'that which is harnessed', i.e. his 'chariot team' drawing the clouds (cf. Hab. 3:8). Cf. J. Aistleitner's translation 'Gespann', *Wörterbuch der Ugaritischen Sprache* (ed. O. Eissfeldt, Berlin, 1967), no. 744a. Note that Hebrew and Ugaritic *ṣmd* are similarly employed both as a verb meaning 'to harness' and as a noun denoting the animals thus yoked together. One may compare the fact that in a hymn to Ishkur, Ishkur, who 'rides the storm' like Baal, is commissioned by Enlil: 'Let the seven winds be harnessed before you like a team, harness the winds before you' (*ANET*, p. 578). According to J.C. Greenfield, 'Ugaritic *mdl* and its cognates', *Biblica* 45 (1964), pp. 527–34, the verbal form *mdl* is to be understood as a metathesis of the root *lmd* 'to bind, tie', which is attested in Mishnaic Hebrew and Syriac.

preted only as referring to the personification of the lightning and is analogous to the seraphim (lit. 'burning ones') of Is. 6, who are likewise personifications of the lightning, as is indicated by the fact that 'the house was filled with smoke' when they called out and also that the foundations of the thresholds shook (cf. Is. 6:4), suggesting that they had thunder-like voices (cf. Ps. 18:8–9, ET 7–8). The personification of the lightning here is also ultimately of Baalistic origin: as I have argued elsewhere, Baal's 'seven lightnings . . . eight storehouses of thunder' (*RS* 24.245, 3b–4 = *KTU* 1.101.3b–4) appear to have been personified at Ugarit as 'seven servitors . . . eight boars' (*CTA* 5.V.8–9 = *KTU* 1.5.V.8–9). In view of the Baalistic nature of the imagery generally in this context such a background is far preferable to the view of P.D. Miller,[94] following D. Shenkel, who suggests that 'fire and flame' derive from the fiery messengers of Baal's opponent Yam in *CTA* 2.I.32–3 (= *KTU* 1.2.I.32–3) *'išt. 'ištm. y'itmr. ḥrb. lṭšt* [*lš*]*nhm.* '(Like) a fire, two fires they appeared, (like) a sharpened sword (was) their to[ngue].'

In view of the psalm's concern with creation and its allusion to the divine conflict with chaos, it is probable that its *Sitz im Leben* is to be sought in the Feast of Tabernacles, as P. Humbert[95] first argued, Mowinckel having surprisingly overlooked its appropriateness in this context. There is insufficient evidence, however, to support the view of P.C. Craigie[96] that this psalm was originally composed for that Feast of Tabernacles in which Solomon dedicated his temple (1 Kings 8). We cannot be so specific. Nevertheless, the psalm is to be regarded as pre-exilic in date, since, as will be noted below,[97] it seems to have been extensively used by the Priestly writer (probably 6th century B.C.) in the creation account in Gen. 1.

Finally, a word on the translation of v. 8 is called for. Some scholars, followed by the *RSV*, have understood the subject of this sentence to be not the waters, as in the above rendering, but rather the mountains and valleys: 'The mountains rose, the valleys sank down to the place which you appointed for them.' This, however, is

94 P.D. Miller, 'Fire in the mythology of Canaan and Israel', *CBQ* 27 (1965), pp. 258 n.9, 259.
95 P. Humbert, 'La relation de Genèse 1 et du Psaume 104 avec la liturgie du Nouvel-An israëlite', *RHPR* 15 (1935), pp. 1–27.
96 P.C. Craigie, 'The comparison of Hebrew poetry: Psalm 104 in the light of Egyptian and Ugaritic poetry', *Semitics* 4 (1974), pp. 10–21.
97 Cf. below, pp. 51–3.

unsatisfactory, since the next verse continues 'You set a boundary which they should not pass, that they might not return to cover the earth', where 'they', clearly the same as the subject of v. 8, can only refer to the waters alluded to in v. 6f.

Psalm 65:7–8 (ET 6–7)

V. 7 (6) By your strength[98] you established the mountains,
being girded with might,
V. 8 (7) you still the roaring of the seas,
the roaring of their waves,
the tumult of the peoples.

V. 7 (ET 6) makes it clear that the stilling of the seas is here related to the control of the waters in connection with the creation. At the same time, however, the last line of v. 8 shows that the waters are also thought of in historicized terms as the hostile nations, though some wish to delete this line. This is clearly a harvest psalm associated with the Feast of Tabernacles, and Yahweh's control of the cosmic waters means that he has control of the fertilizing rains which issue therefrom, to which vv. 10ff. (ET 9ff.) make reference. (Cf. Ps. 144:5–15; Isa. 27:1ff.; Hab. 3:8–19).

Psalm 93

V. 1 The Lord has become king, he is robed in majesty,
the Lord is robed, he is girded with strength.
Yea, the world is established, it shall not be moved.
V. 2 Your throne is established from of old,
you are from everlasting.
V. 3 The floods have lifted up, O Lord,
the floods have lifted up their voice,
the floods lift up their roaring.
V. 4 Mightier than the thunders of many waters,
mightier than the waves of the sea,[99]
the Lord on high is mighty.
V. 5 Your decrees are very sure,
holiness befits your house,
O Lord, for evermore.

In this Enthronement Psalm Yahweh's victory over the chaotic waters is clearly associated with his kingship. At the same time it seems clear that it relates to the time of creation, since v. 2 declares, 'Your throne is established from of old.' This is in keeping with the

98 Reading *b*^{e}*ḵōḥ*^{a}*ḵā* for MT *b*^{e}*ḵōḥō* with LXX^{B}, Old Latin^{G} and Vulgate.
99 Reading *'addīr mimmišb*^{e}*rē yām* for MT *'addīrīm mišb*^{e}*rē yām*.

theme of creation which permeates the Enthronement Psalms (cf. Ps. 95:4–5, 96:10, etc.). It is not impossible, however, that the thought is extended to that of Yahweh's rule over the nations, a motif also occurring in related psalms (cf. Ps. 96:10, 13, 98:9, 99:2).

The name given to the waters in v. 3, 'the floods' (Heb. *nᵉhārōṯ*) recalls Yam's title in the Ugaritic texts, 'Judge River' (*ṯpṭ nhr*). In the Ugaritic texts Baal's victory over Yam results in his enthronement as king (cf. *CTA* 2.IV.32 (= *KTU* 1.2.IV.32), *ym. lmt. bʿlm yml*[*k*] 'Yam is indeed dead! Baal shall be king!'). It is an interesting question whether in v. 1 (cf. Ps. 96:10, 97:1, 99:1, also 47:9, ET 8) *yahweh mālaḵ* should be understood in a comparable way as a declaration of enthronement resulting from his victory over the sea, 'Yahweh has become king', or whether it simply means 'Yahweh is king'.[100] Philologically either is possible. The analogy of declarations of enthronement applied to earthly kings has been adduced in support of the former, e.g. 2 Sam. 15:10, *mālaḵ 'aḇšālōm bᵉḥeḇrōn* 'Absalom has become king in Hebron' and 2 Kings 9:13, *mālaḵ yēhū'* 'Jehu has become king.' More directly relevant, the words *mālaḵ 'ᵉlōhīm* in Ps. 47:9 (ET 8) should probably be translated 'God has become king' rather than 'God is king', since the declaration of Ps. 47:7 (ET 6) that 'God has gone up with a shout, the Lord with the sound of a trumpet' is suggestive of an action rather than an eternal state. There is no evidence that the placing of the subject first in the statement *yahweh mālaḵ* involves a durative as opposed to the ingressive meaning of Ps. 47:9 (ET 8) as is sometimes claimed; 1 Kings 1:13, 18 for example contain both the declaration *mālaḵ 'ᵃḏōniyyāhū* and *'ᵃḏōnīyyāh mālaḵ* in otherwise almost identical sentences. The placing of the subject first simply gives added emphasis to it. The rendering 'Yahweh has become king' need in no way imply that he was not regarded as already king previously. It need mean no more than that his kingship was then being made properly effective over the world. We find the same thing in the New Testament: the book of Revelation can

100 The rendering 'Yahweh has become king' was strongly defended by S. Mowinckel, *Psalmenstudien* 2 (Kristiania, 1922), pp. 6ff., and *The Psalms in Israel's Worship* 2 (ET, Oxford, 1962), pp. 222–4, and has evoked much discussion, both favourable and unfavourable. Cf., for example, L. Koehler, 'Syntactica III. IV. *Jahwäh mālāk*., *VT* 3 (1953), pp. 188f.; J. Ridderbos, 'Jahwäh Malak', *VT* 4 (1954), pp. 87–9; D. Michel, 'Studien zu den sogenannten Thronbesteigungspsalmen', *VT* 6 (1956), pp. 40–68; É. Lipiński, *La royauté de Yahwé dans la poésie et le culte de l'ancien Israël* (Brussels, 1965), pp. 336–91; J. Ulrichsen, 'Jhwh mālak', *VT* 27 (1977), pp. 361–74.

declare to God that 'you have taken your great power and begun to reign (ἐβασίλευσας)' (Rev. 11:17, cf. v. 15) and 'Hallelujah! For the Lord our God the Almighty has become king (ἐβασίλευσεν)' (Rev. 19:6), thus echoing the LXX rendering of *mālaḵ* in the Enthronement Psalms (ἐβασίλευσεν), without in any way denying God's eternal kingship.

Some scholars wish to see a further point of contact with Ugaritic in the use of the expression *doḵyām* 'their roaring', employed in connection with the floods in v. 3, which has been compared with *dkym* in *CTA* 6.V.3 (= *KTU* 1.6.V.3). In *CTA* 6.V.1–3 (= *KTU* 1.6.V.1–3) we read *y'iḫd. b'l. bn. 'aṯrt rbm. ymḫṣ. bktp dkym. ymḫṣ. bṣmd.* Apart from *dkym*, the meaning is clear enough, 'Baal seized the sons of Asherah, the mighty ones he smote with a hatchet, the *dkym* he smote with an axe.' However, whatever *dkym* may mean precisely, the view that it means 'their roaring' analogous to Ps. 93:3 is certainly to be rejected, since, as H. Donner[101] has correctly pointed out, we should expect an ending in *-hm*, not *-ym*, if the third person plural suffix 'their' were really present in the word. Moreover, the parallelism with *rbm* 'mighty ones' in the preceding line, alluding to the sons of Asherah, makes it most probable that *dkym* is a further word describing them, possibly meaning 'the brilliant ones' (cf. Arabic *ḏakīy* 'brilliant'),[102] which might refer to their equation with the stars (*CTA* 10.I.3–4 = *KTU* 1.10.I.3–4) or 'the oppressors' (cf. Heb. *dākāh* 'to crush').[103] Accordingly, Hebrew *doḵyām* is to be distinguished from Ugaritic *dkym*.

Psalm 24 – probable implied battle with the sea

The final psalm to be considered in connection with the divine conflict with chaos at creation is Ps. 24. Unlike the previous psalms discussed, no actual battle with the sea is here described, however. Nevertheless, it is arguable that the psalm implies this background. This conclusion emerges from a correlation of vv.2 and 7–10. V. 2 declares of Yahweh, 'for he has founded it (*sc.* the earth) upon the seas, and established it upon the rivers'. The seas and rivers mentioned here must be the cosmic seas and rivers mentioned else-

101 H. Donner, 'Ugaritismen in der Psalmenforschung', *ZAW* 79 (1967), pp. 346–50.
102 Cf. W.F. Albright, 'The North-Canaanite Epic of 'Al'êyân Ba'al and Môt', *JPOS* 12 (1932), p. 203, n. 2.
103 Cf. É. Lipiński, *La royauté de Yahwé* (Brussels, 1965), p. 99.

where in the Old Testament in connection with the conflict with chaos. However, no actual battle is described. On the other hand, in vv. 7–10 we have the famous 'gate liturgy', repeated in vv. 7–8 and 9–10: 'Lift up your heads, O gates! and be lifted up, O ancient doors! that the King of glory may come in. Who is the King of glory? The Lord, strong and mighty, the Lord, mighty in battle!' Yahweh the King is here clearly returning victorious from a battle, probably being symbolized by the Ark. But we are not explicitly informed what the battle was. However, in the light of v. 2 it is natural to suppose that it was with the waters of chaos at the time of creation, just as in the psalms discussed above.[104]

Chaoskampf in the book of Job

Job 26:5–14

V. 5 The shades below[105] tremble,
the waters and their inhabitants.
V. 6 Sheol is naked before him,
Abaddon has no covering.
V. 7 He stretched out Zaphon[106] over the void,
and hanged the earth upon nothing.
V. 8 He binds up the waters in his clouds,
and the clouds do not burst open under them.
V. 9 He covers the face of the full moon,[107]
and spreads over it his cloud.
V. 10 He marked out a circle on the face of the waters,
at the boundary of light and darkness.
V. 11 The pillars of heaven shook,
and were astounded at his roar.
V. 12 By his power he stilled the sea,
and by his understanding he smote Rahab.
V. 13 By his wind the heavens were made fair,
his hand pierced the twisting serpent.

104 Cf. T.N.D. Mettinger, *The Dethronement of Sabaoth* (Lund, 1982), pp. 70–1.
105 *Mittaḥaṯ* is transferred from the beginning of the second line to the end of the first line.
106 Zaphon here seems to allude to the firmament of heaven comparable to Is. 14:13. This is consonant with the fact that the verb *nṭh* used here in connection with Zaphon is elsewhere used of the stretching out of the heavens, often in parallelism with the earth (cf. Is. 40:22, 42:5, 44:24, 45:12, 51:13; Jer. 10:12, 51:15; Zech. 12:1; without parallelism with the earth in Ps. 104:2; Job 9:8).
107 Reading *kēseh* 'full moon' for MT *kissēh* 'throne'. A reference to the full moon is far preferable to one to a throne in the present context in which God's power over creation is being extolled.

V. 14 Lo, these are but the outskirts of his ways;
and how small a whisper do we hear of him.
But the thunder of his power who can understand?

This chapter, like Job 9:5ff. and 38ff. is probably based on a psalm extolling Yahweh's work in creation, as Westermann[108] has argued. Like these other texts, moreover, the allusion to Yahweh's victory over the chaos monster comes at the very end of the passage lauding his power over creation, cf. Job 9:13, 40:15–41:26 (ET 40:15–41:34), whereas in Ps. 74:13f. and 89:10f. (ET 9f.) it comes first. In view of the evident connection of the *Chaoskampf* here with the creation, it is probable that, as in Ps. 74 and 89, here too we have an allusion to Yahweh's victory at the time of creation. This seems more probable than the view that vv. 12–13 refer to Yahweh's continuous victory over chaos, whilst the views of older scholars such as Hertlein[109] that Rahab denoted Egypt or Heidel[110] that it is 'a real aquatic creature of some kind' have now been generally given up. It would appear that 'the twisting serpent' (v. 13) is identical with Rahab (v. 12). Since 'the twisting serpent' is another name of Leviathan (cf. Is. 27:1, 'Leviathan the twisting serpent, Leviathan the crooked serpent'), it follows that Rahab is probably an alternative name for Leviathan.

Possibly we are to conclude from v. 13a, 'By his wind the heavens were made fair', that the dragon is in the sky, even though the parallelism of Rahab and the sea in v. 12 makes it clear that Rahab is a sea monster. Cf. *KTU* 1.83.3–10 (= *UT* 1003.3–10), where the dragon in the sea reaches up into heaven before being defeated by Anat. However, whether or not this is the case, in Job 26 the association of the dragon with darkness is here clear. Cf. Gen. 1:2, where likewise we have an allusion to Yahweh's wind hovering over the darkness, which is associated with the chaotic watery deep. Also to be compared is Job 3:8 (see below), where it is implied that the rousing up of Leviathan brings darkness in its train. Also cf. *CTA* 6.VI.46ff. (= *KTU* 1.6.VI.47ff.), where it is clear that the dragon is an enemy of the sun.

Job 9:5–14

V. 5 He who removes mountains, and they know it not,
when he overturns them in his anger;

108 C. Westermann, *Der Aufbau des Buches Hiob* (Tübingen, 1956), pp. 58ff.
109 E. Hertlein, 'Rahab', *ZAW* 38 (1919–20), p. 135.
110 A. Heidel, *The Babylonian Genesis* (2nd ed., Chicago and London, 1951), p. 107.

V. 6 who shakes the earth out of its place,
and its pillars tremble;
V. 7 who commands the sun, and it does not rise;
who seals up the stars;
V. 8 who alone stretched out the heavens,
and trampled the waves of the sea;
V. 9 who made the Bear and Orion,
the Pleiades and the chambers of the south;
V. 10 who does great things beyond understanding,
and marvellous things without number.
V. 11 Lo, he passes me by, and I see him not;
he moves on, but I do not perceive him.
V. 12 Behold, he snatches away; who can hinder him?
Who will say to him, 'What are you doing?'
V. 13 God will not turn back his anger;
beneath him bowed the helpers of Rahab.
V. 14 How then can I answer him,
choosing my words with him?

Like the preceding passage discussed this one too is taken from a psalm of praise to Yahweh as creator. Indeed, parts of this particular psalm recur in the doxologies of the book of Amos – cf. Job 9:8, 9 with Amos 4:13, 5:9. The psalm in question would presumably have had its *Sitz im Leben* in the Autumn Festival.

In view of the fact that Rahab personifies the sea (e.g. Job 26:12), it is evident that Yahweh's trampling of the sea (v. 8) and defeat of Rahab's helpers (v. 13) allude to the same event. Although parts of the passage are concerned with Yahweh's continuous power over creation (cf. vv. 5ff.), vv. 8a and 9 are specifically concerned with the original act of the creation of the world, so that the reference in v. 8b, and with it v. 13, must allude to Yahweh's primaeval conflict with the powers of chaos. Furthermore, the view that Rahab here refers to Egypt[111] is now generally given up, for it is quite out of keeping with the context. For the same reason we must reject the suggestion of A. Guillaume[112] that Job 9:13 may contain a thinly veiled allusion to Nabonidus and his allies – a view in any case bound up with Guillaume's claims for a sixth century B.C. Arabian background for the book, which have not found favour with other scholars.

111 A. Heidel, *op. cit.*, p. 105. S.I.L. Norin, *op. cit.*, p. 73 also regards this as possible.
112 A. Guillaume, *Studies in the book of Job* (Leiden, 1968), p. 88.

The reference to the bowing low of Rahab's helpers is particularly interesting. Enuma elish tablet IV, line 107 is usually quoted as a parallel, where the gods who were Tiamat's allies are referred to as 'her helpers'. There can be no doubt that Rahab's helpers are other sea monsters, 'the dragons' mentioned parallel to Leviathan in Ps. 74:13–14 and the 'enemies' referred to alongside Rahab in Ps. 89:11 (ET 10). The book of Job itself describes Behemoth in 40:15–24 before going on to depict Leviathan (probably = Rahab), and this is certainly one of the helpers: indeed, in the next chapter it will be argued that he has his prototype in the oxlike creature of the sea called Arš or *ʿgl ʾil ʿtk* in *CTA* 3.IIID.40–1 (= *KTU* 1.3.43–4) and 6.VI.50 (= *KTU* 1.6.VI.51), where he is in both cases mentioned alongside Leviathan or the dragon, whilst the former passage mentions a whole series of monsters who were defeated by Anat, there being besides the two just mentioned also Yam and *klbt. ʾilm. ʾišt* 'El's bitch the Fire', also called *bt. ʾil. ḏbb* 'El's daughter the Flame'. Here we clearly have authentic Ugaritic testimony to 'Rahab's helpers'. A number of scholars prefer, however, to render *ʿōzᵉrē rāhaḇ* as 'Rahab's cohorts', seeing here a word cognate with Ugaritic *ǵzr* 'hero',[113] but, although it is of little moment to the primary issue discussed above, it is safer to retain the more certainly attested meaning 'helpers', paralleling the allusion to Tiamat's 'helpers' in Enuma elish. One may also note the reference to *ʾil. tʿḏr. bʿl* 'the helper-gods of Baal' in *Ugaritica V*.9.8 *RS* 24.643, line 8 = *KTU* 1.148.8) (also to be restored in *CTA* 29, rev. 4 = *KTU* 1.47.26). That *ʾil* is here plural is confirmed by its presence in the Akkadian Ugaritic Pantheon list as *ilanu*^{M} *til-la-at* ^{d}*adad*.

Another interesting point is the reason given for the specific mention of God's overcoming of Rahab's helpers in this context: Job declares, 'God will not turn back his anger; beneath him bowed the helpers of Rahab. How much less can I answer him, choosing my words with him.' The point is, therefore, that since the mighty sea monster and its associates were defeated by God, how much less can he, the wretched Job, hope to contend with him! Earlier in the chapter (vv. 2–4) Job has already pointed out the futility of contending with God, and this is set in the context of

113 M.H. Pope, *Job* (3rd ed., New York, 1973), p. 68. Cf. the full discussion in P.D. Miller, 'Ugaritic ǴZR and Hebrew ʿZR II', *UF* 2 (1970), pp. 159–75, esp. p. 164.

God's might as displayed in nature (vv. 5ff.). It does not appear to have been noted that we find the very same sequence of ideas in Job 38–42:6: first God's might as displayed in nature (38–9), then the implication that God has overcome the monsters Behemoth and Leviathan (= Rahab) (40:15–41:26, ET 41:34), and finally the consequence that Job is in no position to contend with God (42:1–6). As will be argued in the next chapter,[114] this parallelism provides new evidence both for the authenticity of the second divine speech describing Behemoth and Leviathan and also for the mythological identity of these creatures.

With regard to Job 9:8, some scholars, beginning with W.F. Albright,[115] see a more personal reference to the dragon here also, rendering '... and trampled the back of Yam' instead of 'and trampled the waves of the sea', by understanding *bomoṯē* as 'back' (cf. Ugaritic *bmt*), a meaning probably attested in Deut. 33:29, and *yām* as the name Yam. If the meaning really were 'back', however, one would rather expect the singular form to be used in connection with the singular personified Yam rather than the plural *bomoṯē*, and the occurrence of the parallel expression *weḏāraḵ ʿal-bomoṯē ʾāreṣ* 'and he will tread upon the high places of the earth' (Mic. 1:3; cf. Amos 4:13; Is. 58:14) would appear to support the meaning 'the heights of the sea' in Job 9:8, i.e. the waves. The raising high of the sea is attested elsewhere in the context of Yahweh's conflict with the sea, cf. Ps. 93:3f.

Job 38:8–11
V. 8 Who shut in[116] the sea with doors,
when it burst forth from the womb;
V. 9 When I made clouds its garment,
and heavy clouds its swaddling band,
V. 10 and shut[117] it within its bounds,[118]
and set bars and doors,

114 Cf. below, p. 70f.

115 W.F. Albright, review of G. Hölscher's *Das Buch Hiob*, *JBL* 57 (1938), p. 227, and 'The Psalm of Habakkuk', in H.H. Rowley (ed.), *Studies in Old Testament Prophecy* (Edinburgh, 1950), p. 18; M.H. Pope, *op. cit.*, p. 70; M.K. Wakeman, *God's Battle with the Monster* (Leiden, 1973), pp. 118, 121 n. 3.

116 Reading *mī sāḵ* for MT *wayyāseḵ*, following most commentators.

117 MT reads *wāʾešbōr* 'and I broke', which does not fit the context. The most attractive view is to hold that the text originally read *wāʾeskōr* 'and I shut'. This verb is used in Gen. 8:2 of the shutting in of the waters at the end of the flood.

118 Reading *ḥuqqō* for MT *ḥuqqī*.

V. 11 and said, 'Thus far shall you come, and no further,
and here your proud waves shall cease?'[119]

This is the third passage in Job alluding to Yahweh's control of the sea at the time of creation which appears to be based on a creation psalm. It differs from the other passages in Job considered in this section in that there is no specific reference to the dragon. The reference to 'your proud waves' (*g*^{e}*'ōn gallekā̠*) hints at the personal conflict existing between the sea and Yahweh and the allusion to the sea as a new-born child with swaddling clothes in vv. 8b–9 also hints at the personification of the sea contained in the underlying myth.

If the allusion in v. 7 to the time at creation 'when the morning stars sang together, and all the sons of God shouted for joy' belongs to the same circle of mythical ideas as vv. 8–11 (cf. too the reference to the morning/dawn in v. 12), then we have a further allusion to the idea that the unruly waters were subdued at dawn, a notion attested elsewhere in Ps. 46:6 (ET 5) and Is. 17:12–14.

Job 7:12
Am I the sea or the dragon,
that you set a guard over me?

We have here a reference to two powers, the sea or Yam (*yām*) and the dragon (*tannīn*), i.e. Leviathan. Job complains that God is unfairly treating him like them, giving him no respite, the thought being paralleled in Ps. 44:19–20 (ET 18–19), where the psalmist complains to God, 'Our heart has not turned back, nor have our steps departed from your way, that you should have crushed us instead of the dragon, and covered us with deep darkness.' (For the translation 'instead of the dragon' here, see discussion below.)[120]

With regard to the motif of the imprisoning of the sea and dragon, it is interesting to note that we have similar language used in Enuma elish, tablet IV, lines 110ff. of Marduk's treatment of Tiamat and her allies who are explicitly said to have been imprisoned by Marduk. One may presume that the Canaanite myth used similar language, since the expressions used, *yām* and *tannīn*, indicate that we are in the realm of Canaanite mythology as elsewhere with the Old Testament's dragon and sea conflict allusions; in *CTA* 2.IV.29–30 (= *KTU* 1.2.IV.29–30) Yam is spoken of as the

119 Reading *yīšbōṯ* (or *yiššābēṯ*) *g*^{e}*'ōn* for MT *yāšīṯ big*^{e}*'ōn*.
120 Cf. below, Ch. 3, p. 112f.

captive of Baal and Astarte – *kšbyn. zb[l. ym. k?]šbyn. ṯpṭ. nhr* 'For Prince [Yam] is our captive, [for?] Judge River is our captive', but this is clearly no permanent fate, since Yam is immediately afterwards killed (cf. lines 30–4). There are various other Old Testament passages which may be compared, e.g. Job 38:8, 10–11, discussed above,[121] where God shuts in the unruly sea with doors and bars at the time of creation and so contains them, and Jer. 5:22b, to be discussed below,[122] where the sand serves as a perpetual barrier which the sea cannot pass. M.J. Dahood[123] has proposed that *mišmār* in this verse should be rendered by 'muzzle' rather than 'guard', because the Ugaritic verb *šbm*, which has been widely held to mean 'to muzzle', is applied to the dragon (*tnn*) in *CTA* 3.IIID.37 (= *KTU* 1.3.III.40) (the noun *šbm* being similarly applied in *KTU* 1.83.8 (*UT* 1003.8) and also, according to Dahood, in Ps. 68:23 (ET 22), though on this latter see below Chapter 3.[124] J. Barr[125] has recently shown, however, that the Arabic evidence which has usually been accepted to justify the meaning 'to muzzle' for Ugaritic *šbm* is very weak, and so there are no grounds for believing that *mišmār* in Job 7:12 bears this specific meaning.

There is admittedly nothing in the context of this verse to lead one to assume that the sea and dragon were specifically imprisoned at the time of the creation, but as this is the clear time reference of the comparable mythological passages in Job discussed above, and no other time is plausible, this is surely the case here also.

Job 3:8
Let those curse it who curse the day,
who are skilled in rousing up Leviathan.

These words form part of a passage (Job 3:1ff.) in which the wretched Job is lamenting the day of his birth (cf. Jer. 20:14ff.) and wishing it to be covered with darkness. The rousing up of Leviathan ought therefore to be associated with darkness. That this is in fact the case is supported by another passage in Job in 26:13, where we read in connection with the creation, 'By his wind the heavens were made *fair*; his hand pierced the twisting serpent', and also by Gen. 1:2 where, prior to the creation of light 'darkness was

121 Cf. above, p. 42f.
122 Cf. below, p. 57.
123 M.J. Dahood, 'Mišmār "muzzle" in Job 7 12', *JBL* 80 (1961), pp. 270–1.
124 Pp. 113–19.
125 Cf. above, p. 14, n.32.

upon the face of the deep'. That the connection between Leviathan and darkness goes back to Canaanite mythology may be surmised from the Ugaritic texts, where in *CTA* 6.VI.44ff. (= *KTU* 1.6.VI.45ff.) we read that Kothar-and-Ḫasis, who it is hoped will defeat the dragon (*tnn* = Leviathan), was also the friend of the sun-goddess Shapash, who is apparently threatened by the dragon.

44 špš	Shapash,
45 rp'im. tḥtk[126]	the shades are under you;
46 špš. tḥtk. 'ilnym	Shapash, the ghosts are under you;
47 ʿdk. 'ilm. hn. mtm	the gods (come) to you, behold! the dead
48 ʿdk. kṯrm. ḫbrk	(come) to you. Kothar is your companion
49 wḫss. dʿtk	and Ḫasis your friend.
50 bym. 'arš. wtnn	In the sea are Arš and dragon;
51 kṯr. wḫss. yd	May Kothar-and-Ḫasis drive (them) away,
52 ytr. kṯr. wḫss	May Kothar-and-Ḫasis cut (them) off.

The dragon and the sun, one may deduce from this passage, were enemies, and accordingly the dragon, as the enemy of the light, would have been allied to darkness. Kaiser[127] is therefore mistaken in saying that we have no evidence from the Ugaritic texts to decide whether Leviathan was an enemy of the light or whether this rather goes back to Egyptian influence. The context of this passage, coming as it does at the very end of the Baal cycle, as was noted earlier, is very likely that of the New Year's Eve, corresponding also to the period immediately before the creation which would have occurred at the time of the very first New Year.[128] This Ugaritic passage therefore offers a remarkable parallel to Job 3:8

126 If this is the correct translation, *rp'im*, which is in the oblique case, is an error for *rp'um*, or the oblique case is used for the nominative. The same may be the case in *CTA* 21.A.9 (= *KTU* 1.21.9). Alternatively, assuming *rp'im* to be correct, we might render 'Shapash, you rule (√*ḥtk*) the shades, Shapash, you rule the ghosts'. However, that *tḥt* is here the preposition meaning 'under' rather than part of a verb √*ḥtk* is supported by the text *KTU* 1.161.19–26, where, in a similar underworld context, Shapash is told to go under (*tḥt*) various dead individuals, including *rp'im. qd*[*mym*](?) 'the an[cient] (?) shades'. I cite the passage: *ʿln. špš. tṣḥ 'aṯr.* [*b*]*'lk. l. ks⟨'i⟩h 'aṯr bʿlk. 'arṣ. rd. 'arṣ rd. w. špl. ʿpr. tḥt sdn. w. rdn. tḥt. ṯr ʿ11mn. tḥt. rp'im. qd*[*mym*] (?) *tḥt. ʿmṯtmr. mlk tḥt* (!). *'u. nq*[*md*]. *mlk*, which may be translated 'Unto Shapash you must cry. "After your lord from his throne, after your lord descend to the earth and go down to the dust, under Sdn-w-rdn, under Ṯr ʿ11mn, under the an[cient] (?) shades, under ʿAmiṯtamar, the king, under also Niq[mad], the king."'

127 O. Kaiser, *Die mythische Bedeutung des Meeres* (*BZAW* 78, 1959), p. 151.

128 Cf. J.C. de Moor, *Seasonal Pattern*, p. 244, and *New Year With Canaanites and Israelites* 1 (Kampen, 1972), pp. 5–6.

with its desire for the return of the pre-creation darkness associated with Leviathan, although it is in fact only rarely noted in this connection.[129] The implicit association of Job 3:8 with the creation justifies its consideration at the present point of this monograph. At the same time, however, it is probable that the occurrence of eclipses was regarded as an example of Leviathan's continuing to swallow up the sun – such a connection between dragons and eclipses is widespread throughout the world and is often cited in relation to this verse[130] – and that this is what 'those who curse the day' were believed to be able to bring about.

In view of the fact that the MT of Job 3:8 thus makes good sense as it stands, alluding to Job's desire for the pre-creation darkness associated with Leviathan to cover the day of his birth, it seems wise not to emend the text. Many scholars, however, taking up a suggestion first made by G. Schmidt and publicized by Gunkel,[131] wish to emend *yōm* 'day' to *yām* 'the sea' and to see a parallel to the sea monster Leviathan of the following line – 'Let those curse it who curse the sea (Yam), who are skilled in rousing up Leviathan.' If, however, 'the sea' and Leviathan are here to be regarded as parallel to one another, one should expect the two lines to express parallel thoughts; but this is clearly not the case, since whereas, on this view, the sea is cursed, Leviathan (with his darkness) is roused up, which are surely opposing, not parallel thoughts. The context indicates that Job is wishing that things considered undesirable should take place; whilst the rousing up of Leviathan is consonant with this, the cursing of Yam is not, but would rather be considered

129 It is noted by T.H. Gaster, *Myth, Legend and Custom in the Old Testament* (London, 1969), p. 788, and M. Fishbane, 'Jeremiah IV 23–26 and Job III 3–13: a recovered use of the creation pattern', *VT* 21 (1971), p. 159, but the latter mistakenly says that the Ugaritic text mentions the goddess Asherah: it should, of course, be Shapash.

130 On the widespread belief that eclipses are caused by a dragon swallowing up the sun, cf. T.H. Gaster, *Thespis* (2nd ed., New York, 1966), pp. 228–9.

131 Cf. H. Gunkel, *Schöpfung und Chaos*, p. 59, n. 1; O. Eissfeldt, 'Gott und das Meer', in *Studia Orientalia Ioanni Pedersen septuagenario dicata* (Copenhagen, 1953), p. 78f.; H.H. Rowley, *Job* (London, 1970), p. 44 seems to favour this view; M.H. Pope, *Job* (3rd ed., New York, 1973), pp. 26, 30; M.K. Wakeman, *God's Battle with the Monster* (Leiden, 1973), p. 63. M.J. Dahood, 'Northwest Semitic texts and textual criticism of the Hebrew Bible', in C. Brekelmans (ed.), *Questions disputées d'Ancien Testament* (Louvain, 1974), pp. 24f. also sees a reference to the sea here, though without emending *yōm* to *yām*, since he regards the former here as a Phoenician spelling of the latter. Cf. S.I.L. Norin, *op. cit.*, p. 63.

a good thing.[132] No such problem attaches to the MT reading *yōm* 'day', for the cursing of the day no less than the rousing up of Leviathan is something generally considered undesirable, and both bring darkness in their train. The MT is therefore to be retained; at the same time, however, it is quite possible, as Barr[133] has suggested, that at some stage in the *prehistory* of this verse, there was a reference to Yam parallel to Leviathan.[134]

G.R. Driver[135] has put forward a view, followed, as often, by the *NEB*, in which *yōm* is emended to *yām*, but which is not open to the objection that contradictory things are done to the sea and Leviathan. His rendering is, 'Cursed be it by those whose magic binds even the monster of the deep, who are ready to tame Leviathan himself with spells.' However, Driver gains this parallelism of thought only by translating the verb *ʿōrēr* as 'to tame' on the basis of an alleged Arabic cognate *ʿāra(y)* II 'reviled', VI 'abused one another', Ethiopic *taʿayyara* 'reviled', instead of the usual rendering 'to rouse up'. Driver's translation must surely be rejected since it means introducing a meaning for *ʿōrēr* which is nowhere else attested for this root (*ʿīr* 'reviling', which Driver finds in Hos. 11 : 9 being equally dubious), when the usual meaning makes good sense. Moreover, Driver's overall rendering has the disadvantage compared with that favoured here in that what is done to 'the monster of the deep' and Leviathan would be considered desirable rather than undesirable and is therefore less apposite to the context, besides involving the emendation of MT *yōm* to *yām*.

132 The few scholars making this important point include É. Dhorme, *Le livre de Job* (Paris, 1926), p. 27 (ET *A Commentary on the Book of Job*, London, 1967, p. 29); L. Grabbe, *Comparative Philology and the Text of Job* (Missoula, Mt, 1977), pp. 36–7; R. Gordis, *The Book of Job* (New York, 1978), pp. 34–5. Other scholars who retain the MT, but without noting this point, include A. Weiser, *Das Buch Hiob* (2nd ed., Göttingen, 1956), p. 38; O. Kaiser, *Die mythische Bedeutung des Meeres* (*BZAW* 78, 1959), p. 145; J. Barr, 'Philology and Exegesis', in C. Brekelmans (ed.), *Questions disputées d'Ancien Testament* (Louvain, 1974), p. 57.

133 J. Barr, *loc. cit.*

134 Cf. J.A. Montgomery, *Aramaic Incantation Texts from Nippur* (Philadelphia, Pa., 1913), p. 121, no. 2, lines 3–4. 'I will lay a spell upon you, the spell of the Sea and the spell of the monster Leviathan.'

135 G.R. Driver, 'Problems in the Hebrew text of Job', *SVT* 3 (1955), p. 72. Following on from Driver's proposal J.V. Kinnier Wilson, 'Hebrew and Akkadian philological notes', *JSS* 7 (1962), pp. 181–3 argued for the existence of an Akkadian verb *āru* or *awāru* also meaning 'revile'.

Next, the view of E. Ullendorff[136] may be noted, who translates the verse as follows: 'Let the light-rays of the day pierce it (i.e. the night) apt even to rouse Leviathan.' He arrives at this translation by understanding *yiqq^{e}ḇūhū* as deriving from the verb *nqb* 'to pierce' instead of *qbb* 'to curse' and by taking *'ōr^{e}rē* as plural construct of *'ōr* 'light' (he compares *har^{a}rē* from *har*) instead of from the verb *'rr* 'to curse'. This view, however, is to be rejected, since it involves postulating an otherwise unattested plural construct from *'ōr^{e}rē* for which *har^{a}rē* cannot be quoted in support, since *har* and *'ōr* are derived from different kinds of root (*hrr* and *'wr*). Also it is forced to deny the meaning 'curse' to *yiqq^{e}ḇūhū* and *'ōr^{e}rē* when both are mentioned in such close proximity. Furthermore, Ullendorff's view that the night is to become light contradicts v. 6, which states that it is to become dark. Ullendorff here claims that v. 6 must be corrupt, since one can hardly wish the night to become dark, as it is that already. He therefore holds that v. 6 originally referred to the day, 'that night' having come in from v. 7. This, however, is to forget that the night has the moon and stars as illuminations and it is surely these which are hoped to become dark at night; support for this may be found in v. 9 where reference is made to the stars, 'Let the stars of its dawn be dark . . .' Furthermore, if the wish for light at night were really expressed here, it would be surprising that this chapter makes no other reference to it, whereas the darkness, which on Ullendorff's view constitutes only half the desired misfortune, is mentioned many times (e.g., vv. 4, 5, 6, 9, 20, 23).

I conclude, therefore, that Job 3:8 makes excellent sense if we give every word its most natural meaning and do not resort to emendation, and that it alludes to Job's desire for the return of the pre-creation darkness associated with the chaos monster Leviathan. Further, a not widely recognized passage at the end of the Baal cycle implying that the dragon was the enemy of the sun on the eve of the New Year (creation) provides the most relevant extra-biblical illumination of the background of this verse.

Job 40:15–41:26 (*ET 34*)

A detailed consideration of the interpretation of the passages concerning Behemoth and Leviathan in this section will be deferred to the next chapter.[137]

136 E. Ullendorff, 'Job III 8', *VT* 11 (1961), pp. 350–1.
137 Cf. below, pp. 62–72, 75–84.

The importance of the Chaoskampf motif in Job

The number of allusions to the *Chaoskampf* in the book of Job is most striking – they are found in Job 3:8, 7:12, 9:8, 13, 26:12f., 38:8–11 and 40:15–41:26 (ET 34). How are we to account for this fact ? There appear to me to be two main reasons. First, the creation theme is prominent in the book, as is fitting in a work of Wisdom, the theology of which, as Zimmerli has emphasized, is based on creation,[138] and the dragon motif is bound up with the creation, especially in the cultic psalms on which the book of Job has drawn. Secondly, the imagery is employed because the conflict between the dragon and God provided an apt parallel to the book's theme of Job's conflict with God. This latter reason, to which insufficient attention has previously been paid, is the case in Job 7:12 and 9:13–14 and also provides the motivation for the description of Behemoth and Leviathan (Job 40:15–41:26, ET 34) to be considered in the next chapter.

Yahweh's control of the cosmic waters as simply a job of work

There remain to be considered a few Old Testament passages in which Yahweh's control of the cosmic waters at the time of creation is alluded to but where all thought of conflict has disappeared and in which there is no longer a trace of personality within the waters. That is to say, a process of demythologization has taken place and Yahweh's control of the waters has simply become a job of work. The most prominent example of this is in the well-known account of creation in Genesis 1.

Genesis 1:2, 6–10

V. 2 The earth was without form and void, and darkness was upon the face of the deep; and the wind of God was hovering over the face of the waters.

V. 6 And God said, 'Let there be a firmament in the midst of the waters, and let it separate the waters from the waters.'

V. 7 And God made the firmament and separated the waters which were under the firmament from the waters which were above the firmament. And it was so.

138 W. Zimmerli, 'Ort und Grenze der Weisheit im Rahmen der alttestamentlichen Theologie', in *Les sagesses du Proche-Orient ancien* (Paris, 1963), p. 123 (ET 'The Place and Limit of the Wisdom in the framework of the Old Testament Theology', *SJT* 17, 1964, p. 148.)

V. 8 And God called the firmament Heaven. And there was evening and there was morning, a second day.
V. 9 And God said, 'Let the waters under the heavens be gathered together in one place, and let the dry land appear.' And it was so.
V. 10 God called the dry land Earth, and the waters that were gathered together he called Seas. And God saw that it was good.

V. 2, which describes the primaeval state of the world consisting of the chaos waters, has evinced much discussion. The word translated 'deep', in Hebrew *t^{e}hōm*, is philogically related to the Akkadian Tiamat, the chaos monster whose name means 'sea', defeated by Marduk in connection with the creation of the world as narrated in Enuma elish. It should not be held, however, as Gunkel and many after him have maintained,[139] that Hebrew *t^{e}hōm* is actually derived from Akkadian Tiamat. If this were the case, as Heidel and others have noted,[140] we should expect the second Hebrew radical to be ', not *h*, and the word to have the feminine ending *h*. Rather, both *t^{e}hōm* and Tiamat are derived from a common Semitic root. Moreover, the word occurs similarly as *thm* or *thmt* in Ugaritic to denote the cosmic waters (cf. *Ugaritica V*.7.1 [*RS* 24.244, 1] = *KTU* 1.100.1, *CTA* 3.IIIC.22 = *KTU* 1.3.III.25, etc.). Again, 'the deep' in Gen. 1:2 is not a divine personality hostile to God; rather it is here used to denote the impersonal watery mass which covered the world before God brought about the created order. At the same time, however, it is probable that the fact that the word almost always lacks the definite article in the Old Testament is a remnant of the time long past when the term did denote a mythical personality. The quasi-personal nature of *t^{e}hōm* is most apparent in Gen. 49:25 and Deut. 33:13, where we read of 'the deep (*t^{e}hōm*) that crouches beneath', the verb *rbṣ* 'to crouch' employed here being commonly used elsewhere of animals, including the mythical dragon (Ezek. 29:3). In so far as *t^{e}hōm*'s mythological background is concerned this is not Babylonian at all, but rather Canaanite, as the Old Testament dragon passages

139 Cf. H. Gunkel, *Schöpfung und Chaos, passim*; R.W. Rogers, *The Religion of Babylonia and Assyria* (New York, 1908), p. 137; J. Morgenstern, 'The sources of the creation story – Genesis 1:1–2:4', *AJSL* 36 (1920), p. 197.

140 A. Heidel, *op. cit.*, pp. 99–100; W.H. Schmidt, *Die Schöpfungsgeschichte der Priesterschrift* (Neukirchen, 1964), p. 80, n. 5.

show, a point which some scholars still have not properly grasped.[141]

Moreover, it is improbable that the account of creation in Gen. 1 is dependent on Enuma elish at all. So far as the order of creation is concerned, the parallelism is not very remarkable: in both we have the common order of splitting of the sea (Tiamat/*t^ehōm*), creation of the firmament and the earth, luminaries and man. However, the differences are significant in that the account of creation in Enuma elish makes no reference to the creation of the vegetation, sea creatures or other animals, all of which are mentioned in Gen. 1, whilst Gen. 1 makes no reference to such things as the creation of the clouds and the mountains, which are explicitly alluded to in Enuma elish.

On the other hand, there are striking parallels between Gen. 1 and Ps. 104 in both the order of creation and with respect to verbal similarities, and these are of such a nature as to suggest the dependence of Gen. 1 on Ps. 104. With regard to the common order, this may be illustrated by the following table:

Ps. 104:1–4	Creation of heaven and earth	Cf. Gen. 1:1–5
Ps. 104:5–9	Waters pushed back	Cf. Gen. 1:6–10
Ps. 104:10–13	Waters put to beneficial use	Implicit in Gen. 1:6–10
Ps. 104:14–18	Creation of vegetation	Cf. Gen. 1:11–12
Ps. 104:19–23	Creation of luminaries	Cf. Gen. 1:14–18
Ps. 104:24–6	Creation of sea creatures	Cf. Gen. 1:20–2
Ps. 104:27–30	Creation of living creatures	Cf. Gen. 1:24–31

With regard to verbal similarities, it may be noted that a considerable amount of common vocabulary is shared between Gen. 1 and Ps. 104. Particularly striking are the expression *l^emō^{ca}ḏīm*, found in the Old Testament only in Ps. 104:19 and Gen. 1:14 (both in connection with the luminaries), and the form *ḥay^{e}ṯō*, found in Ps. 104:11, 12 and Gen. 1:24, and apart from the latter passage attested only in poetry in the Old Testament.

141 A point noted by W.G. Lambert, 'A new look at the Babylonian background of Genesis', *JTS* 16 n.s. (1965), p. 290. Cf. O. Eissfeldt, 'Genesis', in *IDB* 2, p. 375; G. von Rad, *Der erste Buch Mose, Genesis* (5th ed., Göttingen, 1958), p. 38 (ET, *Genesis*, London, 1961), p. 48; H.M. Orlinsky, 'The new Jewish version of the Torah', *JBL* 82 (1963), p. 256. My own personal contacts with scholars bear out that this is still the case.

The question is therefore raised: is Gen. 1 dependent on Ps. 104, is Ps. 104 dependent on Gen. 1, or are they both dependent on a common source? Although the last mentioned option is possible, the alternatives are more economical. Various points strongly suggest the priority of the psalm.[142] First, it is noteworthy that Ps. 104 is more mythological than Gen. 1: in Ps. 104:7 we actually have an allusion to the divine conflict with the sea, whereas in Gen. 1:6ff. God's control of the waters is simply a job of work, and in Ps. 104:26 we hear of God's creation of Leviathan, whereas Gen. 1:21 speaks in demythologized terms of 'great sea monsters'. Secondly, as was noted above, the form *ḥayᵉṯō*, which occurs in Ps. 104:11, 12 and Gen. 1:24, is attested in the Old Testament only in poetry apart from the latter passage. This suggests that Gen. 1 is dependent on a poetic passage, presumably Ps. 104.

The apparent dependence of Gen. 1 on Ps. 104 thus suggests the immediate derivation of the allusion to *tᵉhōm* 'the deep' in Gen. 1:2 – like other features, it derives from Ps. 104, for in v. 6 the chaos waters are specifically referred to by this name. This seems to have been overlooked in the general clamour to see evidence of dependence of Gen. 1 on Enuma elish, following Gunkel, or specific polemic against Enuma elish as others, such as A.S. Kapelrud and G.F. Hasel,[143] have supposed.

Moreover, the apparent dependence of Gen. 1 on Ps. 104 enables us to shed light on another disputed question in the interpretation of Gen. 1, namely the meaning of the expression *rūaḥ ʾᵉlōhīm* in Gen. 1:2. Does this refer to the Spirit of God or the wind of God or even a mighty wind?[144] It is significant that in Gen. 1:2 the piel participle of the verb *rḥp* 'to hover'[145] is used of the *rūaḥ*, and is

142 For a detailed presentation of the evidence see A. van der Voort, 'Genèse I, 1 à II, 4ᵃ et le Psaume 104', *RB* 58 (1951), pp. 321–47, *contra* P. Humbert, 'La relation de Genèse 1 et du Psaume 104 avec la liturgie du Nouvel-An israëlite', *RHPR* 15 (1935), pp. 1–27. Cf. too, B.W. Anderson, *Creation versus Chaos. The Reinterpretation of Mythical Symbolism in the Bible* (New York, 1967), pp. 91–2.

143 *Contra* J. Albertson, 'Genesis 1 and the Babylonian Creation Myth', *Thought* 37 (1962), pp. 226–44; A.S. Kapelrud, 'The mythological features in Genesis Chapter 1 and the author's intentions', *VT* 24 (1974), pp. 178–86; G.F. Hasel, 'The polemic nature of the Genesis cosmology', *EQ* 46 (1974), pp. 81–102.

144 On this question cf. H.M. Orlinsky, 'The plain meaning of ruᵃḥ in Gen. 1.2', *JQR* 48 (1957–8), pp. 174–82; S. Moscati, 'The wind in biblical and Phoenician cosmogony', *JBL* 66 (1947), pp. 305–10; O. Eissfeldt, 'Das Chaos in der biblischen und in der phönizischen Kosmogonie', *Kleine Schriften* 2 (Tübingen, 1963), pp. 258–62; W.H. Schmidt, *op. cit.*, pp. 81–4.

employed elsewhere in Bibilical Hebrew and Ugaritic particularly of birds (cf. Deut. 32:11; *CTA* 18.IV.20, 21, 31, 32 = *KTU* 1.18.IV.20, 21, 31, 32). In view of the evidence of the dependence of Gen. 1 on Ps. 104 noted above, it is therefore striking that Ps. 104 : 3 (cf. Ps. 18:11, ET 10 = 2 Sam. 22:11, emended) actually alludes to Yahweh's coming swiftly on the *wings* of the wind (*rūaḥ*), suggestive of a bird, at the time of the confinement of the unruly waters. Accordingly, we are to understand that Gen. 1:2 has taken up a tradition concerning Yahweh's driving of the waters off the earth by his wind. This corresponds to Job 26:13, 'By his wind the heavens were made fair, his hand pierced the twisting serpent', Dan. 7:2, where 'the four winds of heaven were stirring up the great sea' prior to the *Chaoskampf*, and Gen. 8:1, where in order to bring an end to the flood, which represented a kind of re-emergence of the chaos waters, 'God made a wind blow over the earth, and the waters subsided.' The wind of Gen. 1:2 derives ultimately from the wind of Baal employed against the sea monster. *CTA* 5.V.7 (= *KTU* 1.5.V.7) cites the wind as one of the things Baal is commanded by Mot to take with him into the underworld, with which one may compare the winds used by Marduk against Tiamat in Enuma elish (cf. IV.32, 42ff., 96–9, 132).)

Accordingly, unless the Priestly writer intended to alter the meaning of his underlying source (in which case he might have been more specific), Gen. 1:2 refers to the wind and not the Spirit of God, a meaning already detected by the Targums and followed by Saadia, Ibn Ezra and Rashban. That we should understand *rūaḥ 'ᵉlōhīm* as referrring to 'the wind of God' and not 'a mighty wind', the latter interpreting *'ᵉlōhīm* as a superlative use of the divine name and followed by some scholars, including the *NEB*, is supported by the fact that *'ᵉlōhīm* denotes God as the subject of both the preceding and following verses, which makes it difficult to deny all thought of divinity here. Furthermore, if a simple superlative were intended, without divine overtones, this could be expressed less ambiguously by *rūaḥ śᵉʿārāh*, *rūaḥ śᵉʿārōṯ* (Ps. 107:24, 148:8, etc.) or *rūaḥ qāḏīm* (Ps. 48:8, ET 7; Jer. 18:17 etc.).

145 In Jer. 23:9 the verb is used in the qal and the context shows that the meaning is something like 'shake', which definitely indicates that the older rendering 'brood' for *rḥp* in Gen. 1:2 is incorrect, and supports some such meaning as 'hover' for the piel. 'Hover' rather than 'brood' also suits the Ugaritic example better (for references, see text).

Excursus on Genesis 1:26

In Gen. 1:26 we read that 'God said: Let *us* make man in *our* image, after *our* likeness ....' It was Gunkel[146] who first recognized that this was no original notion of the Priestly writer but preserves a mythic fragment, presumably belonging in an underlying source with the same circle of mythical ideas as the *Chaoskampf* motif which has been taken up and transformed in Gen. 1:2ff. Gen. 1:26 is commonly supposed to allude to God's consultation with his divine council ('the sons of God') when creating man in their image,[147] a view already attested in Targum Jonathan and Philo, and supported by the closely related Ps. 8:6 (ET 5), which declares that Yahweh has made man 'little less than *the gods*' (or 'the angels', Heb. *'ᵉlōhīm*; not 'God', referred to elsewhere in this psalm as Yahweh) and the analogy of Is. 6:8, where Yahweh's question '... who will go for *us*?' refers to Yahweh and the angelic seraphim. If so, R.N. Whybray's argument in his book on *The Heavenly Counsellor in Isaiah xl 13–14*[148] is mistaken in claiming that a tradition did not exist in Israel that Yahweh had need of a counsellor when undertaking the creation, a notion against which Is. 40:13f. polemicizes; further, it leads one to question his view that Is. 40:13f. is rejecting the concept specifically found in Enuma elish in which the creation of man, in contrast to the earlier works of creation, involves not only Marduk but also Ea (Enuma elish, VI, lines 1–38). That it is not specifically this concept in Enuma elish against which Deutero-Isaiah is polemicizing is shown by the parallel passage in Is. 44:24, where Yahweh declares, 'I am the Lord, who made all things, who alone stretched out the heavens; when I spread out the earth, who was with me?',[149] which makes explicit what is implicit in Is. 40:13f. (cf. v. 12), namely that the consultation concerned the creation of the heavens and the earth and not simply the creation of man, as in Enuma elish.

Another Old Testament reference, however, Job 38:7, does declare that the time of Yahweh's creation of the earth was one 'when the morning stars sang together, and all the sons of God

146 Cf. H. Gunkel, *Schöpfung und Chaos*, p. 9–11.

147 Cf. most recently the discussion in P.D. Miller, *Genesis 1–11. Studies in Theme & Structure* (Sheffield, 1978), pp. 9–20.

148 R.N. Whybray, *The Heavenly Counsellor in Isaiah xl 13–14* (Cambridge, 1971), pp. 62–3.

149 Reading *mī 'ittī* for MT *mē'ittī*, with kethibh, 31 MSS, Edd LXX, Vulgate.

shouted for joy'. Although this does not state that Yahweh consulted with the sons of God, it does clearly reflect the view that they were present with him at the time of creation. That the ideas in Gen. 1:26 and Job 38:7 belong to the same mythic circle is fortified by the fact that both Gen. 1 and Job 38–41 show other signs of dependence on common material. Thus, as has been argued above, Gen. 1 is dependent on the creation psalm, Ps. 104, and similarly, as Westermann and others maintain, Job 38–41 is dependent on a creation psalm or psalms; I would argue that this included either Ps. 104 or something very much like it, since both begin with Yahweh's creation of the world and control of the chaos waters (Ps. 104:1ff.; Job 38:1ff.), proceed to laud Yahweh's various works of creation beginning with the springs (Ps. 104:10ff.; Job 38:16ff.), and significantly come to a climax (or virtually so) with a reference to Leviathan, with whom Yahweh can play (Ps. 104:26; Job 40:25–41:26, ET 41:1–34, esp. 40:29, ET 41:5).[150] Further, that it should be against the mythic idea reflected in Gen. 1:26 that Deutero-Isaiah is polemicizing is congruous with the fact that, as M. Weinfeld[151] has pointed out, Deutero-Isaiah appears to reject other notions in the Priestly creation story, i.e. that Yahweh created the world a waste (*tōhū*, Is. 45:18, *contra* Gen. 1:2), that darkness preceded the creation (Is. 45:7, *contra* Gen. 1:2), that Yahweh has a physical image (Is. 40:18, 46:5, *contra* Gen. 1:26), and that he grows tired with the result that he needs rest (Is. 40:28, *contra* Gen. 2:2–3). The only point on which I would differ from Weinfeld is that, whereas he thinks Deutero-Isaiah was polemicizing against the Priestly creation account in Gen. 1–2:4a, I would hold that he was rejecting certain ideas in a source underlying it, since Is. 40:13–14 implicitly (cf. v. 12), and 44:24 explicitly, are not rejecting the specific notion that God needed to consult his divine council when creating man in particular, as in Gen. 1:26, but rather when creating the world as a whole.

Accordingly, in the light of all the above, it is attractive to suppose that Gen. 1:26 and Job 38:7 are referring to the same circle of mythic ideas and that these are rejected in Is. 40:13f. and 44:24, ideas according to which the sons of God, the divine council, were present with, and consulted by, Yahweh at the time of the creation of the world and of man. In a source underlying Gen. 1 it

150 Cf. below, pp. 000–00.

151 M. Weinfeld, **האל הבורא בבראשית א ובנבואת ישעיהו השני**, *Tarbiz* 37 (1967–8), pp. 105–32.

is natural to suppose that this divine consultation was closely connected with the conflict with the chaos waters, just as Job 38:7 is followed by the *Chaoskampf* (Job 38:8–11), a factor which accounts for the consideration of this subject in the present monograph. In the Canaanite prototype, however, one may speculate that, as the god who presided over the divine council and created the earth and man, it was El who consulted with the divine council, whereas it was Baal who fought the dragon and the sea.

Psalm 33:7–8

V. 7 By the word of the Lord the heavens were made;
by the breath of his mouth all their host.
V. 8 He gathered the waters of the sea as in a skin-bottle,[152]
he put the deep in storehouses.

The context makes it clear that the control of the waters here is at the time of creation. Job 38:37 also refers to 'the skin-bottles of heaven', where the parallelism makes it clear that they denote the clouds. Meteorological storehouses are also mentioned in Deut. 28:12 (rain), Jer. 10:13, 51:16, Ps. 135:7 (wind) and Job 38:22 (snow and hail), and in Ugaritic the cognate word *'iṣr* is used in connection with the thunder (*Ugaritica V*.1.4 = *KTU* 1.101.4).

Proverbs 8:24, 27–9

V. 24 When there were no depths I was brought forth,
when there were no springs, streams[153] of water.
V. 27 When he established the heavens, I was there,
when he drew a circle on the face of the deep,
V. 28 when he made firm the skies above,
when he fixed fast[154] the foundations of the deep,
V. 29 when he assigned to the sea its limit,
so that the waters might not transgress his command,
when he marked out the foundations of the earth.

These verses are part of a section (Prov. 8:22ff.) in which the antiquity of personified Wisdom is extolled. The above selected

152 Reading *kannō'd̲* 'as in a skin-bottle' for MT *kannēd̲* 'like a heap', which is inappropriate here.

153 Reading *nib̲*^{e}*k̲ē* for MT *nik̲baddē* (cf. LXX τὰς πηγάς), first suggested by G. Beer in *BH3*. In Ugaritic *mbk* and *npk* mean 'source' or 'fountain' and the former is frequently used in connection with El's dwelling where it is mentioned in close association with *thmtm*, just as *nib̲*^{e}*k̲ē* is here closely associated with *t*^{e}*hōmōt̲*, whilst at Qumran we find the expression נבוכי מים (Hodayot III, 15). Cf. *nib̲*^{e}*k̲ē yām* in Job 38:16 and מבכי נהרות in Job 28:11. See M. Mansoor, 'The Thanksgiving hymns and the Massoretic text (part II)', *RQ* 3 (1961–2), pp. 392–4.

154 Reading *b*$^{e\text{'}}$*azz*^{e}*zō* with the Versions for MT *ba*$^{\text{'}a}$*zōz*.

verses make explicit reference to the confinement of the waters in connection with the creation.

Jeremiah 5:22b

I placed the sand as the boundary for the sea,
a perpetual barrier which it cannot pass;
it may toss, though not prevail,[155]
its waves may roar, but cannot pass over it.

The containment of the sea is here set in contrast to the rebellious nature of the people (cf. vv. 23ff.).

Jeremiah 31:35

Thus says the Lord,
who gives the sun for light by day,
the moon[156] and stars for light by night,
who stirs up the sea so that its waves roar,
the Lord of hosts is his name.

Here again the context shows that the allusion to the sea is related to God's work in creation. The last part of the verse is also attested in Is. 51:15.

Yahweh's victory over the sea as a feature of his present lordship over creation

Psalm 29

V. 1 Give to the Lord, O gods,[157]
Give to the Lord glory and strength.
V. 2 Give to the Lord the glory of his name,
worship the Lord in the beauty of holiness.
V. 3 The voice of the Lord is upon the waters,
the God of glory thunders,
the Lord, upon many waters.
V. 4 The voice of the Lord is powerful,
the voice of the Lord is majestic.
V. 5 The voice of the Lord breaks the cedars,
the Lord breaks the cedars of Lebanon.

155 Reading singular verbs *wayyiṯgāʿaš* and *yūḵāl* for MT *wayyiṯgāʿᵃšū* and *yūḵālū*, following LXX, Peshiṭta and Old Latin. The subject is the sea alluded to in the previous verse. The *waw* came in by dittography in both cases.

156 Omitting *ḥuqqōṯ* with 1 MS and LXX, since otherwise the line is one beat too long. Possibly it is a misplaced alternative reading for *ḥuqqīm*, which occurs in the following verse.

157 Lit. 'sons of gods' (*bᵉnē 'ēlīm*). Cf. the expression 'sons of the prophets'.

V. 6 He makes Lebanon skip like a calf,
and Sirion like a young wild ox.
V. 7 The voice of the Lord flashes forth flames of fire.
V. 8 The voice of the Lord shakes the wilderness,
the Lord shakes the wilderness of Kadesh.
V. 9 The voice of the Lord makes the oaks whirl,
and strips the forests bare,[158]
and in his temple all say, 'Glory!'
V. 10 The Lord sits enthroned over the flood,
the Lord sits enthroned as king for ever.
V. 11 May the Lord give strength to his people,
may the Lord bless his people with peace.

This is another psalm connected with the theme of Yahweh's kingship (cf. v. 10) and surely had its *Sitz im Leben* at the Feast of Tabernacles, a fact still attested in the superscription to the psalm in the LXX. Since the thought of the psalm is centred on the lordship of Yahweh over the created order, it seemed appropriate to consider it in this chapter (cf. Nah. 1:4, to be discussed below),[159] although, since there are references to the cedars of Lebanon, etc., it is clearly not speaking about the *Urzeit* but Yahweh's present lordship over creation (cf. v. 11). Yahweh's lordship over the cosmic waters is alluded to in v. 3, and it is most natural to suppose that this is also being referred to in v. 10, rather than that we there have an allusion to Noah's flood.[160]

Yahweh's kingship in this psalm is manifested in the thunder, just like that of Baal, and the thunder is represented as his voice, as was also the case with Baal (cf. *CTA* 4.VII.29–31 = *KTU* 1.4.VII.29–31). Yahweh's lordship over the cosmic waters (vv. 3, 10) and exaltation over the other gods of the divine assembly (v. 1) is also ultimately derived from Baal mythology. In addition, the

158 Reading *'ēlōṯ* 'oaks' for MT *'ayyālōṯ* 'hinds', since this provides a more appropriate parallel to the following line's reference to forests (*y*^{e}*'ārōṯ*). Moreover, if we were to retain the MT and read 'The voice of the Lord makes the hinds to calve', this would be unique in the Old Testament theophany depictions. On the other hand, references to Yahweh's theophanic manifestation against oaks, alongside cedars of Lebanon (cf. Ps. 29:5–6) is well attested (cf. Is. 2:13; Zech. 11:1–2). This also makes one sceptical of G.R. Driver's proposal ('Studies in the vocabulary of the Old Testament. II', *JTS* 32, 1930–1, pp. 255f.) to read the second half of the verse as 'and he causes premature birth of kids', reading *wayyaḥśēp̱* for MT *wayyeḥ*^{e}*śōp̱*.

159 Cf. below, p. 60f.

160 *Contra* A. Weiser, *Die Psalmen* (5th ed., Göttingen, 1959), p. 178 (ET *The Psalms*, London, 1962, p. 265.)

present writer[161] has pointed out a further striking parallel with Baal mythology previously unnoted. This is the sevenfold manifestation of the deity in the thunder, the *qōl Yahweh* (vv. 3a, 4a, 4b, 5, 7, 8, 9). In *Ugaritica V*.3.3b–4 (*RS* 24.245, lines 3b–4 = *KTU* 1.101.3b–4), we read of Baal.

3b	šbʿt. brqm. x[ ]	Seven lightnings . . .
4	ṯmnt. ʾiṣr rʿt. ʿṣ. brq. y[ ]	Eight storehouses of thunder.
		The shaft of lightning . . .

Now, the numerical sequence 7/8 is capable of meaning simply seven in Ugaritic, the second number having the nature of what has been called automatic parallelism[162] (cf. *CTA* 6.V.8–9 = *KTU* 1.6.V.8–9 and *CTA* 19.I.42–4 = *KTU* 1.19.I.42–4). It therefore seems that we have a reference to Baal's seven thunders as well as lightnings (cf. Hab. 3:9), the parallel to Ps. 29 being even closer when we note that in *Ugaritica V*.3.1–3a (*RS* 24.245, lines 1–3a = *KTU* 1.101.1–3a), immediately before the reference to Baal's seven thunders and lightnings, we read of Baal's enthronement like the flood: *bʿl. yṯb. kṯbt. ǵr. hd. r*[*ʿy*][163] *kmdb. btk. ǵrh. ʾil ṣpn. b*[*tk*] *ǵr. tlʾiyt*, 'Baal sits enthroned, like the sitting of a mountain, Hadad (the shepherd) like the flood, in the midst of his mountain, the god of Zaphon in the (midst of) the mountain of victory', just as Ps. 29:10 states, 'The Lord sits enthroned over the flood, the Lord sits enthroned as king for ever.' The fact that the seven thunders of Ps. 29 go back to Baal mythology thus means that they are an integral part of the original psalm, a fact which serves to rebut the recent article of S. Mittmann,[164] who holds that the original psalm consisted of only vv. 1bc (ET 1), 2, 3, 4, 5, 8, 3b, 9bc and 10, which leaves him with only a fivefold *qōl Yahweh* in the thunder.

There can thus be no doubt that Ps. 29 stands remarkably close to the circle of mythological ideas surrounding Baal as they are attested in the Ugaritic texts. A number of scholars, in particular

161 J. Day, 'Echoes of Baal's seven thunders and lightnings in Psalm xxix and Habakkuk iii 9 and the identity of the seraphim in Isaiah vi', *VT* 29 (1979), pp. 143–5.

162 Cf. M. Haran, 'The graded numerical sequence and the phenomenon of "automatism" in biblical poetry', *SVT* 22 (1972), pp. 238–67.

163 Cf. *Ugaritica V*.2.3 *RS* 24.252, line 3 = *KTU* 1.108.3) for the restoration *hd r*(*ʿy*).

164 S. Mittmann, 'Komposition und Redaktion von Psalm XXIX', *VT* 28 (1978), pp. 172–94.

H.L. Ginsberg,[165] T.H. Gaster,[166] F.M. Cross[167] and A. Fitzgerald,[168] go so far as to maintain that Ps. 29 is a Canaanite psalm taken over wholesale, with the simple substitution of the name of Yahweh instead of Baal for the deity concerned (Ginsberg and Cross also maintaining that v. 11 is a Yahwistic addition.). This is possible, but cannot claim to be proved. It is also possible that the Baalistic mythology was mediated through the cult of the Jebusite god El-Elyon, who seems to have appropriated a number of Baalistic features, since the word *ʿelyōn* 'Most High' occurs in the related Enthronement Psalm 97:9, and Ps. 29:3 refers to Yahweh as *'ēl-hakkāḇōḏ* (though admittedly Baal was, on occasion, capable of being referred to as *'il*, cf. *'il ṣpn* in *Ugaritica V*.3, *RS* 24.245 = *KTU* 1.101 cited above).

V. 8 refers to Yahweh's shaking the wilderness of Kadesh in connection with his theophany. If this alludes to Yahweh's theophany at Sinai[169] (cf. Deut. 33:2, which seems to refer to Meribath–Kadesh, cf. LXX; Ex. 19:16–19; Judg. 5:4–5; Ps. 68:8–9, ET 7–8, etc.) widely attested elsewhere in the Old Testament, this would appear to militate against the view that Ps. 29 is nothing more than a Canaanite psalm with the simple substitution of Yahweh for Baal.

Nahum 1:4

V. 4 He roars at the sea and makes it dry,
he dries up all the rivers;
Bashan and Carmel wither,
the bloom of Lebanon fades.

This verse is part of a description of Yahweh's theophany in nature. As part of the introductory acrostic section of the book of Nahum it is not concerned specifically with Yahweh's judgement on Nineveh but rather with his universal power, the cosmic back-

165 H.L. Ginsberg, כתבי אגרית (Jerusalem, 1936), pp. 129–31.
166 T.H. Gaster, 'Psalm 29', *JQR* 37 (1946–7), pp. 55–65.
167 F.M. Cross, 'Notes on a Canaanite Psalm in the Old Testament', *BASOR* 117 (1950), pp. 19–21.
168 A. Fitzgerald, 'A note on Psalm 29', *BASOR* 215 (1974), pp. 61–3.
169 This seems the most probable opinion in view of its prevalence in the Old Testament. The fact that *mdbr qdš* occurs in Ugaritic (*CTA* 23.65 = *KTU* 1.23.65) has led some to see Ps. 29's reference as an allusion to the same Syrian place name (cf. Lebanon and Sirion, vv. 5–6). It is, however, extremely dubious whether the Ugaritic expression *mdbr qdš* is actually a specific place name. Cf. G.R. Driver's rendering 'the glaring wilderness' and J.C.L. Gibson's translation 'a sanctuary . . . of the desert' or 'holy desert'.

ground against which his judgement on Nineveh must be seen. God's conflict with the sea in v. 4a would seem to be alluding to his present power over the chaotic sea within the world of nature, in view of the context, as in Ps. 29:3, 10. It is not therefore alluding to Yahweh's conflict with the sea at the time of creation, but as with Ps. 29 this seems the most appropriate chapter in which to consider it. The reference to the drying up of the sea in connection with its defeat derives from the fact that at creation the unruly waters were driven off the earth.

Summary

In this chapter it has been established that there are passages in the Old Testament which associate Yahweh's conflict with the dragon and the sea with the creation of the world, and that the imagery was appropriated from the Canaanites, not the Babylonians. Although the Baal–Yam text (*CTA* 2 = *KTU* 1.2) is not concerned with the creation of the world, there was also a primordial conflict between Baal and Leviathan, Yam and others, which probably was connected with the creation.

It was also concluded that the dragon and sea conflict had its *Sitz im Leben* in Israel in the Autumn Festival, where it was associated with the theme of Yahweh's enthronement as king. A number of references in the Psalms are to be understood in this light. The author of the book of Job took up the motif from comparable creation hymns and found it an apt parallel to the theme of the conflict between Job and God described in the book. One point of detail that may be noted here is that in Job 3:8 the common emendation of *yōm* 'day' to *yām* 'sea' is to be rejected, and that Job is there wishing for Leviathan to be roused with his pre-creation darkness, in connection with which an interesting Ugaritic parallel may be adduced.

Eventually, the divine conflict with the dragon and the sea underwent a process of demythologization and the control of the waters simply became regarded as a job of work. This is found especially in Gen. 1, but also in several other passages. Contrary to a widespread view, Gen. 1 is neither dependent on, nor polemicizing against, the Babylonian Enuma elish. Rather, as elsewhere, the traditions are ultimately Canaanite, though more immediately Gen. 1 is dependent on Ps. 104, where the order of creation is identical.

2

The alleged naturalization of Leviathan and Behemoth

In the previous chapter I have considered the subject of the divine conflict with the dragon and the sea in so far as it is associated with the creation of the world. The dragon is here clearly a mythological entity. In two places, however, it has been maintained by a considerable number of scholars that Leviathan is an identifiable natural creature (Job 40:25–41:26, ET 41:1–34; Ps. 104:26) and this has similarly been alleged in connection with a beast named Behemoth (Job 40:15–24). In the present chapter I shall focus attention on this question, discussing first Leviathan and then Behemoth.

Leviathan

Job 40:25–41:26 (ET 41:1–34)

40:25 (41:1) Can you draw out Leviathan with a fish-hook,
or press down his tongue with a cord?
40:26 (41:2) Will you put a reed through his nose,
or pierce his jaw with a hook?
40:27 (41:3) Will he make many supplications to you,
or speak softly to you?
40:28 (41:4) Will he make a covenant with you,
will you take him as a perpetual slave?
40:29 (41:5) Will you play with him as with a bird,
or tie him up for your maidens?[1]

1 D.W. Thomas, 'Job XL 29*b*: text and translation', *VT* 14 (1964), pp. 114–16, argues that the second half of the verse should be rendered rather 'or canst thou tie him with a string *like a young sparrow* (or young sparrows)', reading *kannōʿār* (*–āh, –ōṯ*) instead of MT *lᵉnaʿᵃrōṯeḵā*, on the basis of LXX ὥσπερ στρουθίον, which suggests to him that *nōʿār* may be cognate with Arabic *nugharᵘⁿ*, fem. *nugharatᵘⁿ* 'a species of sparrows, young sparrows'. R. Gordis, 'Job XL 29 – an additional note', *VT* 14 (1964), pp. 491–4, seeks to achieve a similar translation

40:30 (41:6) Will traders bargain over him,
will they divide him up among the merchants?
40:31 (41:7) Can you fill his skin with harpoons,
or his head with fish-hooks?
40:32 (41:8) Lay your hand on him,
remember the battle, do not do it again!
41:1 (41:9) Behold, the hope of a man[2] is disappointed,
cast down[3] even[4] at the sight of him.
41:2 (41:10) Is he not fierce when one rouses him,[5]
who is he that can stand before him?[6]
41:3 (41:11) Who has confronted him and remained safe?
There is not one under the whole heaven.[7]
41:4 (41:12) I will not remain silent concerning his limbs,
nor with regard to the might and strength[8] of his
frame.

without resort to emendation. Rather than creating a *hapax legomenon*, however, it is preferable to suppose that the LXX rendering is due to the intrusion of the word *kᵉnaʿᵃnīm* 'merchants' at the end of the following verse into the text here as *kayᵉʿēnīm* 'like sparrows', since the LXX actually renders *kayᵉʿēnīm* in Lam. 4:3 as *ὡς στρουθίον*. Significantly, the Qumran Targum failed to recognize the name of a bird in Job 40:29b.

2 Lit. 'his hope'.

3 Heb. *yūṭāl*. There is no need to emend to *ṯuṭṭāl*, as lapse of concord with the feminine subject could have occurred because of the intervening words.

4 Deleting *hᵃ* (dittography).

5 Reading *yᵉʿīrennū* with the kethibh rather than qere *yᵉʿūrennū* since the suffix requires a transitive verb.

6 Reading *lᵉp̱ānāyw* for *lᵉp̱ānay* with the support of many Heb. MSS and MSS of the Targ. This keeps the thought on Leviathan, which is more natural.

7 Reading *hiqdīmō* for *hiqdīmanī* and *wayyišlām* for *waʼᵃšallēm*, the latter with the support of the LXX. This keeps the thought on Leviathan rather than God, which is more natural. In the second half of the verse I read *lōʼ ʼeḥāḏ* or *lōʼ huʼ* for *lī hūʼ*.

8 MT *ḥīn* is very difficult. Often it is supposed to be related to *ḥēn* and to mean 'grace', but this would seem to be a rather curious expression to use of the dreadful monster Leviathan. M.H. Pope renders it as a proper name Hayyin (reading *hayyin* for *ḥīn* which is found in the Ugaritic texts as a name for Kothar-and-Ḫasis (*CTA* 3.VIF.22–3, 4.I.24, 17.V.18 = *KTU* 1.3.VI.22–3, 1.4.I.23, 1.17.V.18), the smith of the gods who made the weapons with which Baal defeated Yam. His translation runs, 'Did I not silence his boasting, by the powerful word Hayyin prepared?' However, this seems highly questionable: Hayyin is a rare name in the Ugaritic texts and is never mentioned anywhere else in the Old Testament (Albright's attempt, 'The furniture of El in Canaanite mythology', *BASOR* 91 (1943), p. 40, n. 11 to see a reference to Hayyin in Hab. 2:5 being totally unconvincing). Unless a more satisfactory explanation is forthcoming, I follow the suggestion (e.g. in *BH3*) that *ḥīn* should be emended to *ḥēl*. This fits in well with *gᵉḇūrōṯ*.

41:5 (41:13) Who can remove his outer garment,
penetrate his double coat of mail?[9]
41:6 (41:14) Who has opened the doors of his face?
Round about his teeth is terror.
41:7 (41:15) His back[10] is made of rows of shields,
shut up closely as with a seal.
41:8 (41:16) One is so near to another
that no air can come between them.
41:9 (41:17) They cling to one another,
they clasp each other and cannot be separated.
41:10 (41:18) His sneezing[11] flashes forth light,
and his eyes are like the eyelids of the dawn.
41:11 (41:19) Out of his mouth proceed flaming torches,
sparks of fire escape.
41:12 (41:20) Out of his nostrils comes forth smoke,
as from a heated and boiling[12] cauldron.
41:13 (41:21) His breath kindles coals,
and a flame comes forth from his mouth.
41:14 (41:22) In his neck dwells strength,
and dismay dances before him.
41:15 (41:23) The folds of his flesh cleave together,
firmly cast upon him and immovable.
41:16 (41:24) His heart is hard as stone,
hard as the lower millstone.
41:17 (41:25) When he raises himself the angels are afraid,
the waves of the sea[13] pass away from him.[14]
41:18 (41:26) If one reaches him with a sword, it will not avail,
nor the spear, the dart, or the javelin.
41:19 (41:27) He regards iron as straw,
bronze as rotten wood.
41:20 (41:28) The arrow cannot make him flee,
with him sling-stones are turned to stubble.

9 Reading *siryōnō* 'his coat of mail', which forms a good parallel to *lᵉḇūšō*, following the LXX, rather than MT *risnō* 'his bridle', which seems inappropriate here.
10 Reading *gēwōh* 'his back' with LXX, Aquila and Vulgate instead of MT *ga'ᵃwāh* 'pride'.
11 Reading singular *ʿᵃṭīšāṯō* for MT's plural *ʿᵃṭīšāṯāyw*, with LXX, Aquila, Vulgate and Targum. Note the singular verb *tāhel* which supports this.
12 Reading *'ōg̱ēm* 'boiling' with the Vulgate and Peshiṭta instead of MT *'ag̱mōn* 'rushes', the *n* having crept in by dittography.
13 Reading *mišbᵉrē yām* or *mišbārīm* for *miššᵉḇārīm*.
14 The translation 'pass away from him' for *yiṯḥaṭṭā'ū* follows I. Eitan, *A Contribution to Biblical Lexicography* (New York, 1924), pp. 41–2, where he mistakenly refers to this verse as Job 41:12.

41:21 (41:29) The club he regards[15] as stubble,
and he laughs at the whirr of the javelin.
41:22 (41:30) His underparts are like sharp potsherds,
he spreads himself like a threshing-sledge on the mire.
41:23 (41:31) He makes the deep boil like a cauldron,
he makes the sea like a pot of ointment.
41:24 (41:32) He leaves a shining trail behind him,
one would suppose the deep to be a hoary head.
41:25 (41:33) Upon the earth there is none like him,
a creature without fear.
41:26 (41:34) He beholds everything that is high,
he is king over all the sons of pride.

The most popular view of Leviathan in Job 41 is that the description refers to the crocodile. The widespread acceptance of this view goes back to S. Bochart's *Hierozoicon* 2, cols. 769–96, published in 1663. Bochart similarly identified Behemoth (Job 40:15–24) with the hippopotamus.[16] Leviathan has scales on his back (Job 41:7–9, ET 14–16) which is suggestive of the crocodile. However, there are a number of points which strongly suggest that the identification with the crocodile is untenable. (i) Job 40:25 (ET 41:1)ff. clearly imply that it is impossible for man to capture Leviathan. However, we know that the Egyptians did in fact capture the crocodile. Herodotus (II.70) informs us that the crocodile was captured by means of a hook baited with a piece of pork, while a live pig was beaten on the bank to attract the crocodile towards the bait. As soon as the crocodile was landed, its eyes were covered with mud to make it easy to kill. (ii) The first verse of the description (40:25, ET 41:1) makes it clear that Leviathan has a tongue. We know, however, from many writers (Herodotus, Diodorus Siculus, Plutarch, Pliny, Ammianus Marcellinus) that it was widely

15 Reading *neḥšaḇ lō* for *neḥšᵉḇū* in view of the fact that the subject *ṯōṯāḥ* is singular.

16 Among the many scholars who accept the identification of Leviathan here with the crocodile are K. Budde, *Das Buch Hiob* (Göttingen, 1896), pp. 246ff.; B. Duhm, *Das Buch Hiob* (Freiburg, 1897), p. 195; S.R. Driver and G.B. Gray, *A Critical and Exegetical Commentary on the Book of Job* (Edinburgh, 1921), pp. 359ff.; É. Dhorme, *Le livre de Job* (Paris, 1926), pp. 570ff. (ET, *A Commentary on the Book of Job*, London, 1967, pp. 619, 625); G. Hölscher, *Das Buch Hiob* (Tübingen, 1952), p. 94; G. Fohrer, *Das Buch Hiob* (Gütersloh, 1963), pp. 525–31; H.H. Rowley, *Job* (London, 1970), p. 333; R. Gordis, *The book of Job* (New York, 1978), pp. 569–72.

believed in antiquity that the crocodile has no tongue.[17] (iii) The name Leviathan means 'twisting one' and elsewhere in the Old Testament and in Ugaritic it is used of the mythical sea serpent, so that it is most natural to assume that this is its meaning here also. Far from twisting, however, the crocodile has vertebrae which are shaped in such a way that it has great difficulty in turning its body rapidly. That people in the post-exilic period were conscious of the etymology of the name Leviathan is perhaps indicated by Isa. 27:1, where he is called 'the *twisting* serpent'. (iv) Job 41:22 (ET 30) states, 'His underparts are like sharp potsherds, he spreads himself like a threshing-sledge on the mire.' This is inappropriate for the crocodile, whose underside is smooth. (v) The description of Leviathan's breathing out fire and smoke (Job 41:10–13, ET 18–21) is inappropriate of the crocodile and suggests rather a mythical monster.

Sensitive to some of the objections to the identification of Leviathan with the crocodile, G.R. Driver[18] held that Leviathan in Job 41 is the whale, while in a later review of H.H. Rowley's commentary on Job[19] he also expressed the possibility that Leviathan might be the dolphin. The most serious objection to both of these views is the fact that Driver has to transpose a large part of the description of Leviathan (40:31–41:26, ET 41:7–34) and insert it into the passage dealing with Behemoth (which he understands as dealing with the crocodile) because what is there described does not agree with what we know of the whale or dolphin. This view is followed in the *NEB*. It is surely an arbitrary procedure to transpose verses simply because they do not fit in with an *a priori* hypothesis. We should retain the text as it stands and only resort to transposition *in extremis* when there really is no alternative. Moreover, in accounting for the whale's receiving the name Leviathan Driver notes that the whale is a faithful attendant in its care for the young – hence the relevance of the name derived from *lwh* 'to

17 G.R. Driver, 'Mythical monsters in the Old Testament', *Studi orientalistici in onore di Giorgio Levi della Vida* 1 (Rome, 1956), p. 238, n. 1, points out: 'In fact, the crocodile has a tongue, but it is flat and thick and wholly attached to the under-jaw, so that there can be no question of tying it down in making it captive.'

18 G.R. Driver, *op. cit.*, pp. 238–42.

19 G.R. Driver, review of H.H. Rowley's *Job* commentary, *JTS* 22 n.s. (1971), pp. 177–8. The identification of Leviathan with the dolphin had earlier been suggested by B.D. Eerdmans, *Studies in Job* (Leiden, 1939), pp. 27–34 (limited to Job 40:25–32, ET 1–8).

accompany', i.e. 'attend, escort'. However, such an explanation is surely inadmissible, since it is clear that the name Leviathan is derived from *lwh* in the sense of 'to twist' rather than 'to accompany'. Indeed, Driver recognizes that this is the case elsewhere but wants to make an exception for Job 40:25–30 and Ps. 104:26 in order to accommodate the meaning 'whale'. This, however, is forced: if Leviathan means 'twisting one' elsewhere we should reasonably expect this to be the case here also. Finally, against the identification of Leviathan with the whale one may note that the whale was in fact caught in ancient times (Pliny, *Nat. Hist.* IX, v. 12–15).

As for Driver's later argument that Leviathan may be the dolphin we find that here we are presented with a series of *non sequiturs*. I quote Driver: 'Further the question "will it plead with you for mercy...?" recalls the story of the dolphins (a mammal akin to the whale) who, when one of their number was caught and held captive by a Carian king, swam into the harbour and begged *maestitia quādem quae posset intellegi miserationem petens* and not to no purpose for its release, while its *pro voce gemitus humano similis* recalls the question "will he speak to you soft words?"; similarly the question "will it enter into an agreement with you....?" may be compared with the assertion that dolphins assisted fishermen by rounding up the fishes that they were trying to catch and received wages for their services (Pliny, op. cit. IX.vii.23, ix.29–33, x.33).'[20] All this is very learned but splendidly irrelevant, since in Job 40:25ff. (ET 41:1ff.) the whole point of the argument is that Leviathan will *not* plead for mercy, will *not* speak soft words and will *not* enter into an agreement with Job, whereas Driver's classical citations indicate that the opposite would be the case with the dolphin. We may rest assured, therefore, that Leviathan is not the dolphin!

Another scholar who is guilty of a *non sequitur* like that of Driver is E. Ruprecht.[21] He thinks that in Job 40:25–41:3 (ET 41:1–11) Leviathan is the hippopotamus, a continuation of the description of the hippopotamus which he finds in the account of Behemoth in Job 40:15–24. Ruprecht's reason for so thinking is that the method of capturing Leviathan referred to agrees with that used by the Egyptians in capturing the hippopotamus. However,

20 G.R. Driver, *loc. cit.*
21 E. Ruprecht, 'Das Nilpferd im Hiobbuch', *VT* 21 (1971), pp. 209–31.

the whole point of the questions in 40:25–41:3 (ET 41:1–11), as noted above in the criticism of Driver's view, is that Leviathan *cannot* be captured by this method. Consequently, we may rest assured that Leviathan here is not the hippopotamus. The forced nature of Ruprecht's view is brought out further by the fact that having equated Leviathan in Job 40:25–41:3 (ET 41:1–11) with the hippopotamus, he then has to hold that 41:4–26 (ET 41:12–34) are a later addition, since the dragon-like description does not suit his postulated hippopotamus. However, the very name Leviathan in Job 40:25 (ET 41:1) suggests a dragon-like creature, so that the separation of Job 40:25–41:3 (ET 41:1–11) and 41:4–26 (ET 41:12–34) is entirely forced. Furthermore, Ruprecht sees Leviathan = Behemoth as symbolizing political enemies,[22] but this again is unnatural, since, if particular historical enemies were referred to here, one would expect it to be made explicit. As it is, however, the whole tenor of the passage (like the other chaos monster allusions in the book of Job) is entirely against such a view.

One further identification with an actual living creature has been made, *viz.* that with the tunny fish by S. Spinner.[23] However, we know that, though generally netted, the tunny fish was also taken with two pronged hooks of bronze or iron (Oppian, *Halieutica* iii, 285–337), thus contradicting what is said of Leviathan in Job 40:25ff. (ET 41:1ff.).

In view of the absence of any satisfactory identification of Leviathan with an actually existing creature one is led back to the fact, first pointed out by Gunkel,[24] that Leviathan has a number of mythical traits in Job 41. Some of these have already been noted above when dealing with objections to the common equation of Leviathan with the crocodile. There is first the very name Levi-

22 Cf. C. Westermann, *Der Aufbau des Buches Hiob* (Tübingen, 1956), pp. 87f., who had earlier suggested that Leviathan and Behemoth were veiled allusions to political powers.

23 S. Spinner, 'Die Verwendung der Synonymen im AT', *BZ* 23 (1935–6), p. 149.

24 H. Gunkel, *Schöpfung und Chaos*, pp. 48–58, though it is to be noted he later came to accept that Leviathan here refers to the crocodile (cf. *Die Psalmen*, Göttingen, 1925, p. 325). He was followed in the mythological interpretation by T.K. Cheyne, *Encyclopaedia Biblica* 1 (London, 1899), cols. 519ff. Since the discovery of the Ugaritic texts the mythical nature of Leviathan in Job 41 has been recognized by N.H. Tur-Sinai (H. Torczyner), *The Book of Job* (ET, Jerusalem, 1957), p. 558; A. Weiser, *Das Buch Hiob* (2nd ed., Göttingen, 1956), pp. 261–3; M.H. Pope, *Job* (New York, 1973), pp. 329ff.; N.C. Habel, *The Book of Job* (Cambridge, 1975), p. 217.

athan itself, used elsewhere of the mythical sea serpent, both in Ugaritic and in the Old Testament. This is in keeping with the versions, none of which see a specific living creature here, but which either transcribe the name (Aquila, Symmachus, Vulgate, Targum) or render by 'dragon' – thus Septuagint *δράκοντα*, Qumran Targum *tnyn*, Syriac *tnyn'*. Secondly, it is clearly implied that it is impossible for man to capture Leviathan in Job 40:25ff. (ET 41:1ff.), whilst Job 40:9ff. suggests that Job would need divine power to overcome Leviathan (and Behemoth). At the same time there is the implication that God can, or more precisely, has captured Leviathan. Such a conclusion is supported by a consideration of the fact that in chapters 38–9 we have a series of questions in which what is impossible for man is possible for God. The series of questions in Job 40:25ff. (ET 41:1ff.) in which Job is asked whether he is able to subdue Leviathan ought similarly therefore to have the corollary that God has actually done this. This is further borne out by the fact that, whereas in Job 40:29a (ET 41:5a) Job is asked, 'Will you play with him (*haṯᵉśaḥeq bō*) like a bird. . . .?', in Ps. 104:26b we read of 'Leviathan whom you formed to play with (*lᵉśaḥeq bō*)'.[25] One may therefore reasonably conclude that the list of things connected with the subduing of Leviathan mentioned in Job 40:25ff. (ET 41:1ff.), which are impossible for Job, represents what God has actually done. The message therefore presupposes a battle in which God defeated Leviathan. This being the case, one can scarcely dissociate it from the other passages in the Old Testament which speak of God's defeat of the mythical sea serpent Leviathan. Leviathan in Job 41 ought therefore to be the mythical sea serpent. It is no valid argument against this that elsewhere we read of God's *slaying* Leviathan, since Job 7:12 also reflects a tradition that the sea monsters were not slain but captured: 'Am I Sea or Dragon (*tannīn* = Leviathan) that you set a guard over me?'. This view may also be reflected in Is. 30:7 if we render *rahaḇ hēm šāḇeṯ* (reading *rahaḇ hammošbāṯ*) as 'the silenced Rahab'.

Moreover, some of the passages occur in the book of Job itself – cf. 3:8, 7:12, 9:13, 26:12–13. Accordingly, if it can be shown that the second divine speech is an authentic part of the book, we have an even stronger case for the mythological nature of Leviathan. Whilst a majority of scholars reject the second divine speech as inauthentic, the reasons are uncompelling. First, it is alleged that

25 Cf. below, p. 72f.

the style is inferior to that of the rest of the book of Job. This, however, has been disputed, and V. Kubina[26] has recently shown how many are the stylistic and vocabulary parallels shared by the second divine speech and other parts of the book of Job. Secondly, it is alleged that Job has already repented in 40:4–5, so that the following sections on Behemoth and Leviathan must be an addition. It may be argued, however, that Job is only silenced in 40:4–5 and does not actually repent until 42:2–6. Thirdly, it is argued that the descriptions of Behemoth and Leviathan only give us more of the same as in Job 38–9. This, however, is not the case, since, whilst Chapters 38–9 illustrate Job's inability to fathom the mysteries of nature and to preside over creation, Job 40:6ff. rather argue that Job is unable to overcome the wicked creatures in battle. If these are the chaos monsters defeated at the time of the creation, this makes them creatures of a totally different order from those in Chapters 38–9, and also, incidentally, it explains why the description of Leviathan (and to some extent Behemoth) is much longer than those in Chapters 38–9, which has also been alleged against their authenticity. Further, it also makes quite unnecessary G. Fohrer's attempt[27] to divide the Leviathan pericope into two separate halves (40:25–41:4, ET 41:1–12, 41:5–26, ET 41:13–34) on the grounds that it is much too long in comparison with that of Behemoth (32 verses over against 10 verses), since, whilst Leviathan is the chaos monster *par excellence*, Behemoth is merely one of his helpers (cf. Job 9:13), as will be argued later below.

An argument in favour of the authenticity of the second divine speech, provided by two parallel biblical passages, however, appears previously to have been overlooked. Both Job 9:2–14 and Ps. 104 laud Yahweh's power over creation and significantly come to a climax (or virtually the climax in the latter passage) with a reference to Rahab/Leviathan, just as is the case in Job 38ff. Since, moreover, as Westermann[28] has argued, Job 38ff. has its origins in creation psalms – to which group Ps.104 belongs – a strong case can be made that the description of Leviathan inherently belongs with the previously mentioned works of creation in Chapters 38–9. Such a conclusion is also borne out by the other parallel passage, Job 9:2–14, which similarly ends with a reference to the bowing low of the helpers of Rahab (probably = Leviathan) in v. 13, which

26 V. Kubina, *Die Gottesreden im Buche Hiob* (Freiburg, 1979), pp. 115–23.
27 G. Fohrer, *Das Buch Hiob* (Gütersloh, 1963), p. 528.
28 C. Westermann, *Der Aufbau des Buches Hiob* (Tübingen, 1956), p. 85.

significantly leads to Job's declaration, 'How much less can I answer him or find words to dispute with him', thus providing a remarkable parallel to Job 41–2 where Job's inability to answer Yahweh (42:2–6) follows the account of Leviathan.

If we assume, therefore, the authenticity of the second divine speech, it becomes apparent that the Leviathan of Job 40:25ff. (ET 41:1ff.) must be identical with the mythological Leviathan/Rahab/dragon alluded to elsewhere in the book of Job, overcome at the time of creation.

Very striking are the references to Leviathan's breathing out fire and smoke (Job 41:10–13, ET 18–21). Whilst inappropriate to any actually existing creature, this describes a typically dragonesque feature and suits the mythical Leviathan admirably.[29] Another possible allusion to the mythical background of Leviathan here is Job 41:17 (ET 25), where we read, 'When he raises himself the *'ēlīm* are afraid, the waves of the sea pass away from him.' Aquila, Symmachus, the Targum and the Peshiṭta render *'ēlīm* as 'mighty ones' whilst the Vulgate has *angeli*. Pope translates 'gods'[30] and compares the incident in the Baal myth in which the assembly of the gods took fright at the arrival of Yam's fierce emissaries: 'the gods perceived them, perceived the messengers of Yam (and) the embassy of judge River; the gods lowered their heads on to their knees and (on) to their princely seats' (*CTA* 2.1.22–4 = *KTU* 1.2.1.22–4). Although Leviathan is not mentioned here as one of Yam's ambassadors, the fact that he was closely associated with Yam indicates that this passage does provide a relevant parallel to Job 41:17 (ET 25), if the *'ēlīm* really are the gods, or as one should perhaps rather translate, 'angels' (cf. Vulgate and popular Qumran usage), in view of the monotheistic outlook of the book of Job.

In two recent works devoted to the divine speeches in the book of Job, O. Keel and V. Kubina[31] have argued that Leviathan in Job 40:25–41:26 (ET 41:1–34) is the Egyptian god Seth, who was defeated by Horus, and in this role is sometimes represented as a crocodile. Leviathan in this passage can, however, be satisfactorily explained from the Canaanite figure of Leviathan (*ltn*) without

29 For depictions of a fiery dragon on both a Mesopotamian shell plaque and a seal cylinder, cf. *ANEP*, pl. 671, 691. Interestingly, the dragon has seven heads like Leviathan in the Ugaritic texts.

30 M.H. Pope, *op. cit.*, pp. 336–7.

31 O. Keel, *Jahwes Entgegnung an Ijob* (Göttingen, 1978), pp. 143–56; V. Kubina, *op. cit.*, pp. 68–75.

adding Egyptian mythological influence, and, although certain of the objections to the view that Leviathan is a simple crocodile do not hold against the opinion that it was a mythological crocodile, others do, and for this reason it must be rejected.

I conclude, therefore, that Leviathan in Job 40:25–41:26 (ET 41:1–34) is the mythical sea serpent Leviathan/Rahab/dragon mentioned elsewhere in the book of Job and in other books of the Old Testament as having been defeated at the creation, and is not to be equated with a mere crocodile or any other known living creature. It would appear, however, that he now has only one head rather than the original seven (cf. *CTA* 3.IIID.39, 5.I.3 = *KTU* 1.3.III.42, 1.5.I.3, Ps. 74:14), since, if he still had seven heads, such a striking feature would surely have been mentioned in the long, horrendous description given. Whereas in Job 38–9 Yahweh asks Job whether he can preside over the universe and fathom its mysteries, he now taunts Job by asking him whether he is able to overcome the chaos monster Leviathan which was necessary for creation to come into being. Since Job is unable to contend with Leviathan, which Yahweh himself has subdued, how much less is he able to contend with the God who overcame Leviathan! Consequently, his only appropriate action is to repent in dust and ashes in the face of the inscrutable divine power and mystery (cf. Job 42:6).

Before turning to a consideration of Behemoth in Job 40:15–24, we must discuss Leviathan in Ps. 104:26, which is also often understood as simply a natural creature.

Psalm 104:24–6

104:24 O Lord, how manifold are your works!
In wisdom have you made them all;
the earth is full of your creatures.
104:25 There is the sea, great and wide,
with moving creatures beyond number,
living things both great and small.
104:26 There go the ships,
and Leviathan whom you formed to play with.

There are two main problems in the interpretation of this verse. First, are we to translate v. 26b 'and Leviathan whom you formed *to play with*' or 'and Leviathan whom you formed to play *in it*' (i.e. the sea)?[32] Secondly, who is Leviathan here – the chaos monster in depotentized form or some natural creature such as the whale?[33]

As for the first question, the Hebrew (*lᵉśaḥeq bō*) is capable grammatically of bearing either meaning. However, it is interesting that the former rendering is already implied in Job 40:29 (ET 41:5), where God asks Job about Leviathan, 'Will you play with him (*haṯᵉśaḥeq bō*) as with a bird?', the context making it clear that this is something which God can or does do. It is probable that the verse in Job is directly dependent on Ps. 104:26, which is supported by other evidence of the verbal dependence of the second divine speech on Ps. 104, i.e. Ps. 104:1, where the words addressed to God 'You are clothed with honour and majesty' (*hōḏ wᵉhāḏār laḇāštā*) may be compared with Job 40:10, in which Yahweh encourages Job to adopt the divine mantle with the words 'and clothe yourself with honour and majesty' (*wᵉhōḏ wᵉhāḏār tilbāš*). That God plays with Leviathan is also attested in rabbinic literature (Abodah zarah 3b; Pirqe de Rabbi Eliezer 9; Midrash Jonah 98; Ḥasidim 476); according to Abodah zarah 3b this is what God does during the last three hours of the day. Although I have followed above the translation already implicit in Job, it is recognized that the alternative rendering is also possible.

As for the identity of Leviathan here, the allusion to him in the present Psalm implies that he is thought of as one of Yahweh's creatures (cf. 'whom you formed', v. 26) and the context makes it clear that he is regarded as really existing in the sea. But does this make him a natural creature, identifiable, at any rate in principle, with a known species? It is true that Akhenaten's famous hymn to the sun, which is generally accepted to be related to Ps. 104 in some way, speaks in the parallel section simply of the fish in the river, 'The ships are sailing north and south as well, for every way is open at your appearance. The fish in the river dart before your face; your rays are in the midst of the great green sea', a passage, incidentally, which, with its reference to ships, also supports the maintenance of MT 'ships' (*'ᵒniyyōṯ*) as appropriate to the context

32 The former understanding is followed by H. Gunkel, *Schöpfung und Chaos*, p. 57, n. 4; H.-J. Kraus, *Psalmen* 2 (Neukirchen, 1978), p. 878; M.J. Dahood, *Psalms* 3 (New York, 1970), p. 32; A.A. Anderson, *Psalms* 2 (London, 1972), p. 724. The latter rendering is followed by A.F. Kirkpatrick, (Cambridge, 1906), p. 612, as well as most Bible translations, e.g. *AV*, *RV*, *RSV*.

33 Amongst those taking the former view are H.-J. Kraus, *op. cit.*, p. 885; M.J. Dahood, *op. cit.*, p. 45; A.A. Anderson. *loc. cit.* (probably). Those taking the latter view include A.F. Kirkpatrick, *loc. cit.* H. Gunkel, *op. cit.*, p. 58, whilst maintaining that the figure has its origin in the mythological chaos monster, holds that the depotentization has gone so far that the mythological background has been forgotten.

in Ps. 104:26, over against those who wish to emend it.[34] However, against seeing a natural creature here is the name Leviathan itself, for in every other instance in the Old Testament and later Jewish literature this alludes to the mythological sea serpent, and Ps. 104:26 would be painfully isolated if this were not the case here too. The writer of Job certainly saw Ps. 104:26 as referring to a creature transcending any known in the natural world, since the allusion to this verse in Job 40:29 (ET 41:5), forms part of the description of the mythological Leviathan discussed above. Leviathan in Ps. 104:26 may be understood as a remnant of the chaos powers whose conquest is described in highly mythological terms earlier in the Psalm in vv. 6–9. The writer of Gen. 1 rejected the notion of a battle with the chaos waters in favour of seeing the control of the waters as simply a job of work (Gen. 1:6–10), and it was surely the same anti-mythological tendency which led to the substitution of 'great sea monsters' (*hattannīnīm haggᵉḏōlīm*) in Gen. 1:21 for the more mythological term Leviathan of the parallel passage in Ps. 104:26.[35]

It is probably best, therefore, to assume that the mythological chaos monster has been taken up and has undergone a process of depotentization. The fact that Leviathan is now Yahweh's plaything in Ps. 104:26 does not contradict the more horrendous nature which the dragon has elsewhere in the Old Testament. According to the myth, although it was a terrifying monster, Yahweh had subdued it so that it was now humbled and under his control, cf. Job 7:12, the implications of Job 41, Is. 30:7, etc.

This understanding of Leviathan in Ps. 104:26 can be paralleled in Amos 9:3, where we read, '. . . though they hide from my sight at the bottom of the sea, there I will command the serpent, and it shall bite them'. Since the sea is clearly the Mediterranean (cf. Carmel, v. 3a), the allusion cannot be to a crocodile (cf. Qimḥi) or to the venomous sea serpents attested in tropical regions.[36] Rather, as is now generally agreed, it must allude to a mythological sea serpent, and this may well be Leviathan. Interestingly, it is depicted as Yahweh's servant, which agrees well with what is implied of

34 Cf. *ANET*, p. 370. H. Gunkel, *op. cit.*, p. 57, n. 3 emends *'ᵒniyyōṯ* to *'ēmōṯ* or *'ᵃyummōṯ* 'terrors', and W.O.E. Oesterley, *The Psalms* 2 (London, 1939), p. 442 emends it to *tannīnīm* 'sea monsters'.

35 Cf. above, p. 51ff., on the parallelism between Gen. 1 and Ps. 104.

36 Cf. E.B. Pusey, *The Minor Prophets with a Commentary 2. Amos* (London, 1906), pp. 324–5.

Leviathan's relationship to Yahweh in his present defeated state in Job 40:28 (ET 41:4), where God asks Job of Leviathan, '. . . will you take him as a perpetual slave?' In conclusion, therefore, there seems no reason why Leviathan in Ps. 104:26 need not be the mythological sea serpent of that name, here appearing in depotentized form.

Behemoth

Job 40:15–24

15 Behold Behemoth before you,[37]
he eats grass like an ox.
16 Behold his strength in his loins,
and his power in the muscles of his belly.
17 He makes his tail erect[38] like a cedar;
the sinews of his thighs are intertwined.
18 His bones are tubes of bronze,
his limbs are like bars of iron.
19 He is the first of God's works,
He that made him may bring near his sword.[39]
20 Surely the mountains yield him produce,[40]
and the wild beasts play there.
21 Under the lotus he lies,
in the covert of the reeds and in the marsh.
22 The shade of the lotus covers him,
the willows of the wadi surround him.

37 Omitting *'ᵃšer 'āśīṯī* with the LXX, since this line is otherwise too long in relation to the following line. On *'immāḵ* meaning 'before you', cf. Job 17:3, 36:4.

38 The verb *ḥpṣ* here cannot have its usual meaning 'to delight in'. It is clearly a different root, though it is attested nowhere else in the Old Testament. The translation 'makes errect' follows the LXX, Peshiṭta, the Arabic version, and Ibn Ezra.

39 It seems best to follow the translation offered here, which involves no emendation of the text and makes excellent sense, cohering with the idea implicit in Job 40:9ff. and 24 that God, but not man, can overcome Behemoth. It seems unnecessary to emend the text with Gunkel to read *he'āśūī yiggōś ḥᵃrāḇō* 'made that he should rule the dry land' or with Duhm to read *he'āśū nōgēś ḥᵃbērāw* 'made oppressor of his companions'. The former rendering, though comparable to 1 Enoch 60:9 and 2 Esdras 6:51, where Behemoth is associated with the dry ground or desert, is incompatible with the amphibious nature of Behemoth depicted in Job, whilst the latter translation seems to involve excessive emendation of the text. Cf. too below, n. 51.

40 This rendering gives *būl* the meaning which it has in Is. 44:19 (cf. *yᵉḇūl*). The proposal that it means 'tribute', cognate with Aramaic *bᵉlō* and Akkadian *biltu*, is also possible, though it would involve creating a *hapax legomenon*.

23 If the river swells violently,[41] he is not disturbed,
he lies flat[42] though the Jordan surge to his mouth.
24 Who[43] will catch him by his eyes,
or pierce his nose with barbs?[44]

The most common view of modern scholars is that the word Behemoth here refers to a hippopotamus.[45] Like the identification of Leviathan in Job 40:25–41:26 (ET 41:1–34) with the crocodile, the widestread acceptance of this view goes back to S. Bochart's *Hierozoicon* 2, cols. 753–69, published in 1663, which rejected the view then common that Behemoth was the elephant. At one stage it was common to hold that the name itself means 'hippopotamus' and that it is a loan word from the Egyptian *pꜣ-iḥ-mw* 'the ox of the water' (cf. Italian *bomarino*). It is now recognized, however, that no such Egyptian (or Coptic) word ever existed.[46] Even so, it is understandable how the name Behemoth, which probably means 'great ox' (intensive plural of *bᵉhēmāh* 'cattle'), of which it is said that it 'eats grass like an ox' (Job 40:15), taken together with the fact that it lives in and by water (Job 40:21–3), was thought to indicate the hippopotamus. Especially when Leviathan in the following section was equated with the crocodile, it seemed appropriate that Behemoth should be that other typically Egyptian creature, the hippopotamus.

There are, however, a number of important objections to the view that Behemoth is here simply a hippopotamus. Thus, the comparison of the hippopotamus' tail with the cedar would be odd,

41 Following Dhorme (*op. cit.*, p. 569, ET pp. 623–4) there is no need to emend the text here as is often done, and the meaning 'swell violently' can be obtained from the verb *ʿšq*.

42 The translation 'he lies flat' for *yiḇtah* follows G.R. Driver, *Eph. Theol. Lovan.* 26 (1950), p. 342, and 'Difficult words in the Hebrew prophets', in H.H. Rowley (ed.), *Studies in Old Testament Prophecy* (Edinburgh, 1950), p. 60. The root *bṭḥ* here is cognate with Arabic *baṭaḥa*. I 'lay with the face downwards'.

43 The first line as it stands in the MT is clearly too short. As is commonly done, I insert *mī hū'* at the beginning of the line, which could easily have fallen out through haplography with *pīhū* at the end of v. 23.

44 The MT has *mōqᵉšīm* 'snares'. However, since one does not pierce a nose with snares it is better to accept that metathesis has occurred and to read instead *qimmōśīm* 'barbs' (lit. 'thorns'). It is a significant pointer to the correctness of this emendation that v. 26 speaks of piercing Leviathan's nose with a *ḥōaḥ* (hook, brier) since *ḥōaḥ* and *qimmōś* are found parallel in Is. 34:13 and Hos. 9:6.

45 E.g. K. Budde, *op. cit.*, pp. 242ff.; B. Duhm, *loc. cit.*; S.R. Driver and G.B. Gray, pp. 352ff.; É. Dhorme, *op. cit.*, pp. 564ff. (ET, pp. 618ff.); G. Hölscher, *loc. cit.*; G. Fohrer, *op. cit.*, pp. 521ff.; R. Gordis, *loc. cit.*

46 Cf. E. Ruprecht, *op. cit.*, pp. 217–18 for full details.

since, whereas the former is extremely short and curled, the latter is noted for its height and stateliness (cf. Is. 2:13; Amos 2:9; Ezek. 31:3). Again, the reference to the creature's bones and sinews (vv. 16–18) is surprising, since none of them is visible in the case of the hippopotamus. Furthermore, it is important to note that Behemoth is described as 'the first of God's works (*rē'šīṯ darᵉḵē 'ēl*) in v. 19. It is arguable whether this means that it was created first before everything else or whether it is first in importance. The analogy of Prov. 8:22, where Wisdom is similarly described as created 'at the beginning of his work' (*rē'šīṯ darkō*), supports the former interpretation. The fact that Leviathan is described as 'king over all the sons of pride' (Job 41:26, ET 34) might be felt to leave no room for Behemoth as first in importance, so that this too favours the interpretation that Behemoth was rather created first. In any case, on either interpretation the words seem inappropriate of a hippopotamus. Moreover, the implication of v. 24 is that man cannot capture this animal (cf. Leviathan), and this is further borne out by Job 40:9ff., which indicates that Job would need to possess divine attributes in order to overcome Behemoth (as also Leviathan), whose description immediately follows. Cf. too v. 19, 'He that made him may bring near his sword.' We know, however, that the hippopotamus was hunted in the ancient near east,[47] and the author of Job would surely have known this, especially if he was as knowledgeable of the hippopotamus as many supporters of the identification of Behemoth with the hippopotamus suppose. Moreover, if Behemoth were simply the hippopotamus here, the whole point of God's argument would be destroyed, since Job would have been able to retort that it was perfectly feasible to capture a hippopotamus. Rather, the whole thrust of the argument requires a creature which, though able to be overcome by God, cannot be captured by man.

In recent years a number of scholars have suggested that Behemoth is not an ordinary hippopotamus, but rather the Egyptian god Seth, who was defeated by Horus, and in this role is sometimes represented as a hippopotamus.[48] Although this circumvents the problem that ordinary hippopotamuses could be defeated by human captors, it nevertheless comes up against some of the other

47 Cf. Diodorus Siculus, I.35.10 and T. Säve-Söderbergh, *On Egyptian Representations of Hippopotamus Hunting as a Religious Motive* (Uppsala, 1953).

48 E. Ruprecht, *op. cit.*, p. 228; O. Keel, *op. cit.*, pp. 127–41; V. Kubina, *op. cit.*, pp. 68–75; B. Lang, 'Job xl 18 and the "bones of Seth"', *VT* 30 (1980), pp. 360–1.

objections which the ordinary hippopotamus theory has to face. At the same time, the fact that it has been shown above that Leviathan is not the Seth animal, the crocodile, but rather derives from the Canaanite dragon Leviathan, makes less plausible the suggestion that Behemoth is a Seth hippopotamus and renders more attractive the view that his origin is to be sought in a Canaanite sea ox, a companion of Leviathan known from the Ugaritic texts, if I may anticipate a conclusion that will be argued in detail below.

G.R. Driver,[49] noting some of the difficulties besetting the identification of Behemoth with the hippopotamus, argued that the passage rather refers to the crocodile, and this view is followed by the *NEB*. In v. 15 Driver reads *ʿemśāḵ* which he takes to mean 'crocodile'[50] on the analogy of supposedly cognate words in other Semitic languages, Egyptian, Coptic and Greek, in place of MT *ʾᵃšer ʿāśīṯī ʿimmāḵ* and translates *bᵉhēmōṯ* simply as 'beasts', so achieving the rendering, 'lo! now the chief of the beasts, the crocodile'. Against this, however, it may be noted that, whilst the line in the MT is admittedly overloaded, the correct metre may be more easily obtained by simply omitting *ʾᵃšer ʿāśīṯī* with the LXX. This is surely preferable to Driver's expedient of creating a *hapax legomenon ʿemśāḵ*, one moreover without any versional support. Furthermore, having discovered the word 'crocodile' in the text, he has to emend the words 'he eats grass like an ox' – words entirely appropriate of a creature named Behemoth (lit. 'great ox') – to read 'he eats cattle like grass' (again without any versional support), since the crocodile is carnivorous and does not eat grass. All this seems too conjectural a way of treating the text in the interests of a dubious theory, when the text makes good sense as it stands. Again, it seems odd for the crocodile to be called 'the first of God's works' (v. 19). Finally, since the crocodile was captured in the ancient near east, this view is open to the same objection as that which pertains to the hippopotamus noted above.

A different view has been put forward by B. Couroyer, who has recently argued that Behemoth is to be identified with the buffalo.[51] He maintains that what is said about Behemoth fits the

49 G.R. Driver, *op. cit.*, pp. 234–7. (Work cited in n. 17.)

50 The view that the text originally read *ʿemśāḵ* 'crocodile' had previously been suggested by G. Richter, *Textstudien zum Buche Hiob* (Stuttgart, 1927), p. 86f.

51 B. Couroyer, 'Qui est Béhémoth?', *RB* 82 (1975), pp. 418–43. In a subsequent article, 'Le "glaive" de Béhémoth: Job XL, 19–20', *RB* 84 (1977), pp. 59–79, Couroyer argues that *ḥereḇ* means 'sickle' and alludes to the set of teeth of the wild ox. However, Couroyer's view involves two assumptions whose problem-

buffalo better than the hippopotamus. Against such an identification, however, it may be objected, as Couroyer himself has to admit, that the buffalo or wild ox has already been referred to in Job 39:9–11. If, as has been argued above, the second divine speech is authentic, this objection has even greater force than it has on the assumption that the second divine speech is a later addition. Again, it seems odd for the buffalo to be called 'the first of God's works' (v. 19). Further, it may be noted that the implication of Job 40:9ff., 19 and 24 that man cannot capture Behemoth, a feat which rather demands divine power, holds also against its equation with the buffalo, since we know that the wild ox was in fact hunted in the ancient near east.[52]

Here is perhaps the best place to mention another theory on the nature of Behemoth which has been put forward by J.V. Kinnier Wilson.[53] Retaining the words *'ᵃšer 'āśîṯî* which, as has been noted above, should probably be rejected on metrical grounds in agreement with the LXX, he translates Job 40:15a as '(So) behold now "Behemoth" which I have made with thy help.' He holds that Behemoth was created by Job with a little help from God, but that Job proved quite unable to play the role of God and the resultant creature was a botched up job! If this really were the case, however, one might rather expect to read '(So) behold now "Behemoth" which *thou* hast made with *my* help.' The main point against Kinnier Wilson's theory, however, is to be found in those verses which he holds give most support to his view, *viz.* Job 40:8–14. He lays stress on the fact that in these verses God challenges Job to play the role of God and he therefore assumes that vv. 15–24 describing Behemoth reflect the result of Job's having attempted to do so by trying to create something. However, Kinnier Wilson overlooks the fact that vv. 8–14 say nothing about Job's adopting God's role as creator; rather, the divine role which Job is there challenged to adopt is that of vanquisher of the proud and wicked. This indeed fits perfectly with the fact that in Job 40:25ff. (ET 41:1ff.) God rhetorically asks Job whether he can vanquish Leviathan, who was certainly proud (cf. Job 41:26, ET

atic nature makes the whole thesis very tenuous: (i) the fact that *ḥereḇ* nowhere else in Biblical Hebrew means 'sickle' but rather 'sword', and (ii) *ḥereḇ* would be a very indirect way of alluding to the creature's set of teeth.

52 Cf. A.T. Olmstead, *A History of Assyria* (Chicago, 1923), fig. 49.

53 J.V. Kinnier Wilson, 'A return to the problems of Behemoth and Leviathan', *VT* 25 (1975), pp. 1–14.

34) and wicked, and whom God defeated. Since the description of Behemoth comes between 40:8–14 and 40:25–41:26 (ET 41:1–34) it is only natural to suppose that Behemoth is another proud and wicked creature whom God had vanquished and whom he here challenges Job to overcome by assuming the divine mantle. This is in keeping with 40:24, where God indeed asks Job whether he is able to subdue Behemoth.[54]

Who, then, was Behemoth? Both the name Behemoth (lit. 'great ox') and the fact that 'he eats grass like an ox' (v. 15) suggest an ox-like creature and vv. 21–3 indicate that it lived both in and near water. It possessed much might (cf. vv. 16–18), so much so that it was apparently impossible for man to capture it (cf. v. 24). This, together with the fact that one apparently needed divine power to do so (cf. vv. 9ff., 19), makes it difficult to equate Behemoth with any known existing creature, and, as has been shown above, those that have been suggested are in any case open to objection on other grounds. This suggests that Behemoth may be a mythological creature, and the probability of such a supposition is increased when we recall that Leviathan, described immediately after Behemoth, is mythical in nature, making it natural to suppose that Behemoth is a creature of the same order. On this view it becomes understandable why Behemoth should be described as 'the first of God's works' (v. 19), since the powers of chaos were primaeval in origin (cf. Gen. 1:2, etc.). On the other hand, as we have seen, this description seems odd for those natural creatures such as the hippopotamus that some scholars have equated with Behemoth.

Since Leviathan was taken over by Yahwism from Canaanite mythology, the question may therefore be raised whether Behemoth does not have a comparable origin. This would in fact be the case if we assume that Behemoth derives from a creature named Arš and *ʿgl ʾil ʿtk*, 'El's calf Atik', who is mentioned in Ugaritic mythology. In *CTA* 3.IIID.40–41 (= *KTU* 1.3.III.43–4) Anat lays claim to having defeated this creature. It is interesting to note that the creature mentioned immediately before this as having been defeated by Anat is 'the crooked serpent, the tyrant with the seven heads', i.e. Leviathan.

54 It may also be noted that Kinnier Wilson claims that Job 40:19a states that Behemoth's ribs are of copper, a soft metal, which is inappropriate. *Nᵉḥūšāh*, however, is not only copper but also bronze, which is frequently associated with strength (cf. Job 40:24; Ps. 18:35, ET 34), and the *ʿᵃṣāmāyw* are not ribs but bones. I owe these observations to O. Keel, *op. cit.*, p. 128, n. 353.

37 l'ištbm.[55] tnn. 'ištm[ ]	Surely I lifted up the dragon, I . . .
38 mḫšt. bṯn. ʿqltn	(and) smote the crooked serpent,
39 šliyṭ. d. šbʿt. r'ašm	the tyrant with the seven heads.
40 mḫšt. mdd 'ilm. 'ar[š]	I smote Ar[š] beloved of El,
41 ṣmt. ʿgl. 'il. ʿtk	I put an end to El's calf Atik

We thus have here an ox-like creature mentioned alongside Leviathan, which provides a good parallel to Job 40–1 where the ox-like Behemoth and the serpent Leviathan are described together.

The suggestion that Arš or El's calf Atik is to be equated with Behemoth has already been made by M.H. Pope.[56] But Pope also suggests[57] a comparison with the *ʿqqm* 'devourers' and *'aklm* 'eaters', bovine creatures which seized Baal and caused him to fall into a miry swamp, thereby bringing a seven or eight year drought on to the world (*CTA* 12 = *KTU* 1.12); he also suggests a comparison with the 'Bull of Heaven', which in Mesopotamian mythology was overcome by Gilgamesh and Enkidu. Moreover, Pope also claims that El's calf Atik is nowhere else mentioned in Ugaritic. All these claims by Pope, however, are mistaken. Thus, taking the last point first, it is to be noted that El's calf Atik's other name Arš *is* mentioned elsewhere in Ugaritic, in *CTA* 6.VI.50–2 (= *KTU* 1.6.VI.51–3) in a context which is highly significant for the present subject:

50 bym. 'arš. wtnn	In the sea are Arš and the dragon,
51 kṯr. wḫss. yd	May Kothar-and-Ḫasis drive (them) away,
52 ytr. kṯr. wḫss	May Kothar-and-Ḫasis cut (them) off.

This passage is significant not only for the fact that the bovine creature Arš (= *ʿgl 'il ʿtk*) is here again closely associated with the dragon (*tnn* = Leviathan), but also for the fact that the bovine creature Arš here dwells in the sea, just as Job 40:23 makes it clear that Behemoth could live in the water. In the light of this passage it is very probable that it is El's calf Atik (Arš) who lies behind the biblical Behemoth and not the *ʿqqm* and *'aklm* of *CTA* 12 (= *KTU* 1.12) or the Bull of Heaven of the Gilgamesh epic, since these latter are mentioned neither in connection with the sea nor as associates of Leviathan. Thus the evidence strongly supports the view that Behemoth derives from the Ugaritic creature named Arš or *ʿgl 'il*

55 See above, Ch. 1, n. 32.
56 M.H. Pope, *op. cit.*, p. 321.
57 M.H. Pope, *op. cit.*, pp. 321–2.

'tk, 'El's calf Atik', which was an associate of Leviathan. It will be noted that the Ugaritic texts referred to above assign the defeat of Arš, as also of Leviathan, to both Anat and Kothar-and-Ḫasis. In *CTA* 5.I.1–3 (*KTU* 1.5.I.1–3) the defeat of Leviathan is ascribed to Baal. This suggests that all three deities are involved in the conflict. As argued above in Chapter 1, *CTA* 6.VI.50–2 (= *KTU* 1.6.VI.51–3) probably reflects the period around the New Year corresponding to the time of the creation. There seems every reason to believe that Baal too was involved in the defeat of Arš as well as Anat and Kothar-and-Ḫasis.[58]

The evidence thus supports the derivation of Behemoth from a mythological ox-like creature twice mentioned alongside Leviathan in the Ugaritic texts. Like Leviathan it is probable that his defeat was associated with the creation of the world, cf. especially *CTA* 6.VI.50–2 (= *KTU* 1.6.VI.51–3), *bym. 'arš. wtnn kṯr. wḫss. yd ytr. kṯr. wḫss* 'In the sea are Arš and Dragon, may Kothar-and-Ḫasis drive (them) away, may Kothar-and-Ḫasis cut (them) off', words coming at the very end of the Baal cycle, probably corresponding to the time immediately preceding the New Year, when Creation would have taken place. It is interesting that in later Jewish writings the defeat of Behemoth as well as Leviathan is associated with the *Endzeit*,[59] thus suggesting an original association with the *Urzeit*, in the light of the *Urzeit wird Endzeit* principle.

58 There is a reference to *'gl 'il* in *Ugaritica V*.2.11 (*RS* 24.252, line 11 = *KTU* 1.108.11) but the allusion is obscure: *'il ǵnṯ. 'gl 'il.* De Moor, 'Studies in the new alphabetic texts from Ras Shamra', *UF* 1 (1969), pp. 175, 178, rendered this as 'the god who subdued the heifer of Ilu', connecting *ǵnṯ* with Akkadian *ḫanāšu*, *ḫanšu*, by-forms of *kanāšu* 'to submit' and *kanšu* 'humble' which he then understands as being the causative D stem 'to subdue'. Similarly, in line 9, where we read of Anat *'aklt. 'gl 'l* (or rather *ṯl*, according to Prof. D. Pardee), de Moor emends the last word to *'il* and renders 'who devoured the heifer of Ilu'. If this is correct, it would be attractive to see mythological allusions to the conflict with *'gl 'il 'tk.* However, as the text depicts a banquet scene, one wonders whether simple allusions to eating calf might not rather be contained here paralleling the allusions to drinking. Possibly *'il* goes not with *'gl* but with the following word in the next line, but the text is broken there.

59 It lies outside the purpose of this chapter to discuss the later references to Leviathan and Behemoth in the Apocrypha and Pseudepigrapha (1 Enoch 60:7–9; 2 Baruch 29:4; 2 Esdras 6:49–52) and in other Jewish writings (for references to which, cf. L. Ginzberg, *The Legends of the Jews* 5, Philadelphia, 1925, p. 26, n. 73, and pp. 43–6, n. 127; I. Jacobs, 'Elements of Near-Eastern Mythology in Rabbinic Aggadah', *JJS* 28 (1977), pp. 1–11. Also, see A. Caquot, 'Léviathan et Behémoth dans la troisième "Parabole" d'Hénoch', *Semitica* 25 (1975), pp. 111–22. The fact that Behemoth (together with Leviathan) was associated with the *Endzeit* in some of these writings is consonant with the view expressed above

However, in arguing that Leviathan and Behemoth in Job 40–1 are mythological creatures, I do not wish to deny that the writer of these chapters thought that they actually existed. The reference to the river Jordan in 40:23 in connection with Behemoth suggests that he is thought of as actually existing. The fact that Leviathan is described alongside Behemoth would suggest that he is a creature of the same type, and therefore actually existing, and this can also claim support from the fact of Job's dependence on Ps. 104:26 in the description, noted above, where Leviathan is clearly one of God's creatures in the earth's sea. Since, as has already been argued, the Leviathan of Job 41 is to be equated with the chaos monster mentioned elsewhere in the book of Job (Leviathan, Rahab, dragon) overcome at creation, it must be concluded that for the writer of Job the mythology surrounding the conflict with the dragon was still living. However, since the writer of Job was clearly a monotheist, we must regard Leviathan and Behemoth as demonic creatures rather than deities in Job.

Finally, it may be noted that a correct understanding of Behemoth and Leviathan enables us to see the purpose of their description and an important point which the book of Job is making about its central theme: since Job is unable to engage successfully in conflict with the chaos monsters Leviathan and Behemoth which God overcame at the time of creation, how much less can he hope to contend with the God who defeated them! His only right attitude towards God must therefore be one of humble submission in the face of the inscrutable divine will.[60] This motif is precisely

that his defeat was originally associated with the creation events of the *Urzeit*. Cf. too Rev. 13, where the two beasts (vv. 1–10 and 11–18), clearly representing Leviathan and Behemoth respectively (the former having seven heads and the latter, as in 1 Enoch 60:8 and 2 Esdras 6:51, a land beast), are associated with the *Endzeit*. For later depictions of Leviathan and Behemoth in art, cf. J. Gutman, 'Leviathan, Behemoth and Ziz: Jewish Messianic symbols in art', *HUCA* 39 (1968), pp. 219–30.

60 Cf. E. Jones, *The Triumph of Job* (London, 1966), p. 108. It follows from this that there is a certain implied parallelism between Leviathan and Behemoth on the one hand and Job on the other – both are unable to overcome God. However, I find unconvincing the arguments adduced by J.G. Gammie to support the thesis that Leviathan and Behemoth represent 'didactic images' for Job. See J.G. Gammie, 'Behemoth and Leviathan: on the didactic and theological significance of Job 40:15–41:26', in J.G. Gammie, W.A. Brueggemann, W.L. Humphreys and J.M. Ward (edd.), *Israelite Wisdom: Theological and Literary Essays in Honor of Samuel Terrien* (New York, 1978), pp. 217–31. According to Gammie, Behemoth and Leviathan were 'intended by the author as caricatures of Job himself, images put forth not only to put him down, but also to instruct

paralleled in Job 9:13–14, where we read 'God will not turn back his anger; beneath him bowed the helpers of Rahab. How then can I answer him, choosing my words with him?' As we have seen, Behemoth (El's calf Atik) is twice mentioned alongside Leviathan (= Rahab) in the Ugaritic texts. In view of all this it is clear that Behemoth is one of those helpers to which Job 9:13 refers.

Excursus: M.K. Wakeman's theory of an earth monster

M.K. Wakeman[61] has argued that, in addition to the sea monster (known as Leviathan, etc.), the Old Testament knows of an earth monster Ereṣ and that it is also called Behemoth. She sees the background of this in the Ugaritic texts in an earth monster *'arṣ* (usually seen as simply an impersonal reference to the earth), whom she identifies with Mot, and in turn she equates *'arṣ* with Arš/El's calf Atik. Her whole line of reasoning is, however, unconvincing.

To begin with, none of the allusions to *'ereṣ* in the Old Testament which she sees as referring to the monster requires this interpretation (Ex. 15:12; Num. 16:32; Ps. 46:7, ET 6, 114:7, etc.), the normal simple rendering 'earth' which is otherwise universally accepted being quite acceptable; similarly in the Ugaritic texts, *'arṣ* is not mentioned in parallel with the name of the god Mot, so that there is nothing to suggest that it is another proper name denoting him. On the other hand, where the context makes it clear that we do have the name of a monster, it is spelled *'arš*, also called *'gl 'il*

and console' (p. 218). I cannot deal with all Gammie's points here but will simply cite three in order to indicate the dubious and fanciful type of argumentation employed. (i) He claims that Job 40:24 implies that God can pierce the *anger* (*'ap̱*) of Behemoth and that there is a definite connection with Job's anger (*'ap̱*) alluded to in Job 40:8, 11. But *'ap̱* in Job 40:24 can only mean 'nose' and it is far-fetched to see any connection with Job 40:8, 11. (ii) Gammie claims in support of his thesis that Job identifies himself with Leviathan in Job 3:8, which is rendered 'Let those who curse the day curse it, those midwives who laid bare Leviathan.' However, no justification is given for this highly unusual translation, and footnote 36 simply informs us, 'Reading *'orrê* (*sic!*) instead of *'ōrēr*.' (iii) It is claimed that there is a deliberate parallelism between Job's dwelling in the dust (*'āp̱ār*, Job 30:19, 42:6; cf. 2:8) and the fact that we read of Leviathan, 'On *'āp̱ār* there is not his like' (Job 41:25, ET 33). However, in the latter passage *'āp̱ār* seems to be simply a poetic way of referring to the earth generally rather than specifically dust, whereas Job's dwelling 'in dust and ashes' is something quite different.

61 M.K. Wakeman, 'The biblical earth monster in the cosmogonic combat myth', *JBL* 88 (1969), pp. 313–20, and *God's Battle with the Monster* (Leiden, 1973), pp. 106–17.

ʿ*tk* ʿEl's calf Atik', neither of which names is mentioned in parallelism with *mt* (Mot), of which latter personality, moreover, nothing in the Ugaritic texts suggests that he had the form of a calf.[62] Again, the word *'arṣ* is feminine, whereas Arš is masculine, since it is called ʿ*gl*, not ʿ*glt*, just as Mot is masculine. There are therefore important gender discrepancies in Wakeman's equations. Furthermore, as we have seen, in one place (*CTA* 6.VI.50 = *KTU* 1.6.VI.51), it is clear that Arš's habitat is in the sea alongside *tnn* (the dragon), so that it is difficult to see how Wakeman can be right in maintaining that Arš – in distinction from the dragon – is an earth monster. This is also the case with Behemoth, which can live in water (cf. Job 40:23), even though in later Judaism it became regarded as a land creature in contrast to Leviathan (1 Enoch 60:7–9; 2 Esdras 6:49–52; cf. Rev. 13:1–18, esp. v. 11). Finally, it may be noted that she fails to convince in her attempt to see a reference to Behemoth in Hab. 2:17, which she translates ,[63] 'Lebanon's violence will overwhelm you; Behemoth's destruction will terrify you, (for the blood of men) and the violence of *Ereṣ*.' The comparable oracle against

62 S.E. Loewenstamm and others, however, have held that the description of Mot's destruction in *CTA* 6.II.30ff. (= *KTU* 1.6.II.30ff.) provided the model for the description of Moses' destruction of the golden calf in Ex. 32:20, where we read, 'And he took the calf which they had made, and burnt it with fire, and ground it to powder, and scattered it upon the water, and made the people of Israel drink it.' Cf. S.E. Loewenstamm, 'The Ugaritic fertility myth – the result of a mistranslation', *IEJ* 12 (1962), pp. 87–8, 'The making and destruction of the golden calf', *Biblica* 48 (1967), pp. 481–90, 'The making and destruction of the golden calf – a rejoinder', *Biblica* 56 (1975), pp. 330–43; F.C. Fensham, 'The burning of the golden calf and Ugarit', *IEJ* 16 (1966), pp. 191–3; O. Hvidberg-Hansen, 'Die Vernichtung des goldenen Kalbes und der ugaritische Ernteritus', *Acta Orientalia* 33 (Copenhagen, 1971), pp. 5–46. This view, however, is to be rejected, since, as L.G. Perdue has pointed out, in 'The making and destruction of the golden calf – a reply', *Biblica* 54 (1973), pp. 237–46, the parallel, on examination, is not a very close one. Thus, three of the verbs used in the account of the destruction of Mot in *CTA* 6.II.30ff. (= *KTU* 1.6.II.30ff.: *'aḫd*, *bq*ʿ and *'akl*) have no equivalent in the description of the destruction of the golden calf, and two verbs (*dqq* and *hšqh*) used in the latter have no equivalent in the former. Furthermore *dr*ʿ 'to sow' and *zrh* 'to scatter' are not strictly equivalent. Rather, the description of the destruction of the golden calf has its closest analogues in descriptions of the destruction of cultic objects in the Deuteronomistic history. For example, in 2 Kings 23:6b we read of Josiah's treatment of the Asherah that 'he burned (*śrp*) it at the brook Kidron, and beat it to dust (*dqq*)'. Also the water motif is present, for in 2 Kings 23:12 we read that the dust of the destroyed altars was cast into the brook Kidron. It may safely be concluded, therefore, that the description of the destruction of the golden calf by Moses does not reflect an early literary pattern employed in the Ugaritic texts to describe the destruction of Mot.

63 M.K. Wakeman, *God's Battle with the Monster*, pp. 114–15.

the king of Babylon in Is. 14:8 makes it clear that the violence is done *to* Lebanon by the king, not *by* Lebanon – 'The cypresses rejoice at you, the cedars of Lebanon, saying, "Since you were laid low, no hewer comes up against us"', with which one may also compare Nebuchadrezzar's own account of his activities in Lebanon.[64] Consequently, the parallel *šōḏ bᵉhēmōṯ* refers to 'the destruction of the beasts' and not 'Behemoth's destruction'. In view of all this it is clear that Wakeman's theory of an Old Testament earth monster is to be rejected.

Summary

In this chapter attention has been concentrated on the second divine speech in the book of Job, which concerns the beasts Behemoth and Leviathan. It has been argued that the common identification of these creatures with the hippopotamus and the crocodile is to be rejected, as also are the view of G.R. Driver (followed by *NEB*) that the descriptions relate to the crocodile and the whale and all other identifications of Behemoth and Leviathan with animals actually existing in the real world. Rather the presence of mythological features and the fact that it is implied that only God can overcome them suggest that we have to do with chaos monsters subdued by Yahweh at the time of creation. Just as Leviathan ultimately derives from the Ugaritic dragon *ltn*, so Behemoth has its origin in an ox-like creature of the water called Arš or *'gl 'il 'tk* 'El's calf Atik', who is twice actually mentioned alongside the dragon *ltn* in the Ugaritic texts, and with whose defeat the deities Baal, Anat and Kothar-and-Ḫasis were associated. The grounds which have frequently been alleged against the authenticity of the second divine speech in Job are inadequate. Various factors support its authenticity, including the fact that its placing of Leviathan at the climax of a series of works of the universe in Job 38–41 is paralleled by the similar placing of Leviathan in Ps. 104:26 and Rahab in Job 9:13 (9:14 likewise paralleling Job 42:1ff.). This in turn supports the equation of the Leviathan of the second divine speech with the chaos monster Leviathan or Rahab mentioned elsewhere in the book. However, although Leviathan

64 Cf. J.P. Brown, *The Lebanon and Phoenicia. Ancient Texts Illustrating their Physical Geography and Native Industries* 1 (Beirut, 1969), p. 199, and discussion on pp. 196–9; pp. 175–212 give a useful compilation of a whole series of ancient texts relating to the deforestation of Lebanon.

and Behemoth are mythological, their presence in subdued form within the earth's seas seems to be presupposed, and this also is the case with Leviathan in Ps. 104:26 and the sea serpent in Amos 9:3. They are perhaps best understood as demonic creatures. The reason for the inclusion of the sections on Behemoth and Leviathan in Job 40–1 is to drive home the point that, since Job is unable to overcome them, how much less can he hope to overcome in argument the God who defeated them. Finally, in an excursus, M.K. Wakeman's theory of an Old Testament earth monster (equated with Behemoth) was rejected.

3

The historicization of the divine conflict with the dragon and the sea and the origin of the 'conflict with the nations' motif

The historicization of the divine conflict with the dragon and the sea

In the first two chapters I have considered passages in the Old Testament where the defeat of the dragon or dragons and the sea is associated with the creation of the world, whether explicitly or implicitly. In the present chapter I shall be considering what I have called the historicization of the divine conflict with the dragon and the sea, that is, instances where various names for the dragon and the sea are applied to a nation or nations hostile to Israel. That this could be done is indicative of the fact that the powers of chaos, though subdued at the creation, were still liable to manifest themselves in the present on the historical plane. The passages to be considered, in order, are as follows: Is. 30:7, Ps. 87:4, Is. 51:9–11, Ezek. 29:3–5, 32:2–8, Ps. 77:17–21 (ET 16–20), Ex. 15:1–18, Is. 17:12–14, 8:5–8, Hab. 3, Jer. 51:34, Jonah 2, Ps. 44:19–20 (ET 18–19), 68:23 (ET 22), 30 (ET 29), 46:3–4 (ET 2–3), 18:5–18 (ET 4–17), and 144:5–7. Following the consideration of these passages there will be a section at the end of the chapter discussing the origin of the 'conflict with the nations' motif and the question whether it represents a historicization of the motif of the divine conflict with the dragon and the sea.

The dragon as a designation for Egypt

Most commonly where a particular foreign nation is intended, Egypt (or its Pharaoh) is denoted (cf. below refs. in Is. 30:7; 51:10; Ps. 87:4; Ezek. 29:3–5, 32:2–8; and note also Ps. 77:17–21, ET 16–20, and Ex. 15). The reason for this is probably because of the oppressive role which Egypt had played *vis à vis* Israel before the Exodus, aided by the fact that the heart of the deliverance actually took place at the sea (Ex. 14–15). Although the imagery was applied, for example, to Babylon (cf. Jer. 51:34; Is. 27:1) and the Seleucids (cf. Dan. 7) when these represented the dominant world power, it was still used of Egypt long after the Exodus had taken place and when Egypt was no longer the dominant world power. This should not surprise us when we recall how prominent the Exodus faith was in the Old Testament, with its attendant consciousness of the oppressive role that Egypt had played.

> Isaiah 30:7
> Egypt's help is worthless and empty,
> therefore I have called her
> 'the silenced Rahab'.

The translation 'the silenced Rahab' involves reading *rahaḇ hammošbāṯ*[1] for MT *rahaḇ hēm šāḇeṯ*, which is patently without sense. This seems preferable to other renderings which have been proposed, such as 'Rahab sind sie? Untätigkeit!', proposed by H. Donner,[2] which retains the MT but gives a dubious sense, or other translations such as 'die zurückgebrachte Rahab' (reading *rahaḇ hammušāḇeṯ*) proposed by K.-D. Schunck,[3] 'Rahab der Wüsten' (reading *rahaḇ hamm^{e}šammōṯ*) advocated by B. Duhm,[4] or 'sein Gelärm hört auf' (reading *rohbāh mušbāṯ*) suggested by O. Procksch.[5] The reading *rahaḇ hammošbāṯ* is to be preferred in view of the fact that in Is. 14:4 *marhēḇāh*,[6] from the same root as *rahaḇ*, is associated with the verb *šbt* 'to cease' (*šāḇ^{e}ṯāh marhēḇāh* 'the insolent fury ceased'). (However, one does not need to go as far as M.K. Wakeman,[7] who says that the root *rhb* means 'to act like Rahab'.)

1 Cf. H. Gunkel, *Schöpfung und Chaos*, p. 39, n. 1, who cites 'Hensler bei Dillmann' for this view.
2 H. Donner, *Israel unter den Völkern* (*SVT* 11, 1964), p. 158.
3 K.-D. Schunck, 'Jes 30 6–8 und die Deutung der Rahab im Alten Testament', *ZAW* 78 (1966), p. 52.
4 B. Duhm, *Das Buch Jesaia* (4th ed., Göttingen, 1922), p. 218.
5 O. Procksch, *Jesaia* 1 (Leipzig, 1930), p. 387.
6 MT has *maḏhēḇāh* and this is supported by H.M. Orlinsky, 'Studies in the St. Mark's Isaiah Scroll, IV' *JQR* 43 n.s. (1952–3), pp. 334–7. However, the emendation to *marhēḇāh* has the support of 1Q Is^{a}, LXX, Peshiṭta and Targum, and is further supported by the fact that the word is parallel to *nōgēś* 'the oppressor', the piel of which verb (*niggaś*) is itself parallel to *yirh^{a}ḇū* in Is. 3:5.
7 M.K. Wakeman, *God's Battle With the Monster* (Leiden, 1973), p. 59.

It has been argued that v. 6 refers to Behemoth and that therefore Rahab (v. 7) and Behemoth are here equated. Thus, Gunkel[8] translates the beginning of v. 6 as 'Oracle on the monster of Egypt'. However, *bahᵃmōṯ negeḇ* is more naturally rendered 'beasts of the Negeb', since we should require strong evidence that the name of the monster Behemoth, attested only in Job 40:15 elsewhere in the Old Testament, is specifically intended here, and in any case, it has been observed earlier that Rahab is quite likely to be equated with Leviathan, which therefore rules out its equation with Behemoth.

Is. 30:7, almost certainly dating from the period 705–1 B.C., expresses the view found elsewhere in Isaiah, that Judah is unwise to form an alliance with Egypt, since its help is useless. This is significant, since it is a pointer to the fact that the imagery of the dragon is not restricted to Old Testament literature of the exilic and post-exilic periods, contrary to what T.H. Gaster and one or two others have supposed.[9]

Psalm 87:4
I reckon Rahab and Babylon as those that know me;
behold Philistia and Tyre with Ethiopia –
'This one was born there.'

In this 'ecumenical psalm' Rahab is here mentioned alongside Babylon, Philistia, Tyre and Ethiopia as one of Zion's citizens. It is generally accepted that Rahab here indicates Egypt, in view of the fact that Egypt is so called elsewhere in the Old Testament (cf. Is. 30:7, 51:9), which is the case with no other nation. It may also be noted that the non-mention of Egypt would be surprising in a list which includes the less significant country of Ethiopia, whilst Egypt also balances the more northerly world power Babylon very well.

There is uncertainty amongst scholars, however, whether Egypt and the other nations alluded to here form part of an eschatological vision of Zion as the world centre of Yahweh's worship, or whether the reference is to proselytes who had come to the festival

8 H. Gunkel, *op. cit.*, p. 66.

9 Cf. T.H. Gaster, *Thespis* (2nd ed., New York, 1966), p. 142, who, referring to Old Testament allusions to the sea monster, states that 'Without exception, the passages in question are of exilic or post-exilic date . . .' This, at any rate, is surely one exception, since a post-exilic context does not seem feasible, whereas it fits readily into the schema of Isaiah's other oracles about Egypt. Even O. Kaiser, *Der Prophet Jesaja Kapitel 13–39* (Tübingen, 1973), p. 230 (ET *Isaiah 13–39*, London, 1974, p. 289) accepts the authenticity of this passage.

cult in Jerusalem, perhaps symbolic of the future eschaton, or whether the Jews of the Diaspora are in mind.[10] In my opinion the first view is the most likely. It is surely improbable that Jews who were merely in exile in Egypt would themselves be referred to by the name of the defeated sea monster Rahab, and much more natural to suppose that actual Egyptians are in mind. Moreover, that it is not simply a few proselytes in the cult but an eschatological vision of worldwide worship that is here in mind is supported by the fact that this is clearly what many other Old Testament passages related to the Zion tradition reflected in Ps. 87 refer to – cf. Is. 2:2–4 (= Mic. 4:1–3); Zech. 8:22f.; Jer. 3:17; Is. 25:6; Ps. 47:10 (ET 9), etc.

Isaiah 51:9–11

V. 9 Awake, awake, put on strength, O arm of the Lord, awake as in days of old, the generations of long ago.
Was[11] it not you who hewed Rahab in pieces,[12] who pierced the dragon?

V. 10 Was it not you who dried up the sea, the waters of the great deep,
who made the depths of the sea a way for the redeemed to pass over?

V. 11 So the ransomed of the Lord will return and come to Zion with singing,
everlasting joy shall be on their heads; they shall obtain joy and gladness, and sorrow and sighing shall flee away.

In this passage from Deutero-Isaiah, which takes the form of a lament, we have a blending of God's victory over chaos at the

10 Thus, for example, A.F. Kirkpatrick, *The Book of Psalms* (Cambridge, 1906), pp. 519, 521, supports the future eschatological interpretation, A. Weiser, *Die Psalmen* (5th rev. ed., Göttingen, 1959), p. 397, (ET *The Psalms*, London, 1962, p. 583), the proselyte view, whilst H.-J. Kraus, *Psalmen* 2 (5th ed., Neukirchen, 1978), pp. 769–70, favours the view that the Jewish Diaspora is alluded to.

11 P.R. Ackroyd, *Exile and Restoration* (London, 1968), pp. 129–30, thinks that this and the following participles in vv. 9–10 require translation by the present rather than the past tense. However, the participle in Hebrew can also represent past actions, cf. *GK* §116 o.

12 Vulgate and 1Q Is^a read *hammōḥeṣeṯ* but this is probably by assimilation to Job 26:12 (*māḥaṣ rahaḇ*). It is much more likely that an original occurrence of the verb *ḥṣb* has been substituted by *mḥṣ* than the reverse, since *ḥṣb* occurs only rarely with a meaning equivalent to 'to kill'. That it could bear this meaning is shown by *CTA* 3.IIB.5–6, 29–30 (= *KTU* 1.3.II.5–6, 29–30), where *mḫṣ* and *ḫṣb* occur as a parallel pair in Ugaritic, and Hebrew *ḥṣb* occurs parallel to *hrg* in Hos. 6:5. See the discussion in E.Y. Kutscher, *The Language and Linguistic Background of the Isaiah Scroll* (*IQIsa^a*) (Leiden, 1974), pp. 33, 255.

creation, at the Exodus and in the coming deliverance from the Babylonian exile. Rahab is both the monster defeated at creation and Egypt at the time of the Exodus and also, by implication, it may be argued, the thought is extended to Babylon at the time of the prophet himself. The return from exile in Babylon is both a new creation and a new Exodus.[13]

Like Ps. 74:12ff. Is. 51:9–11 dates from the exilic period and similarly appeals to God's defeat of the dragon in the past as a basis of confidence in God's deliverance in the present lamentable situation. This fact supports the view that the dragon mythology was well-known in pre-exilic Israel, since the fact that it could be appealed to in this way in the hour of need during the exile implies that it was deeply rooted in the people's consciousness. This reference to the defeat of the dragon is not an isolated allusion in Deutero-Isaiah, but belongs to a wide nexus of motifs associated with the Autumn festival in pre-exilic Israel which have greatly influenced his message, motifs connected with the theme of the kingship of God (cf. Is. 52:7, 'Your God reigns').[14]

Is. 51:9–11 stands particularly close to Ps. 89:10f. (ET 9f.), where again Yahweh's acts in defeating the sea monster and creating the world are appealed to as a ground of hope in Yahweh's gracious intervention in the present distress. In fact, the verbal parallels are so close that it is quite possible, as H.L. Ginsberg[15] has argued, that Is. 51:9–11 is actually dependent on Ps. 89:10f. (ET 9f.) – cf. *'att*, *'ōz*, *z^erōa'*, *rahaḇ* and *m^eḥōleleṯ* in Is. 51:9 with *'attāh*, *biz^erōa' 'uzz^ekā*, *rahaḇ* and *keḥālāl* in Ps. 89:11 (ET 10). The dependence of Deutero-Isaiah on Ps. 89 here is further supported by the fact that there are a number of other striking parallels between the two works, such that to list them all took up a whole page of one of O. Eissfeldt's articles.[16]

13 The theme of the return from the exile in Babylon as a new Exodus is frequent in Deutero-Isaiah. B.W. Anderson, 'Exodus Typology in Second Isaiah', in B.W. Anderson and W. Harrelson (edd.), *Israel's Prophetic Heritage* (London, 1962), pp. 181–2, cites the following passages as alluding to the return from Babylon as a new Exodus: Is. 40:3–5, 41:17–20, 42:14–16, 43:1–3, 43:14–21, 48:20–1, 49:8–12, 51:9–10, 52:11–12, 55:12–13.

14 Cf. now, J.H. Eaton, *Festal Drama in Deutero-Isaiah* (London, 1979).

15 H.L. Ginsberg, 'The arm of YHWH in Isaiah 51–63 and the text of Isa 53 10–11', *JBL* 77 (1958), p. 153, followed by A. Schoors, *I am God your Saviour* (*SVT* 24, 1973), p. 123.

16 O. Eissfeldt, 'The promises of grace to David in Isaiah 55:1–5', in B.W. Anderson and W. Harrelson (edd.), *Israel's Prophetic Heritage* (London, 1962), pp. 199–200.

The view that Rahab is here simply a term for Egypt with all thought of creation absent is now generally rejected.[17] That the thought of the creation is here included, which might claim support from Is. 51:13, 16, where it is explicitly mentioned, is further suggested by the passage's possible dependence on Ps. 89:10f. (ET 9f.), where the context is clearly that of creation. On the other hand, it is also probable that one should reject D.M. Gunn's attempt[18] to see an additional reference to Noah's flood here (which he finds also in Is. 44:27 and 50:2), since not only is it unnecessary – 51:10a carries on the thought of the creation in 51:9, and 51:10b clearly refers to the Exodus (Gunn himself admits that the reference to the redeemed passing through the depths of the sea more appropriately fits the Exodus) – but also, unlike the many allusions to the creation and the Exodus in Deutero-Isaiah, there is only one obvious reference to the flood, i.e. Is. 54:9–10.[19]

Ezekiel 29:3–5

V. 3 Behold, I am against you, Pharaoh king of Egypt,
the great dragon[20] that lies in the midst of his streams, that says, 'My own are my streams,[21] I made them.'

V. 4 I will put hooks[22] in your jaws, and make the fish of your streams stick to your scales;
and I will draw you up from the midst of your streams with all the fish of your streams which stick to your scales.

V. 5 And I will cast you forth into the wilderness,
you and all the fish of your streams;
you shall fall upon the open field, and not be gathered and buried.[23]
To the beasts of the earth and to the birds of the air I have given you as food.

17 Those seeing Rahab here as simply denoting Egypt include J. Fischer, 'Das Problem des neuen Exodus in Isaias c. 40–55', *Theologische Quartalschrift* 110 (1929), p. 116; A. Heidel, *The Babylonian Genesis* (2nd ed., Chicago and London, 1951), p. 109f.; W. Schmidt, *Königtum Gottes in Ugarit und Israel* (*BZAW* 80, 2nd ed., 1966), p. 48.

18 D.M. Gunn, 'Deutero-Isaiah and the Flood', *JBL* 94 (1975), pp. 501–3.

19 Gunn's attempt (*op. cit.*, pp. 503–8) to see an allusion to Noah's messenger-bird in Is. 55:11 and to Noah's rainbow in 55:13b savours more of eisegesis than exegesis.

20 Reading *hattannīn* 'dragon' for MT *hattannīm* 'jackals'.

21 Reading *yᵉʾōray* 'my streams' for MT *yᵉʾōrī* 'my stream'.

22 Reading qere *ḥaḥīm* for kethibh *ḥaḥīyīm*.

23 Reading *ṯiqqāḇēr* with some MSS and Targum for MT *ṯiqqāḇēṣ*.

Ezekiel 32:2–8

V. 2 You are like a lion among the nations,
and you are like a dragon[24] in the seas and you burst forth in your streams,[25]
and you make the waters turbid with your feet and you foul their streams.
V. 3 Thus says the Lord God,
I will throw my net over you in the company of many peoples, and I will draw you up in my dragnet.
V. 4 And I will cast you upon the ground, on the open field I will fling you,
and I will cause all the birds of the air to settle on you, and I will gorge the beasts of the whole earth with you.
V. 5 I will strew your flesh upon the mountains, and fill the valleys with your carcass.[26]
V. 6 I will drench the land with your flowing blood[27] even to the mountains, and the watercourses will be full of you.
V. 7 When I extinguish you I will cover the heavens and darken their stars;
I will cover the sun with a cloud, and the moon shall not give its light.
V. 8 All the bright lights of heaven I will make dark over you, and I will put darkness upon your land, says the Lord God.

In both of the above oracles from Ezekiel the Pharaoh of Egypt (Hophra, 589–70 B.C.) is likened to a dragon (*tannīn*). As has been noted above,[28] both at Ugarit and in the Old Testament this is found as an alternative designation of Leviathan, as also of Rahab in the Old Testament. Many scholars think that the *tannīn* here simply refers to the crocodile rather than the mythological dragon.[29] However, the following points may be noted in support of the mythological interpretation.[30] First, the term *tannīn* is

24 Reading *kattannīn* with 2 MSS^{Ken} for MT *kattannīm*.
25 There seems no need to emend MT *b^{e}nah^{a}rōṯeḵā* to *bin^{e}ḥirōṯeḵā* (a proposal first made by Ewald) or to *bin^{e}ḥīrōṯeḵā* or *b^{e}naḥ^{a}rāṯ^{e}ḵā* (cf. *BHS*, *NEB*, etc.) with the resulting translation 'and you snort *with your nostrils*'. Not only is there no versional support for these emendations but the MT makes excellent sense and *yammīm* and *nah^{a}rōṯ* make a good parallel.
26 Reading *rimmāteḵā* with Symmachus, Peshiṭta and Vulgate for MT *ramūṯeḵā*.
27 Reading *ṣō'āṯ^{e}ḵā* with LXX and Symmachus for MT *ṣāp̄āṯ^{e}ḵā*.
28 Cf. above p. 6.
29 E.g., G. Fohrer, *Ezechiel* (Tübingen, 1955), p. 166; O. Kaiser, *Die mythische Bedeutung des Meeres* (*BZAW* 78, 1959), p. 148.
30 First argued by H. Gunkel, *Schöpfung und Chaos*, pp. 73ff. It has recently been followed by L. Boadt, *Ezekiel's Oracles against Egypt. A Literary and Philological Study of Ezekiel 29–32* (Rome, 1980), pp. 27–8, 131–2.

employed elsewhere in the Old Testament to describe the chaos monster but is never certainly applied to the crocodile. Secondly, the creature is said to dwell 'in the seas' (Ezek. 32:2), which does not suit the crocodile in the Nile but aptly suits the mythological dragon. Thirdly, as we have seen, there is a clear tradition in the Old Testament linking the chaos monster with Egypt, cf. Is. 30:7, 51:9, Ps. 87:4, where it is called Rahab, which was also known as *tannīn* (cf. Is. 51:9). Fourthly, the fact that the dragon is said to have made the streams (Ezek. 29:3) is readily explicable when we consider that the chaos monster was the personification of the primaeval deep which feeds the streams, but does not fit the crocodile.[31] Fifthly, the darkening of the luminaries by the clouds at the time of the defeat of the dragon (Ezek. 32:7–8) may be paralleled by the connection between the drying up of the sea and the darkening of the heavens in Is. 50:2–3 and by Ps. 18:10 (ET 9), where 'thick darkness was under his feet' at the time of God's conflict with 'mighty waters' (v. 17, ET 16), a motif ultimately attributable to the fact that it was the storm god Baal who overcame the chaos waters. Sixthly, the dragon's being given to the wild beasts as food (Ezek. 29:5, 32:4) may be compared with Ps. 74:14, where this is said of Leviathan.

It is to be admitted that the dragon's possession of scales (Ezek. 29:4) derives from the crocodile, but in Job 41:7–9 (ET 15–17) Leviathan is said to possess scales, and, as has already been argued above in detail in Chapter 2,[32] there can be no doubt that Leviathan is there a mythical creature and no crocodile. One crocodile feature therefore does not subvert the total impression that the dragon of Ezek. 29 and 32 is mythological. Ezekiel's use of this mythological imagery is comparable to his employment of mythical motifs elsewhere in the oracles against foreign nations to depict the judgement that befalls hubris (Ezek. 28:1–19 and 31).

31 O. Kaiser, *loc. cit.*, notes that the Egyptians could say to the Pharaoh, 'If you yourself were to speak of your father, the Nile, to the father of the gods, "Let water flow down on to the mountains!" – then they would do all that you said' and, following G. Fohrer, *Ezechiel* (Tübingen, 1955), p. 166, quotes the words of Amon-Re to Thutmose III in the victory hymn at Karnak, 'I cause them to see thy majesty as a crocodile, the Lord of fear in the water, who cannot be approached' (*ANET* p. 374). However, it is to be noted that, though in the above passages we find the Pharaoh on the one hand regarded as the creator of the water and on the other hand compared to a crocodile, the Pharaoh is nowhere spoken of as the creator of water in virtue of his being a crocodile.

32 Cf. above, pp. 62–72.

The Chaoskampfmythos and the Exodus from Egypt

It was noted earlier that the Old Testament allusions to Egypt as Rahab or the dragon probably arose as a result of the oppressive role that Egypt played towards Israel before the Exodus, and that the use of this imagery was also conditioned by the fact that the heart of the Exodus deliverance actually took place at the sea (Ex. 14). In addition to Is. 51:10, already discussed above, two passages actually employ imagery derived from the chaos-conflict myth in the depiction of the Exodus, *viz.* Ps. 77:17–21 (ET 16–20) and Ex. 15. In the former the conflict is with the sea, though in the latter a further demythologization has occurred in that the conflict is at the sea rather than specifically with the sea.

O. Eissfeldt[33] held that the association of the *Chaoskampfmythos* with the Exodus in the Old Testament was due to the fact that the miracle at the Reed Sea occurred near the shrine of Baal Zaphon (Ex. 14:2), where the myth of the dragon conflict would have been known, and was originally ascribed to this god and only subsequently to Yahweh. There is, however, no evidence to suggest that Israel ever ascribed her remarkable deliverance at the Exodus to anyone but Yahweh. J. Gray,[34] whilst not holding that Israel's deliverance was originally ascribed to the god Baal Zaphon, holds that the elaborations of the narrative, such as the control of the sea, are accretions and reflect the cult legend of the neighbouring shrine of Baal. It is doubtful, however, whether Israel was long enough in the vicinity of Baal Zaphon during the flight from Egypt for the Baal myth there to have influenced her in the way that this view presupposes. It is possible, however, as F. Eakin has argued,[35] that the heightening of the water-separation motif in Ex. 14 (absent in J but present in P) may reflect the mythological conflict with chaos.[36]

Psalm 77:17–21 (ET 16–20)

V. 17 When the waters saw you, O God,
when the waters saw you, they were afraid,

33 O. Eissfeldt, *Baal Zaphon*, pp. 66–71.

34. J. Gray, 'Canaanite Mythology and Hebrew tradition', *TGUOS* 14 (1950–2), pp. 54–5.

35 F. Eakin, 'The Reed Sea and Baalism', *JBL* 86 (1967), pp. 378–84.

36 R. de Vaux, *Histoire ancienne d'Israël* 1 (Paris, 1971), p. 364 (ET *The Early History of Israel* 1, London, 1978, p. 388), has criticized Eakin on the ground that Baal is never represented as parting the sea. However, Ps. 74:13 (cf. Gen. 1), does speak of Yahweh dividing the waters in the context of *Chaoskampf*.

yea, the deep trembled.
V. 18 The clouds poured out water;
the skies gave forth thunder;
your arrows flashed on every side.
V. 19 The crash of your thunder was in the wheels;[37]
your lightnings lit up the world;
the earth trembled and shook.
V. 20 Your way was in the sea,
your path through the mighty waters;
yet your footprints were unseen.
V. 21 You did lead your people like a flock by the hand of Moses
and Aaron.

In this Lament Psalm we here find Yahweh's victory over the sea at the Exodus appealed to as a ground for hope in the present, which thus parallels Is. 51:9–11, as it also does Ps. 74:12ff. and 89:10f. (ET 9f.), where the victory over the sea is confined to the creation. The fact that the conflict is *with* the sea at the time of the Exodus, and not simply *at* the sea, goes beyond Ex. 15, to be considered shortly. Parallels with other Old Testament passages on various points may be noted: v. 17 recalls Hab. 3:10–11 and has sometimes actually been employed in reconstructing the latter passage. The whole of vv. 12 (ET 11)ff. seems to relate to the Exodus, and v. 14 (ET 13) 'Your way, O God, is holy, What god is great like our God?', recalls Ex. 15:11, 'Who is like you, O Lord, among the gods? Who is like you, majestic in holiness. . . .?', whilst v. 15 (ET 14) '. . . who works wonders' recalls Ex. 15:11 '. . . worker of wonders'.

V. 17 (ET 16) is a notable example of repetitive parallelism, 'When the waters saw thee, O God, when the waters saw thee, they were afraid, yea, the deep trembled.'

Isaiah 51:9–11

The dual reference to the creation and Exodus here has already been discussed above.[38]

Exodus 15:1–18

Ex. 15:1–18, referred to as the Song of Moses in v. 1, but often known otherwise as 'the Song of the Sea' or 'the Song of Miriam'

37 I.e. the wheels of the cloud-chariot, cf. Ezek. 10:2, 6, 13. Alternatively, the translation 'whirlwind' has been suggested.
38 Cf. above, pp. 91ff.

(cf. v. 21) to distinguish it from the Song of Moses in Deut. 32, differs from the passages discussed above in that there is here no divine conflict with the waters, nor do the waters symbolize a foreign nation or nations; rather, Yahweh's victory at Yam Suph is over Pharaoh and his armies, and the waters, which are in no way personified, are merely the passive instrument used by Yahweh in accomplishing his purpose.[39] Nevertheless, it is very clear that the description has been shaped and influenced by motifs deriving from the myth of the divine conflict with the waters. Thus, the motif of the victory at the sea is associated with Yahweh's eternal kingship (v. 18, 'The Lord will reign for ever and ever'), just as was Baal's victory over Yam (cf. *CTA* 2.IV.10, 32 = *KTU* 1.2.IV.10, 32; cf. Marduk in Enuma elish II. 122ff., III. 59ff., 115ff., IV. 2ff., 28), and it issues in the building of his Temple (v. 17, 'You will bring them in and plant them on the mount of your inheritance, the place which you made for your abode, O Lord, the sanctuary, O Lord, which your hands established'), just as was the case with Baal (*CTA* 3–4 = *KTU* 1.3.–4; cf. Marduk in Enuma elish VI. 49ff.). (The fact that this common ideological background indicates that v. 17 belongs with the earlier part of the poem is an important point to be set against Hyatt's view[40] that vv. 1b–12 and 13–18 were originally separate poems of different date.) The expressions used of Yahweh's dwelling in v, 17 (*har naḥ*ᵃ*lāṯ*ᵉ*ḵā, māḵōn l*ᵉ*šiḇt*ᵉ*ḵā* and also *miqdāš*) are indeed so similar to those used of Baal and other gods in the Ugaritic texts[41] that there can be no doubt that they were derived from the Canaanites. This has been used as an argument in favour of a very early dating of Ex. 15 by Albright and Cross and

39 This point is emphasized by F.M. Cross and D.N. Freedman, 'The Song of Miriam', *JNES* 14 (1955), p. 239 and F.M. Cross, 'The Song of the Sea and Canaanite Myth', in *Canaanite Myth and Hebrew Epic* (Cambridge, Mass., 1973), pp. 131–2 (originally published in *JThC* 5, 1968).

40 J.P. Hyatt, *Exodus* (London, 1971), p. 163.

41 Cf. *CTA* 3.IIIC. 26–7 (= *KTU* 1.3.III.29–30), where we read that Baal's dwelling is *btk. ģry. 'il. ṣpn bqdš. bģr. nḥlty* 'within my mountain divine Zaphon, in the holy place, in the mountain of my inheritance', which is also to be restored in *CTA* 3.IV.63–4 (= *KTU* 1.3.IV.19–20). Similarly, Mot's dwelling is described as *ks'u ṯbth* 'the throne on which he sits' and *'arṣ nḥlth* 'the land of his inheritance' in *CTA* 4.VIII.12–14 and 5.II.15–16 (= *KTU* 1.4.VIII.12–14 and 1.5.II.15–16), and likewise Kothar-and-Ḫasis' dwelling in *CTA* 3.VIF.14–16 (= *KTU* 1.3.VI.14–16) is *kptr ks'u. ṯbth. ḥkpt 'arṣ. nḥlth* 'Caphtor, the throne on which he sits, Memphis, the land of his inheritance', which should also be restored in *CTA* 1.III.1–2 (= *KTU* 1.1.III.1–2). It is noteworthy that in the case of the dwellings of Mot and Kothar-and-Ḫasis, we find the two expressions *'arṣ. nḥlth* and *ks'u. ṯbth* combined, just like Ex. 15:17.

Freedman[42] and against seeing here a reference to Mt Zion. Ugaritic parallels, however, are in no way confined to very early parts of the Old Testament (cf. Is. 27:1, etc.), and since Zion is specifically referred to as Zaphon (the name of Baal's mountain) in Ps. 48:3 (ET 2), we should not be surprised that other language originally used of Baal's dwelling was also applied to Jerusalem. (Cf. too Is. 25:6–8, where imagery drawn from Baal's feast for the gods on Zaphon is taken over and reapplied to Zion.) The fact that the one other place in the Old Testament where the expression *mākōn lᵉšibṯᵉkā* is employed of an earthly sanctuary is in connection with the Temple on Mt Zion (1 Kings 8:13; cf. 2 Chron. 6:2; a quotation from the book of Jashar – cf. LXX and Vulgate), strongly supports the contention that this is the case here also.[43] The main alternative to this view, namely that it is Canaan as a whole,[44] rather than Jerusalem and the Temple which is alluded to in v. 17, is opposed by the fact that Canaan is never spoken of elsewhere in the Old Testament as Yahweh's dwelling place, nor is it described as his sanctuary (*miqdāš*), whereas this expression is used a considerable number of times of the Jerusalem Temple (cf. Ps. 78:69, 96:6; Lam. 1:10, etc.). It is probable, therefore, that these and the parallel expression 'mountain of your inheritance' refer to Jerusalem[45] rather than the Canaanite hill country generally. I would also note that the apparent statement of this verse that Yahweh would plant the people in the Temple – and not simply on the mountain (besides *miqdāš*, note that *mākōn lᵉšibṯᵉkā* in 1 Kings 8:13, the only other instance of this expression, is explicitly used of the Temple building and not simply Jerusalem) – may be accepted, since this is paralleled in Ps. 92:14 (ET 13), where the righteous are 'planted in the house of the Lord, they flourish in the courts of our God' (Cf. Ps. 52:10, ET 8). This thus refutes Hyatt's statement,[46] in his commentary on Ex. 15:17, that planting in the Temple is an

42 W.F. Albright, *The Archaeology of Palestine* (rev. ed., Harmondsworth, 1960), p. 233; F.M. Cross and D.N. Freedman, *op. cit.*, p. 250.

43 The very similar expression *mᵉkōn šibṯekā* is used of heaven in 1 Kings 8:39, 43, 49 (cf. 2 Chron. 6:30, 33, 39); also cf. Ps. 33:14 *mᵉkōn šibṯō*.

44 Cf. M. Noth, *Das zweite Buch Mose, Exodus* (Göttingen, 1959), p. 100 (ET *Exodus*, London, 1966, pp. 125–6); this view has recently been revived by A.R. Johnson, *The Cultic Prophet and Israel's Psalmody* (Cardiff, 1979), pp. 36–8. It should be noted, however, that Cross thinks rather in terms of another sanctuary, namely that at Gilgal, cf. *Canaanite Myth*, p. 142.

45 In this conclusion I agree with such scholars as R.E. Clements, *God and Temple* (Oxford, 1965), pp. 53–4.

46 J.P. Hyatt, *op. cit.*, p. 168.

impossible concept. It presumably alludes to the continuous participation of the people in the Jerusalem cult. The parallel to Ex. 15:17 adduced in Ps. 92:14 (ET 13) is, moreover, yet a further piece of evidence supporting the claim that Ex. 15:17 is indeed alluding to the Temple at Jerusalem.

Accordingly, if v. 17 refers to the Jerusalem Temple, the extremely early dates posited for Ex. 15:1–18 by Albright[47] (thirteenth century B.C.), Cross and Freedman[48] (twelfth–eleventh centuries B.C.) and Robertson[49] (twelfth century B.C.) cannot be maintained, and a tenth century date becomes the *terminus a quo*.

As Mowinckel[50] has emphasized, the Song bears marked resemblances to the Enthronement Psalms, e.g. the references to Yahweh's kingship[51] (v. 18; cf. Ps. 47:9, ET 8, 93:1, 96:10, 97:1, 99:1), his victory at the sea (*passim*; cf. Ps. 93:3–4), his exaltation over the gods (v. 11; cf. Ps. 95:3, 96:4–5, 97:7, 9),[52] and the pre-

47 W.F. Albright, *loc. cit.*

48 F.M. Cross and D.N. Freedman, *op. cit.*, p. 240.

49 D.A. Robertson, *Linguistic Evidence in Dating Early Hebrew Poetry* (Missoula, Mt., 1972), p. 155 and *passim.* Robertson sees it as the oldest Hebrew poetry in the Old Testament, followed by Judg. 5, Ps. 18, Deut. 32, Hab. 3 and Job. According to Robertson the earliest Hebrew poetry can be isolated by the criterion of its similarity to Ugaritic (and Canaanite Amarna glosses). Archaizing poetry is distinguished from the archaic by the degree to which later forms are also present. On this basis Robertson holds Ex. 15 to be the earliest poetic piece in the Old Testament. However, Robertson's method is clearly fraught with uncertainty, since there is no proof that the earliest Hebrew poetry can be isolated on the basis of its closeness to Ugaritic – Hebrew and Ugaritic are, after all, separate languages. (Similarly, the presence of Ugaritic mythological themes in Hebrew is no criterion of antiquity, since some of the most impressive examples occur in late works, e.g. Is. 27:1, Dan. 7.) That caution is needed in applying Robertson's approach is indicated by the early date which he ascribes to Job, since on other grounds this is generally dated to the post-exilic period. This suggests that the attempt to date Hebrew poetry in this way is in danger of imposing a linguistic straitjacket on it which does not accord with reality. In spite of what has been said, however, it is still possible that Ex. 15 is *relatively* early, since the reference to Solomon's temple in v. 17 is compatible with a date in the tenth century B.C.

50 S. Mowinckel, *Psalmenstudien* 2 (Kristiania, 1922), *passim*; *The Psalms in Israel's Worship* 2 (ET, Oxford, 1962), p. 247 and *passim.*

51 The view of G. Fohrer, *Überlieferung und Geschichte des Exodus* (*BZAW* 91, 1964), p. 115, that the words *Yahweh yimlōḵ* in v. 18 indicate that the work must be later than Deutero-Isaiah is now out of the question. It is clear that Deutero-Isaiah himself was dependent on the language of the Enthronement Psalms.

52 Note that the motif of the incomparability of Yahweh amongst the gods is also found specifically in the context of the conflict with the sea, namely Ps. 77:14 (ET 13) and 89:7–9 (ET 6–8).

sence of the same key words. This supports the view that at Jerusalem the Song had its *Sitz im Leben* in the Autumn Festival,[53] and the contrary view that it was recited at the Passover is to be deemed improbable.[54]

The chaotic sea as a designation for Assyria

Isaiah 17:12–14

12 Ah, the raging of many peoples,
they rage like the raging of the sea!
Ah, the roar of nations,
they roar like the roaring of the great waters!
13 The nations roar like the roaring of mighty waters,
but he will roar at them,
and they will flee far away,
chased like chaff on the mountains before the wind
and whirling dust before the storm.
14 At evening time, behold, terror!
Before morning, they are no more!
This is the portion of those who despoil us,
and the lot of those who plunder us.

Here we find the hostile nations compared with the unruly waters, from which Yahweh will deliver Israel. The imagery here is very similar to Ps. 46. In addition to the common comparison of the nations with the waters, the root *hmh* 'rage' being used in both cases (Ps. 46:4, 7, ET 3, 6; Is. 17:12), the deliverance from the enemy comes at dawn (Ps. 46:6, ET 5; Is. 17:14). R.E. Clements,[55]

53 In addition to Mowinckel, this view is held by such scholars as A. Weiser, *Einleitung in das Alte Testament* (4th ed., Göttingen, 1957), pp. 90–1 (ET *Introduction to the Old Testament*, London, 1961, p. 106); J. Muilenburg, 'A liturgy on the triumphs of Yahweh', in *Studia Biblica et Semitica Theodoro Christiano Vriezen . . . dedicata* (Wageningen, 1966), p. 236.

54 *Contra* J. Pedersen, *Israel: its Life and Culture* 3–4 (London and Copenhagen, 1940), p. 726, and additional note 1, pp. 728–37, and 'Passahfest und Passahlegende', *ZAW* 52 (1934), pp. 161–75, who regards the whole of Ex. 1–15 as the cult legend of the Passover, a view made difficult, however, by the presence of various sources in these chapters; G. Beer, *Exodus* (Tübingen, 1939), p. 84; R. Tournay, 'Recherches sur la chronologie des Psaumes. 2 Le chant de victoire d'Ex. XV', *RB* 65 (1958), pp. 335–57, who specifically connects the Song with Josiah's Passover of 621 B.C.; S.I.L. Norin, *Er spaltete das Meer* (Lund, 1977), p. 105, who thinks that the Song is ancient, nevertheless holds that it received a Deuteronomistic redaction in the 7th century B.C. and became associated with the Passover in Josiah's time; F.M. Cross, *Canaanite Myth*, p. 123, associates it with what he refers to as the old spring New Year festival.

55 R.E. Clements, *Isaiah and the Deliverance of Jerusalem* (Sheffield, 1980), pp. 46–7.

however, who regards this passage as a product of that Josianic redaction which, following H. Barth,[56] he believes to have had a pervasive influence on the work, holds that the origin of the comparison of the Assyrians with the waters should be sought in Is. 5:30 and possibly Is. 8:7. It should be noted though that, unlike Ps. 46:4, 7 (ET 3, 6), neither Is. 5:30 nor 8:7 use the verb *hmh* 'to rage' of the waters or enemy, which is found in Is. 17:12. In addition, the reference in Ps. 46:6 (ET 5) to the deliverance at dawn parallels Is. 17:14, and the fact that the nations are spoken of in the plural in Ps. 46:7 (ET 6) helps explain why nations in the plural are mentioned in Is. 17:12, even though only Assyria is apparently in view. It therefore seems to me that Ps. 46 is the main influence behind Is. 17:12–14. The use of the verb *gʿr* 'to roar' in v. 13, a term used especially in connection with God's reaction against the chaos waters (cf. Ps. 18:16, ET 15, = 2 Sam. 22:16, 104:7; Job 26:11; Is. 50:2; Nah. 1:4), also attests the influence of *Chaoskampf* material related to Ps. 46 (cf. too the Zion Psalm 76:7, ET 6). It is clear from Is. 7:14, where the name Immanuel 'God is with us' is employed in the context of the threat to Zion, that the prophet Isaiah was familiar with Ps. 46, since there too we find the refrain 'the Lord of hosts is with us' (*Yahweh ṣᵉḇāʾōṯ ʿimmānū*) in vv. 8, 12 (ET 7, 11) in the setting of Zion under siege. There seems to me no reason why Is. 17:12–14 should not similarly go back to Isaiah, as is generally held.[57]

It is clear from Is. 17:14 that the enemy poses a threat at night. The same notion is implied in Ps. 46:6 (ET 5). Since both passages equate the enemy with the chaos waters one might conjecture that the night threat derives from the myth of the conflict with the chaos waters. Such a supposition finds confirmation from the Ugaritic texts, for at the very end of the Baal cycle (*CTA* 6.VI.44–52 = *KTU* 1.6.VI.45–53), we find that the chaos monsters of the sea, Arš and the dragon, pose a threat precisely at the time when the sun-goddess Shapash is in the underworld, i.e. at night. The relevance of this passage for the understanding of Is. 17:14 and Ps. 46:6 (ET 5) has not hitherto been noted, so far as I am aware.

44	špš	Shapash,
45	rpʾim. tḥtk	the shades are under you;
46	špš. tḥtk. ʾilnym	Shapash, the ghosts are under you;

56 H. Barth, *Die Jesaja-Worte in der Josiazeit* (Neukirchen, 1977).
57 Cf. H. Wildberger, *Jesaja* 2 (Neukirchen, 1978), pp. 669–71.

47 ʻdk. ʼilm. hn. mtm	the gods (come) to you, behold! the dead
48 ʻdk. kṯrm. ḥbrk	(come) to you. Kothar is your companion
49 wḫss. dʻtk	and Ḫasis your friend.
50 bym. ʼarš. wtnn	In the sea are Arš and the dragon;
51 kṯr. wḫss. yd	May Kothar-and-Ḫasis drive (them) away,
52 ytr. kṯr. wḫss	May Kothar-and-Ḫasis cut (them) off.

Isaiah 8:5–8

5 The Lord spoke to me again: Because this people have refused the
waters of Shiloah that flow gently, melting in fear before the pride
of[58] Rezin and the son of Remaliah;
7 therefore, behold, the Lord is bringing up against them the waters
of the River, powerful and mighty, the king of Assyria and all his
glory; and it will rise over all its channels and go over all its
banks;
8 and it will sweep on into Judah, it will overflow and pass on,
reaching even to the neck; and its outspread wings will fill the
breadth of your land, O Immanuel.

Although this passage is not actually referring to a divine conflict with the chaos waters, the imagery of the divine conflict with the waters of Ps. 46 has here been taken up and given a new twist, in that here the waters, symbolizing the king of Assyria, are not defeated but are victorious (vv. 7-8). That the reference is here taking up Ps. 46 is shown by the fact that in addition to the waters (v. 4, ET 3), we also have an allusion to Immanuel 'God is with us' (v. 8), reflecting the influence of Ps. 46:8, 12 (ET 7, 11) (*Yahweh ṣ^{e}ḇāʼōṯ ʻimmānū* 'the Lord of hosts is with us') – though it now symbolizes judgement rather than salvation – and we also read of 'the waters of Shiloah that flow gently' as a ground of hope in the divine protection over against the chaos waters, just as in Ps. 46:5 (ET 4) we learn that 'There is a river whose streams make glad the city of God', and this seems to be a ground of confidence set over against the chaos waters of v. 4 (ET 3).

It is probable that Is. 8:5–8 has its *Sitz im Leben* in the Syro-Ephraimite crisis of 734–2 B.C., reflected in Is. 7.[59] The common

58 The MT *ūm^{e}śōś ʼeṯ r^{e}ṣīn* 'and the joy with Rezin' is widely recognized to be both syntactically difficult and nonsensical. As is generally recognized, the first word should be understood as bearing the meaning 'melt', like Heb. *mss* (cf. Is. 10:18), here 'melt in fear'. We could then read *māśōś* 'melting'. With K. Budde, 'Jes 8 6b', *ZAW* 44 (1926), pp. 65–7, we might then read after this *miśś^{e}ʼēṯ r^{e}ṣīn* 'before the pride of Rezin' for MT *ʼeṯ r^{e}ṣīn*, the letters *mś* having fallen out by haplography.

59 Cf. H. Wildberger, *Jesaja* 1 (2nd ed., Neukirchen, 1980), pp. 322–3.

background of Is. 7 and 8:5–8, rooted as they both are in Ps. 46 with reference to the Syro-Ephraimite crisis, leads me to make a novel suggestion regarding the reason for the location of Isaiah's preaching in Is. 7:3 at the 'conduit of the upper pool'. It was noted above that in Ps. 46:5 (ET 4), the mythological river in Jerusalem is a ground of confidence in the divine protection of Zion from hostile invaders, a protection signified by the refrain *Yahweh ṣ^{e}ḇā'ōṯ ʿimmānū* 'the Lord of hosts is with us', and that in Is. 8:6 the mythological river is taken up to refer to 'the waters of Shiloah that flow gently', i.e. the canal system transferring the waters of the Gihon spring south as far as the lower pool (birket el-ḥamra).[60] The fact that in Is. 7 it is 'at the end of the conduit of the upper pool'. i.e. part of the previously mentioned canal system,[61] that Isaiah delivers his message of deliverance of Zion from hostile invaders, signified by the name Immanuel (Is. 7:14) – provided the people have faith (Is. 7:9b, cf. Is. 8:5–8) – suggests that Isaiah proclaimed his message where he did because of the mythological overtones of divine protection associated with it as the paradisiacal river (cf. Gihon as the name of one of the rivers of Paradise in Gen. 2:13).

The chaotic sea as a designation for Babylon

Habakkuk 3:8–10, 15

V. 8 Is your wrath against the rivers, O Lord?
Is your anger against the rivers,
or your indignation against the sea,
when you ride upon your horses,
upon your chariot of victory?
V. 9 Utterly laid bare are your bow
and seven arrows with a word.[62] Selah.
You cleave the earth with rivers.

60 Cf. J. Simons, *Jerusalem in the Old Testament* (Leiden, 1952), pp. 175ff.; L.H. Vincent and M. Steve, *Jérusalem de l'Ancien Testament* 1 (Paris, 1954), pp. 289ff.

61 Probably near the place in the lower Kidron valley where Canal II (bringing water from Gihon to the upper pool) was diverted by a short tunnel to the lower pool in the central valley. Cf. M. Burrows, 'The conduit of the upper pool', *ZAW* 70 (1958), pp. 221–7.

62 Reading *ʿārōh ṯ^{e}ʿārēh* for MT *ʿeryāh ṯēʿōr* and *šiḇʿaṯ* for MT *š^{e}ḇūʿōṯ*. See below, p. 106f.

V. 10 The mountains see you and writhe;
a torrent of rain descends;[63]
the deep gives forth its voice.
on high it lifts its hands.
V. 15 You trample the sea with your horses,
the seething mass of mighty waters.

The fact that Hab. 3 has musical notations (cf. vv. 1, 19) indicates that it was sung in the cult, and there can be no doubt that this was the Feast of Tabernacles,[64] since this was where the theme of the divine conflict with the chaotic waters had its *Sitz im Leben.* Evidence for its independent circulation is also provided by its absence from the Qumran Habakkuk commentary, but it is still possible that it is a genuine work of the prophet Habakkuk.

The chapter depicts the theophany of Yahweh in the storm coming up from the south and engaging in conflict with the unruly waters, which he overcomes. The conflict with the powers of chaos here enacted clearly involves their identification with a hostile political power which has invaded Judah (cf. vv. 12–14, 16), which, in view of the probable date of Habakkuk, is presumably the Babylonians, the deliverance of the Lord's Anointed associated with the victory (v. 13) being closely parallel to that depicted in Ps. 18 and 144. The connection of Yahweh's control of the cosmic waters with the bringing of rain so as to provide agricultural bounty is also hinted at in v. 17f., which is similarly paralleled in Ps. 144:12–15. One may also compare Ps. 65:8–14 (ET 7–13). V. 2 makes it clear that the present conflict with chaos is simply the renewal of Yahweh's earlier victory, presumably the primaeval conflict at the time of creation.

This chapter is of great interest for our theme, containing a number of mythological allusions not so explicitly expressed elsewhere.[65] One of these is contained in v. 5, where in the midst of Yahweh's storm theophany coming up from the south we read: *l^e^p̱ānāyw yēlēḵ deḇer w^e^yēṣē' rešep̱ l^e^raḡlāyw*, 'Before him went Pestilence, and Plague went forth behind him.' Plague and Pesti-

63 It seems unnecessary to emend MT *zerem mayim ʿāḇār* to *zōr^e^mū mayim ʿāḇōṯ*, simply to bring it into agreement with Ps. 77:18 (ET 17).

64 Cf. esp. J.H. Eaton, 'The origin and meaning of Habakkuk 3', *ZAW* 76 (1964), pp. 158–70.

65 For a survey of the views of various scholars on the mythological elements in Hab. 3, see P. Jöcken, *Das Buch Habakuk* (Cologne and Bonn, 1977), pp. 290–313.

lence are here clearly personified and behind the latter there certainly lies the Canaanite plague-god Resheph. As the present writer was the first to point out,[66] the allusion to Resheph's participation in the conflict with chaos has its ultimate background in the Ugaritic text *KTU* 1.82.1–3 (*UT* 1001.1–3).

(1) [ ] *mḫṣ. bʿl*[ ]*y. tnn. wygl. wynsk.* ʿ[ ]
(2) [ ] *y. lʾarṣ* [*.i*]*dy. ʾalt. lʾaḥš. ʾidy. ʾalt. ʾin ly*
(3) [ ] *t. bʿl. ḫẓ. ršp. bn. km. yr. klyth. wlbh*
(1) Baal smote . . . the dragon and rejoiced and poured out . . .
(2) . . . on the earth . . . support . . . I have no support
(3) . . . the archer Resheph, son of *Km* shot his kidneys and his heart.

In Hab. 3:5 the god Resheph has been demoted to a kind of demon in Yahweh's entourage. Since the Ugaritic parallel shows that Resheph belongs with the *Chaoskampf*, it is clear that Albright[67] is wrong in separating Hab. 3:3–7 (where Resheph occurs, v. 5) and 3:8–15 (where the *Chaoskampf* is described) as originally two separate poems.

Another interesting mythological allusion is contained in v. 9. The MT here reads *ʿeryāh ṯēʿōr qašteḵa šᵉḇūʿōṯ maṭṭōṯ ʾōmer*, which I have proposed to render, 'Utterly laid bare are your bow and seven arrows with a word.' As I have argued elsewhere,[68] the problem of the well-known crux *šᵉḇūʿōṯ* may be solved if it is emended to *šiḇʿaṯ* 'seven', so that we have here a reference to Yahweh's seven shafts or arrows of lightning, comparable to his seven thunders depicted in Ps. 29. This parallelism with Ps. 29 is in keeping with the close relationship between them generally: both refer to Yahweh's theophany in the storm (Hab. 3:3–4, 9, 11, and *passim*; Ps. 29:3–9), including an allusion to the Sinai theophany (Hab. 3:3; Ps. 29:8)[69], Yahweh's exaltation over the cosmic sea (Hab. 3:8–10, 15; Ps. 29:3, 10) and the upheaval of nature at Yahweh's appearing (Hab. 3:6–7, 10–11; Ps. 29:5–9). That the MT

66 J, Day, 'New light on the mythological background of the allusion to Resheph in Habakkuk iii 5', *VT* 29 (1979), pp. 353–5. This contains a discussion of alternative translations of part of the Ugaritic.
67 W.F. Albright, 'The Psalm of Habakkuk', in H.H. Rowley (ed.), *Studies in Old Testament Prophecy* (Edinburgh, 1950), pp. 8–9.
68 J. Day, 'Echoes of Baal's seven thunders and lightnings in Psalm xxix and Habakkuk iii 9 and the identity of the seraphim in Isaiah vi', *VT* 29 (1979), pp. 146–7.
69 Cf. above, Ch. 1, n. 169.

originally read *šibʿat maṭṭōṯ* rather than *šᵉḇūʿōt maṭṭōṯ* can claim support from the LXX which has ἐπὶ (τὰ) σκῆπτρα, which, as was first pointed out by Grevius and has been accepted by such distinguished LXX scholars as J.F. Schleusner, E. Nestle, F.X. Wutz and J. Ziegler, must represent an internal LXX corruption from ἑπτὰ σκῆπτρα or ἐπὶ ἑπτὰ σκῆπτρα. Yahweh's seven thunders and lightnings, attested in Ps. 29 and Hab. 3:9, have their background in Baal mythology. Thus, in *Ugaritica V*.3.3b–4 (*RS* 24.245 lines 3b–4 = *KTU* 1.101.3b–4) we read of Baal.

3b	šbʿt. brqm. x[ ]	Seven lightnings . . .
4	ṯmnt. ʾiṣr rʿt. ʿṣ. brq. y[ ]	Eight storehouses of thunder.
		The shaft of lightning . . .

A further mythological allusion is to be found in Hab. 3:8, 15. There we read of Yahweh's horses drawing his (cloud-) chariot in connection with his victory over the sea: '. . . when you ride upon your horses, upon your chariot of victory?' (3:8) and 'You trample the sea with your horses. . .' Previously only the Babylonian Enuma elish's account of Marduk's horses (Enuma elish IV, 51) has been noted in this connection. However, since it is probably rather Baal mythology which underlies the mythological allusions in Hab. 3, it is interesting to note the evidence that Baal too had horses drawing his (cloud-) chariot. Apollodorus (*The Library* I.6.3) records that in the battle between Zeus and the serpent or dragon Typhon, 'Zeus. . . suddenly appeared in the sky on a chariot drawn by winged horses.' The fact that part of the battle takes place on 'Mt Casius, which overhangs Syria' (Apollodorus, *loc. cit.*), i.e. precisely the Mt Zaphon where Baal's conflict with the dragon and the sea would have been localized (cf. *CTA* 3.IIID.43–IV.46 = *KTU* 1.3.III.46–IV.2), indicates that we here have to do with traditions going back ultimately to Baal.[70] The explicit reference to the chariot itself recalls Baal, but the reference to the winged horses is particularly interesting as a parallel to Hab. 3:8, 15. Since the horses draw the cloud-chariot, it is probable that they symbolize the winds. It is therefore extremely interesting that Ps. 18:11 (ET 10) and 104:3 speak of Yahweh's riding on the *wings* of the wind in the context of his conflict with the sea (cf. Gen. 1:2). It may be conjectured that Baal, like Zeus in the Typhon conflict, had winged horses drawing his cloud-chariot, the horses being reflected in Hab.

70 Cf. above, Ch. 1, n. 92.

3:8, 15 and the wings in Ps. 18:11 (ET 10) and 104:3. I have elsewhere argued that the Ugaritic texts actually allude to the team of horses drawing Baal's chariot.[71]

A number of other mythological allusions have been sought in Hab. 3 which are unconvincing. Thus, F.J. Stephens[72] emended Hab. 3:13b so as to obtain a reference to Behemoth, *māḥaṣtā rō'š bᵉhēmōṯ* 'you smote the head of Behemoth', whilst Albright[73] found in this verse an allusion to Mot, *māḥaṣtā rō'š māweṯ rāšā'* 'you smote the head of wicked Death (Mot)'. It is, however, simpler to retain the MT *māḥaṣtā rō'š mibbēṯ rāšā'* 'you smote the top off the house of the wicked', continuing at the end of the verse *'ārōṯ yᵉsōḏ 'aḏ ṣūr* (for MT *ṣawwā'r*) 'laying bare the foundation as far as the rock'. Again, in Hab. 3:9 U. (M.D.) Cassuto[74] implausibly found an allusion to Baal's club *'aymr*, with which he defeated Yam in *CTA* 2 (= *KTU* 1.2), in the word *'ōmer* at the end of the problematic Hab. 3:9. Cassuto's suggestion, however, would involve seeing here a *hapax legomenon*, and I have suggested above a more probable rendering of this verse which retains the normal meaning of *'ōmer* 'word'.

The description of the effect of the theophany in Hab. 3:11 is interesting: 'The sun and moon stood still in their habitation at the light of your arrows as they sped, at the flash of your glittering spear.' The theophany clearly takes the form of lightning and it is surely by its brightness that the sun and moon are here blotted out. In this there is a parallel with Is. 24:23. What is particularly interesting about Hab. 3:11a, 'The sun and moon stood still in their habitation', is the verbal parallel with Josh. 10:12b–13a, where Joshua declared, 'Sun, stand still at Gibeon, and moon in the valley of Aijalon. And the sun stood still, and the moon stayed, until the nation took vengeance on their enemies' (*šemeš bᵉgiḇ'ōn dōm wᵉyārēaḥ bᵉ'ēmeq 'ayyālōn wayyiddōm haššemeš wᵉyārēaḥ 'āmāḏ 'aḏ yiqqōm gōy 'ōyᵉḇāyw*). R. Tournay[75] has even suggested

71 J. Day, 'Echoes of Baal's seven thunders and lightnings in Psalm xxix and Habakkuk iii 9 and the identity of the seraphim in Isaiah vi', *VT* 29 (1979), p. 147, n. 18. Also see above, Ch. 1, n. 93.

72 F.J. Stephens, 'The Babylonian Dragon Myth in Habakkuk 3', *JBL* 43 (1924), pp. 291–2.

73 W.F. Albright, *op. cit.*, pp. 11, 17, n. oo.

74 U. (M.D.) Cassuto, 'Chapter iii of Habakkuk and the Ras Shamra texts', *Biblical and Oriental Studies* 2 (ET, Jerusalem, 1975), p. 11.

75 R. Tournay, review of A. Deissler and M. Delcor, *Les Petits Prophètes* 2, in *RB* 72 (1965), p. 428.

that Hab. 3:11a is alluding to the battle of Gibeon, but this is improbable. The parallel does, however, add credence to the view that Josh. 10:12–13 is describing the disappearance of the sun and moon as a result of an early morning storm, suggesting a connection with the hail storm alluded to in v. 11. What seems to add striking confirmation to this view is that Ps. 18, which Westermann[76] has shown to have a structure remarkably close to that of Hab. 3, actually mentions hailstones in the section corresponding to Hab. 3:11a, namely in Ps. 18:13 (ET 12).

Finally, it should be noted that in view of the parallels noted above, as well as the Canaanite background of the Old Testament chaos and chaos monster imagery generally, Hab. 3 should be understood as deriving from Canaanite and not Babylonian mythology.[77]

The dragon as a designation for Babylon

Jeremiah 51:34

> Nebuchadrezzar king of Babylon has devoured me[78] and discomfited me;[79] he has made me an empty vessel, he has swallowed me like a dragon; he has filled his belly with my delicacies, he has spewed me out.

That the dragon (*tannīn*) is here a sea monster is supported by v. 36, where we read, 'I will dry up her sea and make her fountain dry.' The imagery of the sea monster is taken up again in v. 44, where it is applied to Babylon's god Bel, i.e. Marduk: 'And I will punish Bel in Babylon, and take out of his mouth what he has swallowed. The nations shall no longer flow to him;[80] the wall of Babylon has fallen.'

76 Cf. the comparison of the form critical structure of Hab. 3:3–15 and Ps. 18:8–16 (ET 7–15) in C. Westermann, *The Praise of God in the Psalms* (ET, London, 1966), pp. 94–5.

77 *Contra* W.A. Irwin, 'The Psalm of Habakkuk', *JNES* 1 (1942), pp. 10–40, and 'The mythological background of Habakkuk, chapter 3', *JNES* 15 (1956), pp. 47–50.

78 Reading with qere MSS Vrs. *'ᵃḵālanī* instead of kethibh *'ᵃḵālanū*.

79 Reading with qere *hᵃmāmanī* instead of kethibh *hᵃmāmanū*.

80 Omitting *gam* (dittography).

The great fish in the book of Jonah: not a symbol for Babylon

Some scholars[81] have imagined that the imagery of Jer. 51:34 has given rise to the depiction of the great fish in the book of Jonah which first swallowed Jonah (2:1, ET 1:17) and subsequently vomited him out on the dry land (2:11, ET 2:10). In keeping with this a number of scholars have argued that the swallowing up of Jonah by the fish and his subsequent deliverance are an allegory of the exile of the Jews in Babylon and their subsequent restoration.[82] It is improbable, however, that Jonah is dependent on Jer. 51:34, 44:[83] although the lack of common vocabulary apart from the use of the verb *bl'* is not decisive,[84] it may be noted that, whereas the great fish vomits out Jonah, it is Yahweh himself who directly draws Israel out of Bel's mouth in Jer. 51:44. Moreover, a point which appears to have been overlooked is that if the swallowing and vomiting of Jonah represent the exile and restoration of the Jews in Babylon, the allegory is highly confused, since immediately after the alleged depiction of the restoration from exile in Babylon Jonah is called to preach against Nineveh, the capital of the *Assyrian* empire, which is still flourishing after the 'exile' just as it did before the 'exile'! It is true that we find a comparable chronological confusion in the book of Judith (1:1), where Nebuchadrezzar is said to have reigned over the Assyrians in Nineveh, but this work is generally dated two centuries later than Jonah; further, such confusion would be surprising if Jonah were dependent on Jer. 51:34, since Nebuchadrezzar there is expressly called 'king of *Babylon*'. In any case, the writer of Jonah was surely aware of 2

81 Cf. A.D. Martin, *The Prophet Jonah: the Book and the Sign* (London, 1926), p. 33; J.D. Smart, in *The Interpreter's Bible* 6 (New York and Nashville, Tenn., 1956), p. 874. This view also appears to be implicit in G.A.F. Knight, *Ruth and Jonah* (London, 1950), pp. 52, 65, 66–7.

82 Apart from the works cited in the previous note, this view is followed by P. R. Ackroyd, *Exile and Restoration* (London, 1968), pp. 244–5. The first British scholar to develop this view at length was C.H.H. Wright, *Biblical Essays* (Edinburgh, 1886), pp. 34–98.

83 So rightly, H.W. Wolff, *Dodekapropheton 3 Obadja und Jona* (Neukirchen, 1977), p. 114.

84 For an example of the dependence of one biblical passage on another, *viz.* parts of Is. 26–7 on Hos. 13–14, in which the parallels are of a thematic rather than a strictly literal character, cf. my article, 'A case of inner Scriptural interpretation. The dependence of Isaiah xxvi. 13–xxvii. 11 on Hosea xiii. 4–xiv. 10 (Eng. 9) and its relevance to some theories of the redaction of the "Isaiah apocalypse"', *JTS* 31 n.s. (1980), pp. 309–19, and note the observation on other examples of this on p. 316.

Kings 14:25, where the prophet is depicted as a historical personage, which makes it unlikely that he would have been interpreted simply as an allegorical figure. The allegorical interpretation is to be rejected and we must conclude that the imagery of the great fish in Jonah is not dependent on that of the dragon in Jer. 51:34.

Nevertheless, it is probable that the 'great fish' of the book of Jonah is derived ultimately from the sea monster of Baal mythology. That there is indeed a wider mythological background to the 'great fish' of Jonah is supported by the fact that the story of Perseus' deliverance of Andromeda from the sea monster, which Morenz[85] even attempts to derive from the story of Baal's (Seth's) deliverance of Astarte from the sea recounted in the Astarte papyrus, was associated by a strong ancient tradition with Joppa (so Pseudo-Scylax, *Periplus*;[86] Strabo, *Geography*, 16.2.28; Pausanias, *Description of Greece*, 4.35.9; Josephus, *Jewish War*, 3.9.3; Pliny, *Natural History*, 5.14 and 9.4), the very place at which Jonah boarded the ship before being swallowed by the great fish.[87] The earliest of these references, that in Pseudo-Scylax, dates from the 4th century B.C., about the same time as the book of Jonah was composed. The common location of the incidents involving Jonah and Perseus and Andromeda was already alluded to by Jerome and Cyril of Alexandria in their commentaries on Jonah, and the deduction that the two stories must therefore have a common origin was already concluded by O. Gruppe[88] in 1889.

85 S. Morenz, 'Die orientalische Herkunft der Perseus-Andromeda-Sage. Ein Rekonstruktionsversuch', *Forschungen und Fortschritte* 36/10 (1962), pp. 307–9, reprinted in his collected essays, *Religion und Geschichte des alten Ägypten* (Weimar, 1975), pp. 441–7.

86 See C. Müller, *Geographi Graeci Minores* 1 (Paris, 1855), p. 79.

87 Other ancient writers associated the event with Ethiopia, but the antiquity of the Joppa tradition is supported by the fact that some of the above writers were able to point to definite places in the environs of Joppa connected with the Andromeda myth by the local inhabitants. Cf. H. Schmidt, *Jona. Eine Untersuchung zur vergleichenden Religionsgeschichte* (Göttingen, 1907), pp. 12–22. Schmidt's whole work, although old, contains a mass of interesting information still worthy of study.

88 O. Gruppe, 'Aithiopenmythen. 1. Der phönikische Urtext der Kassiepeialegende. Zusammenhang derselben mit anderen Aithiopenmythen', *Philologus* 47 (1889), pp. 93f. On Perseus and Andromeda, see most recently, M. Avi-Yonah, פרסאוס ואנדרומדיה ביפו, *Yediot* 31 (1967), pp. 203–10.

The dragon as an uncertain political enemy

Isaiah 27:1

In my view Leviathan in Is. 27:1 most probably denotes Egypt but it could be Babylon or Persia. In view of its eschatological context I shall consider it below in Chapter 4.[89]

Psalm 44:19–20 (ET 18–19)

V. 19 (ET 18) Our heart has not turned back,
nor have our steps departed from your way,
V. 20 (ET 19) that you should have crushed us in place of the dragon,[90]
and covered us with deep darkness.

These words form part of a communal lament in which the people bemoan their military defeat by an unnamed foreign enemy. The main problem of Ps. 44:20 (ET 19) is in deciding whether we should read 'that you should have crushed us in the place of *jackals*' or 'that you should have crushed us in place of the *dragon*'. The former view, reading *tannīm* 'jackals', can claim the support of the MT, but too much weight should not be attached to this, since Ezek. 29:3 and 32:2, where the MT wrongly has *tannīm*, show how easily *tannīn* could be corrupted to *tannīm*, whilst the reverse process occurs in Lam. 4:3. Of course, the MT ought to be preferred if it makes good sense, but though it is not impossible, it is a little odd. Although 'jackals' aptly serve to represent desolation (cf. Is. 34:13, 35:7; Jer. 9:11, 10:22, 49:33, 51:37) and are actually associated with darkness in this connection in Job 30:26, 28, 29, this does not fit Ps. 44:20 (ET 19), since in the latter the reference to the defeat 'in the place of jackals' would rather suggest the presence of the jackals already before the defeat, rather than as a consequence of it.[91]

Accordingly, it eases matters if we follow the suggestion first made by Gunkel[92] and emend MT *tannīm* 'jackals' to *tannīn* 'dragon' (which can claim the support of Peshiṭta's *tnyn*'), and thus render 'that you should have broken us *in place of the dragon*, and

89 Cf. below, pp. 142–5.
90 Reading *tannīn* 'dragon' for MT *tannīm* 'jackals' (cf. Pershiṭta). See discussion below.
91 It could be argued that the verse indicates that the defeat took place in a desolate place, but this seems less likely.
92 H. Gunkel, *Schöpfung und Chaos*, pp. 70–1.

covered us with deep darkness'. That *bim^eqōm* can mean 'in place/instead of' in Biblical Hebrew is indicated by Hos. 2:1 (ET 1:10), 'And it shall be that *instead of* being said to them "You are not my people", it shall be said to them, "Sons of the living God."'[93] Ps. 44:20 (ET 19) then provides an excellent parallel to the thought in Job 7:12, where Job complains to God, 'Am I the sea, or dragon (*tannīn*), that you set a guard over me?' Furthermore, it may be noted that the use of the verb *dikkāh* 'crush' in Ps. 44:20 (ET 19) is paralleled in Ps. 89:11 (ET 10), where *dikkā'* 'crush' is employed in connection with the slaying of Rahab, whilst the motif of darkness associated with the defeat of the dragon in Ps. 44:20 (ET 19) is paralleled in Ezek. 32:7–8, where darkness similarly appears as part of the punishment of the dragon (*tannīn*).

If we assume that we do have here a reference to the dragon, symbolizing the enemy nation defeating Israel, to which nation does it allude? Unfortunately we cannot be sure, since the date of the psalm is uncertain. A.A. Anderson[94] notes that two probable dates are the time after the death of Josiah in 609 B.C., or less likely, during Sennacherib's invasion of Judah in the time of Hezekiah (701 B.C.). In that case, the dragon might refer to Babylon or Egypt (symbolism already encountered above) or possibly Assyria.[95]

Bashan: not a name for the mythical sea serpent

> Psalm 68:23 (ET 22)
> The Lord said, 'I will bring (them) back from Bashan,
> I will bring (them) back from the depths of the sea.'

The reason for the inclusion of this section is that a considerable number of scholars hold that the word rendered 'Bashan' is in reality yet another name for the mythical sea serpent or dragon, serving here perhaps as a poetical name for some foreign nation or nations, e.g. Egypt. The inspiration for this view derives from the fact that the Ugaritic equivalent of Hebrew *peṯen* is *bṯn* and is used of Leviathan in *CTA* 3.IIID.38 (= *KTU* 1.3.III.41) and 5.I.1–2 (= *KTU* 1.5.I.1–2), so that Hebrew Bashan could be a more

93 *BDB* gives this meaning for *m^eqōm* in Is. 33:21, a view still followed by J. Gray, *The Biblical Doctrine of the Reign of God* (Edinburgh, 1979), p. 74, n. 149, but this is most improbable.

94 A.A. Anderson, *The Book of Psalms* 1 (London, 1972), p. 337.

95 On pp. 336–7 Anderson cites a number of reasons why the Maccabaean dating of the psalm favoured by the early Church Fathers and some later exegetes should be rejected.

Canaanitizing form of normal Hebrew *peṯen*. It also derives from the fact that in Ps. 68:23 (ET 22) Bashan is parallel to 'the depths of the sea' (*m^{e}ṣūlōṯ yām*), on which basis it is alleged that Bashan must be a name for the mythical sea serpent.

Quite a number of variants of this view exist, almost all of which involve either emendation or some repointing or redivision of the MT. It was U. (M.D.) Cassuto[96] in 1940 who first suggested tentatively that Bashan might here refer to the mythical sea serpent, and this view was also taken by S. I. Feigin in 1943.[97] In 1950 W.F. Albright[98] incorporated this view into his translation of the verse, reading *'mr yhw mi⟨m^{e}ḥōṣ⟩ bšn 'āšūḇ 'āšūb-m mṣ[m]t ym* 'The Lord said, "From smiting the Serpent I return, I return from destroying Sea!"' Other variants of this which have been proposed are the following: retaining the MT, S. Mowinckel[99] proposed 'Spricht Jahwe: "Ich bringe zurück (selbst) von der Schlange, von Meerestiefen bringe ich zurück"', F.C. Fensham[100] reads *'āmar '^{a}ḏōnāy miḥōr bāšān 'āšīḇ 'āšīḇ mim^{e}ṣūlōṯ yām* 'The Lord said, "From the hole of the Snake I will bring back, I will bring back from the depths of the Sea"', M.J. Dahood[101] proposed *'āmar '^{a}ḏōnāy-m bāšān 'aššīḇ 'ešbam m^{e}ṣūlōṯ yām* 'The Lord said, "I stifled the serpent, muzzled the deep sea"', P.D. Miller[102] suggested *'āmar '^{a}ḏōnāy 'ešbam bāšān 'ešbam m^{e}ṣūlōṯ yām* 'The Lord said, "I muzzled the Serpent, I muzzled the Deep Sea"', F.M. Cross[103] orally proposed *'āmar '^{a}ḏōnāy 'ešbam bāšān 'ešbammennōh ⟨māḥaṣtī⟩ m^{e}ṣūlōṯ yām* 'The Lord said, "I muzzled the dragon, I muzzled him, I smashed the Deep Sea"', the *NEB*[104] ventured

96 U. (M.D.) Cassuto, **תהלים ס"ח**, *Tarbiz* 12 (1940), p. 18, n. 69 (ET, 'Psalm LXVIII', *Biblical and Oriental Studies* 1, Jerusalem, 1973, p. 269, n. 71.)

97 S.I. Feigin, **מסתרי העבר** (New York, 1943), p. 407. (Inaccessible to me.)

98 W.F. Albright, 'A Catalogue of early Hebrew lyric poems (Psalm LXVIII)', *HUCA* 23 Part 1 (1950–1), pp. 14, 27–8, 38.

99 S. Mowinckel, *Der achtundsechzigste Psalm* (Oslo, 1953), p. 48.

100 F.C. Fensham, 'Ps. 68:23 in the light of the recently discovered Ugaritic tablets', *JNES* 19 (1960), pp. 292–3.

101 M.J. Dahood, 'Mišmār "muzzle" in Job 7:12', *JBL* 80 (1961), pp. 270–1. In this article Dahood only gives us his view of the text in the second half of the verse; for the first half we must refer to *Psalms* 2 (New York, 1968), pp. 131, 145–6. Note that whereas in the former place Dahood reads *'ešbam*, in the latter he proposes *'ešbōm*. As noted earlier (above, p. 14, n. 32 and p. 44) *šbm* does not in fact mean 'to muzzle'.

102 P.D. Miller, 'Two critical notes on Psalm 68 and Deuteronomy 33', *HTR* 57 (1964), p. 240.

103 So according to P.D. Miller, *op. cit.*, p. 240, n. 3.

104 Cf. L.H. Brockington, *The Hebrew Text of the Old Testament* (Oxford and Cambridge, 1973), p. 137.

'āmar 'ᵃdōnāy mibbāšān 'ašūḇ 'ašūḇ mimᵉṣūlōṯ yām 'The Lord says, "I will return from the Dragon, I will return from the depths of the sea"', and finally, J. Gray[105] has suggested that we read *'mr 'dny-m bšn hšb 'šyb 'šb mmṣwlwt ym* 'My Lord has declared, "I shall assuredly bring back the Serpent, I shall bring back Sea from the abyss."'

All these views, however, which seek to find a reference to the dragon in Ps. 68:23 (ET 22) are, in spite of their popularity, open to serious criticism. First of all, as noted above, they almost all involve either emendation or repointing and redivision of the text. Such expedients should be entertained only when it is impossible to obtain good sense from the text as it stands. Secondly, since the mountain of Bashan (presumably Mt Hermon) is twice mentioned only a few verses earlier (v. 16, ET 15), it is natural to suppose that this is the meaning of the reference to Bashan in v. 23 (ET 22), especially since the term for Bashan as a name for the serpent is nowhere else attested in Hebrew.[106] Furthermore, a disadvantage to the view that *bāšān* here means 'serpent' and is cognate with Ugaritic *bṯn* lies in the fact that Hebrew already has the word *peṯen* 'snake' cognate with Ugaritic *bṯn*.

Understanding *bāšān* to refer to the mountainous region of that name, as elsewhere in the Old Testament, we therefore obtain the translation, 'The Lord said, "I will bring (them) back from Bashan, I will bring (them) back from the depths of the sea."' Bashan and the depths of the sea are thus not terms standing in synonymous parallelism to one another but rather in antithetical parallelism, i.e. Bashan (Hermon) represents the highest spot, in contrast to the depths of the sea which form the lowest spot, from both of which God will smite the enemies mentioned in the preceding verse (v, 22, ET 21) should they flee there.

As noted above, it is most natural to equate the Bashan of v. 23 (ET 22) with the mountain of Bashan of v. 16 (ET 15). This latter is spoken of as *har 'ᵉlōhīm*: *har 'ᵉlōhīm har bāšān har gaḇnunnīm har bāšān*. Although *har 'ᵉlōhīm* is often rendered 'the mountain of God',[107] this can hardly be correct, since it is directly set in oppo-

105 J. Gray, 'A cantata of the Autumn Festival: Psalm lxviii', *JSS* 22 (1977), pp. 9–10, 24.

106 The suggestion of F.M. Cross and D.N. Freedman, 'The blessing of Moses', *JBL* 67 (1948), pp. 195, 208, that *bāšān* refers to the serpent in Deut. 33:22 is unconvincing. It is probable that we simply have here the comparison of Dan with a lion of Bashan: 'Dan is a lion's whelp that leaps forth from Bashan.'

107 Cf. H.-J. Kraus, *Psalmen* 2 (5th ed., Neukirchen, 1978), p. 625.

sition to Mt Zion in v. 17 (ET 16) (*lāmmāh tᵉraṣṣᵉḏūn hārīm gaḇnunnīm hāhār ḥāmaḏ ʼᵉlōhīm lᵉšiḇtō ʼap̱ yhwh yiškōn lāneṣaḥ*), the mountain where Yahweh dwells, and of which it is clearly represented as being envious. Nor is the superlative rendering of *har ʼᵉlōhīm* as 'mighty mountain'[108] probable, since the fact that it is clearly a sacred mountain makes it dubious that all thought of divinity is lacking from *ʼᵉlōhīm* in the expression *har ʼᵉlōhīm*, and furthermore, D.W. Thomas, who has undertaken the most thorough study of the superlative use of the divine name in the Old Testament,[109] concluded that the superlative use of the divine name does not eliminate the thought of divinity: quite the contrary, it is because something is brought into association with divinity that it has superlative value.[110] My proposal is that *har ʼᵉlōhīm* should rather be rendered 'mountain of the gods'.[111] This both accounts for the note of envy which the mountain has towards Zion in v. 17 (ET 16) as well as the fact that it is associated with the sea in v. 23 (ET 22) as a place connected with Yahweh's enemies: both the sea and the gods are elsewhere set over against Yahweh in Enthronement Psalms related in theme to Ps. 68 (cf. Ps. 29:1, 82, 95:3, 96:4–5, 97:7, 9). The most likely view of the identity of the mountain of Bashan is that held by the majority of scholars, namely that it is probably to be equated with Mt Hermon,[112] since this latter, on the northern boundary of Bashan (cf. Deut. 3:8), is the highest and grandest of the mountains in the area, indeed in the whole of Palestine (it is 2,814 metres high), and is therefore the one most appropriately contrasted with the depths of the sea in v. 23 (ET 22).[113] It is also the one most appropriately designated *har*

108 Cf. M.J. Dahood, *Psalms* 2 (New York, 1968), p. 131.

109 D.W. Thomas, 'A consideration of some unusual ways of expressing the superlative in Hebrew', *VT* 3 (1953), pp. 209–24, and 'Some further remarks on unusual ways of expressing the superlative in Hebrew', *VT* 18 (1968), pp. 120–4.

110 D.W. Thomas, *VT* 3 (1953), pp. 215–16, 218–19.

111 This translation is followed by B.D. Eerdmans, 'Psalm lxviii', *Exp. Times* 46 (1934–5), p. 170, and is noted as a possibility by A.A. Anderson, *The Book of Psalms* 1 (London, 1972), p. 490, but nowhere have I come across a serious discussion of the merits of this view.

112 Cf. J. Vlaardingerbroek, *Psalm 68* (Amsterdam, 1973), p. 75.

113 I have traced this view as far back as J.D. Michaelis. The main alternative view is that the reference is to Jebel Druze (Hauran), cf. W.F. Albright, 'A catalogue of early Hebrew lyric poems (Psalm LXVIII)', *HUCA* 23, part 1 (1950–1), p. 24, a view which I have traced as far back as J.G. Wetzstein, *Das batanäische Giebelsgebirge* (Leipzig, 1884).

'ᵉlōhīm, since its sanctity is well-known, as its very name ($\sqrt{}$*ḥrm*) attests.[114] Two further pieces of evidence, adduced by E. Lipiński,[115] support the view that Mt. Hermon actually was regarded as the mountain of the gods in Canaanite religion. First, in an Old Babylonian version of the Gilgamesh epic[116] we read that after Enkidu's slaying of Ḫuwawa 'at whose noise Hermon[117] and Lebanon [trembled]' (rev., line 13), Gilgamesh and Enkidu penetrated within the forest and Enkidu 'opened the secret dwelling of the Anunnaki' (rev., line 20). Lipiński notes that in later texts it is the Antilebanon-Hermon especially which is the cedar's country and that it is Mt Hermon which is the highest of these mountain ranges and therefore most likely the dwelling place of the Anunnaki who, in the Old Babylonian period, represented the great gods in general.[118] Accordingly, Mt Hermon would have been the dwelling place of the gods. Since the location is in Canaan it is natural to suppose that this reflects a Canaanite tradition, and it may here be noted that this is further supported by the fact that it is not a normal Sumero-Babylonian idea that gods dwell on mountains, in contrast to the Canaanites. Secondly, it is interesting that in 1 Enoch 6:6 it is on Mt Hermon that the sons of God descended when they went to have sexual intercourse with the daughters of men. These angelic sons of God, the *bᵉnē 'ēl*, *bᵉnē 'ēlīm* or *bᵉnē 'ᵉlōhīm* of the Old Testament, derive ultimately from the Canaanite gods of the divine assembly (the *bn 'ilm*) and their association with Mt Hermon may, as Lipiński suggests, reflect an old tradition

114 That Is. 14:13 identifies the mount of the divine assembly with Zaphon does not constitute a difficulty for the view that the Canaanites regarded Mt Hermon as the mount of the gods, since it is clear that the former equation is not original: in the Ugaritic texts Mt Zaphon (the dwelling place of Baal) and the mount of the divine assembly are clearly distinguished.

115 Cf. E. Lipiński, 'El's abode. Mythological traditions related to Mount Hermon and to the mountains of Armenia', *Orientalia Lovaniensia Periodica* 2 (1971), pp. 15–41.

116 Originally published by T. Bauer, 'Ein viertes altbabylonisches Fragment des Gilgameš-Epos', *JNES* 16 (1957), pp. 254–62 (see pp. 256–7). A more recent translation by A.K. Grayson appears in *ANET*, pp. 504–5.

117 Akkadian *saria*, cognate with Hebrew *śiryōn* (cf. Deut. 3:9), etc. For the information that the preceding word should be rendered 'noise' and not 'name' as T. Bauer read it, I am indebted to a private communication from Prof. W.G. Lambert.

118 In fact, the Ninevite version actually speaks here of *mušab ilāni*^{pl} (tablet V, col. I, 6) instead of *mušab Enunaki*. See R. Campbell Thompson, *The Epic of Gilgamesh* (Oxford, 1930), p. 36 (and plate 17).

holding that mountain to be the dwelling place of the gods.[119] Accordingly, I suggest that Ps. 68 further supports Lipiński's view.

Whether or not the understanding of Bashan adumbrated above be accepted, there can be no doubt that Bashan is not the mythical sea serpent but rather the mountainous region of that name, and that it stands in antithetical, not synonymous parallelism, with the depths of the sea. Bashan and the depths of the sea represent the highest and lowest spots to which Yahweh's enemies might flee and from which he has power over them. One may compare Amos 9:3, where we read, 'Though they hide themselves on the top of Carmel, from there I will search out and take them; and though they hide from my sight at the bottom of the sea, there I will command the serpent, and it shall bite them.' Ps. 139:8 may also be compared, though here it is not a question of the flight of an enemy of God: 'If I ascend to heaven, you are there! If I make my bed in Sheol, you are there!' The same motif is also known from the El-Amarna letters, 'If we ascend into heaven, if we descend into the earth (hell), our head is in your hands' (Knudtzon, no. 264, lines 15–19).

However, it is possible that the allusions to Bashan and the depths of the sea are not *merely* synonyms for the highest and lowest places of refuge but also represent places of hostility to Yahweh. That Yahweh's enemies should seek refuge in the depths of the sea is understandable when we recall the role which the sea plays as a symbol of the forces of chaos opposed to Yahweh in Enthronement Psalms related in theme to Ps. 68 (cf. Ps. 29:3, 10; 93:3–4). If the depths of the sea in Ps. 68:23 (ET 22) represent forces hostile to Yahweh, then so should (the mountain of) Bashan mentioned alongside it, and such a supposition is strengthened when we recall the note of hostility to Zion on the part of the mountain of Bashan in v. 17 (ET 16). All this is readily understandable in the light of the view argued above that the mountain of Bashan (Mt Hermon) represents the mount of the gods, especially when we recall that the gods, like the sea, are in fact set over against Yahweh in the Enthronement Psalms (cf. Ps. 29:1, 82, 95:3, 96:4–5, 97:7, 9).

Finally, it is possible that the depths of the sea in Ps. 68:23 (ET

119 In addition to Lipiński, M. Delcor has also suggested this, 'Le mythe de la chute des anges et de l'origine des géants comme explication du mal dans le monde dans l'apocalyptique juive. Histoire des traditions', *RHR* 190 (1976), p. 26.

22) are to be equated with the depths of the river Jordan, whose source rises at the base of Mt Hermon. This would then be comparable to Ps. 42:7–8 (ET 6–7), where the river deeps of Sheol seem to be located by Mt Hermon. The conjunction of the high mountain of Hermon with the source of the Jordan would have made it admirably suited to be the dwelling place of El (and his assembly of the gods), whom the Canaanites believed dwelt on a mountain 'at the source of the rivers, amid the springs of the two oceans' (cf. *CTA* 4.IV.21ff., 6.I.33ff. = *KTU* 1.4.IV.21ff., 1.6.I.33ff.)[120]

The beast of the reeds in Ps. 68:30 (ET 29) – probably not a chaos monster

> Roar against the beast of the reeds,
> the herd of bulls with the calves of the peoples.
> Trample[121] under foot those who lust after[122] silver,
> Scatter[123] the peoples who delight in war.

It has sometimes been supposed that Ps. 68:31 (ET 30) alludes to the conflict with chaos.[124] Since the context (vv. 30–32, ET 29–31)

120 In maintaining with Lipiński that the dwelling of El and the gods was localized on Mt Hermon, I do not imply that this was the only place where it was localized or that this is where the Ugaritic texts located it. Lipiński himself gives plausible reasons for thinking that it was also localized in Armenia at the source of the Tigris and Euphrates (as in the Elkunirša myth). In the view of M.H. Pope, *El in the Ugaritic Texts* (*SVT* 2, 1955), pp. 72–81, El's dwelling is to be sought in Khirbet Afqa at the source of the Nahr Ibrāhīm, whilst F.M. Cross, *Canaanite Myth*, pp. 24–39, locates it on Mt Amanus. However, whilst not impossible, the evidence which they produce is not overwhelmingly convincing. Pope's argument rests on the similarity of the word *'apq* 'spring', used in connection with El's dwelling in the Ugaritic texts (cf. *CTA* 6.I.34, etc. = *KTU* 1.6.I.34, etc.), to the name Afqa, and on the appropriateness of the setting. Ugaritic *'apq* is, however, not a proper name, nor is there any ancient documentary evidence associating this site with El and the assembly of the gods. Cross's case for Mt Amanus largely depends on the equation of the god *Baal Ḥammôn*, understood as meaning 'lord of Amanus', with El. However, whether or not Ḥammon = Amanus, which is certainly questionable, Baal Ḥammon is certainly a form of the god Baal, not El. The deity in question is sometimes spoken of simply as Baal in the Punic texts (e.g. *KAI* 86, 87, 94), indicating that Baal is the name of the god and not just an epithet. In fact, he is not once called El. The fact that classical writers referred to Baal Ḥammon as Kronos does not militate against this, since it is known that Kronos could sometimes denote Baal. I shall be dealing with the question of the identity of Baal Ḥammon in greater detail in a forthcoming book on the Molech cult.

121 Read *hiṯrappēs* for MT *miṯrappēs*.

122 Read *bᵉrōṣē* for MT *bᵉraṣṣē*.

123 Read *bazzēr* for MT *bizzar*. Cf. LXX, Peshiṭta and Jerome.

124 Cf. H. Gunkel, *Schöpfung und Chaos*, pp. 66–9; S. Mowinckel, *Der achtundsechzigste Psalm* (Oslo, 1953), p. 60.

is that of Yahweh's victory over the nations, this would then be a case of historicization of the imagery, and because of the reference to Egypt in v. 32 (ET 31) it has sometimes been thought that the bestial imagery alludes to Egypt. The fact that the psalm is one concerned with Yahweh's kingship and that the verb *g'r* is used in v. 31 (ET 30) gives this view a certain attraction, as does the reference to 'the beast of the reeds', which calls to mind Behemoth, who in Job 40:21 is said to dwell 'in the covert of the reeds and in the marsh'. However, doubt is shed on this interpretation by the fact that not simply one 'beast of the reeds' but a 'herd of bulls with the calves of the peoples' is mentioned, whereas Behemoth and his Ugaritic prototype denote a single ox-like creature. Though this may have had comparable companions, there is nothing to suggest this. Accordingly, the most natural interpretation is that we have in Ps. 68:31 (ET 30) an example of the use of animal titles to denote leaders and warriors attested elsewhere in the Old Testament (e.g. *'attūḏē 'āreṣ* 'rulers of the earth', lit. 'he-goats of the earth'). For the use of *'abbīr* 'bull' and *'abbīrīm* 'bulls' in this sense, see 1 Sam. 21:8; Job 24:22, 34:20; Lam. 1:15. Other examples of the use of animal names as titles in Hebrew and Ugaritic have been documented by P.D. Miller.[125]

The cosmic waters as the nations in general

Psalm 46:3–4 (ET 2–3)

3 Therefore we will not fear though the earth should change,
though the mountains totter in the heart of the sea;
4 though its waters rage and foam,
though the mountains tremble with its tumult.

In this psalm, one of those expressing faith in Zion's inviolability (Ps. 46, 48, 76), it is clear that the divine conflict with the nations attacking Zion is represented as a historicization of the mythological divine conflict with the waters. The two verbs used to describe the nations in v. 7 (ET 6), *hmh* and *mwṭ*, 'the nations *rage*, the kingdoms *totter*', are precisely the ones employed in vv. 3–4 (ET 2–3) of the chaos waters and their effects, cf. v. 4 (ET 3), 'though its waters *rage* . . . .' and v. 3 (ET 2), 'though the mountains *totter* in the heart of the sea', suggesting that the one is a historicization of

125 P.D. Miller, 'Animal names as designations in Ugaritic and Hebrew', *UF* 2 (1970), pp. 177–86.

the other. The imagery of the divine conflict with the chaos waters is also apparent in the cosmic scope of the conflict, cf. v. 10 (ET 9), 'He makes wars cease to the end of the earth', and in the thunderstorm as the mode of God's intervention, cf. v. 7 (ET 6), 'he utters his voice, the earth melts'. I shall argue in detail below[126] in the section on 'The origin of the "conflict with the nations" motif' in favour of its being a historicization of the divine conflict with the chaos waters, defending the view that it reflects an old Jebusite tradition over against rival views which have recently been expressed.

At the moment I simply wish to discuss the question of the timing of Yahweh's deliverance of Zion from its enemies in v. 6 (ET 5) 'at break of day' (*lipnōṯ bōqer*), which is also attested in connection with Yahweh's conflict with the chaos waters in Is. 17:14, 'At evening time, behold, terror! Before morning, they are no more!' What is the reason for this particular timing? In an article expressly devoted to the subject of 'Die Hilfe Gottes "am Morgen"', J. Ziegler[127] expresses various possibilities which could account for the prevalence of this theme in the Old Testament. He enumerates (i) the fact that the night is full of terrors and dangers; (ii) the fact that judgements in law were made at the city gate in the morning; (iii) the fact that God's help was experienced in the morning at certain points in Israel's history, e.g. the passing through the Reed Sea and the deliverance of Jerusalem in the time of Sennacherib. (In fact, Ziegler thinks that Ps. 46 could have been written to celebrate Sennacherib's defeat, a view now generally given up.) None of these reasons, however, would appear to be the correct reason why deliverance comes at dawn in Ps. 46 or Is. 17. This is surely to be connected with the fact that the chaos waters were associated with darkness and their conquest or control with the coming of light, cf. Gen. 1:2–3, '.. and darkness was upon the face of the deep . . . And God said, 'Let there be light" . . .', Job 26:12–13, 'By his power he stilled the sea, and by his understanding he smote Rahab. By his wind the heavens were made fair, his hand pierced the twisting serpent', and the implications of Job 3:8, 'Let those curse it who curse the day, who are skilled to rouse up Leviathan.' I have noted above, when discussing Is. 17:12–14, that the notion of the night as the time when the chaos monsters of the

126 Cf. below, pp. 125–138.
127 J. Ziegler, 'Die Hilfe Gottes "am Morgen"', *Alttestamentliche Studien* (F. Nötscher Festschrift), *Bonner bilblische Beiträge* 1 (Bonn, 1950), pp. 281–8.

sea posed a threat, is already attested in the Ugaritic texts at the very end of the Baal cycle (*CTA* 6.VI.44–52 = *KTU* 1.6.VI.45–53). It is this concept that probably lies behind the idea expressed in Ps. 46:6 (ET 5), as well as Is. 17:14, rather than any of the options posed by Ziegler.

Psalm 18:5–18 (ET 4–17)
V. 5 The waves[128] of death encompassed me,
the torrents of perdition assailed me;
V. 6 the cords of Sheol entangled me,
the snares of death confronted me.
V. 7 In my distress I called upon the Lord;
to my God I cried for help.
From his temple he heard my voice,
and my cry to him reached his ears.
V. 8 Then the earth reeled and rocked;
the foundations also of the mountains trembled and quaked,
because he was angry.
V. 9 Smoke went up from his nostrils,
and devouring fire from his mouth;
glowing coals flamed forth from him.
V. 10 He bowed the heavens, and came down;
thick darkness was under his feet.
V. 11 He rode on a cherub, and flew;
he came swiftly upon the wings of the wind.
V. 12 He made darkness his covering around him,
his canopy thick clouds dark with water.
V. 13 Out of the brightness before him
there broke through his clouds
hailstones and coals of fire.
V. 14 The Lord also thundered in the heavens,
and the Most High uttered his voice.[129]
V. 15 And he sent out his arrows, and scattered them;
he flashed forth lightnings, and routed them.
V. 16 Then the channels of the waters were seen,
and the foundations of the world were laid bare,
at your roar,[130] O Lord,
at the blast of the breath of your nostrils.

128 Reading *mišbᵉrē* for MT *ḥeḇlē* with the parallel passage in 2 Sam. 22:5. *Ḥeḇlē* seems to have crept in from the following verse, where it is more appropriate.

129 Omitting the last line of the MT, *bārāḏ wᵉgaḥᵃlē 'ēš* with some manuscripts, the LXX and the parallel passage in 2 Sam. 22:14. The line probably crept in from the end of v. 13, where the identical words occur.

130 Cf. Ch. 1, n. 82.

V. 17 He reached from on high, he took me,
he drew me out of mighty waters.
V. 18 He delivered me from my strong enemy,
and from those who hated me;
for they were too mighty for me.

Psalm 144:5–7

V. 5 Bow your heavens, O Lord, and come down!
Touch the mountains that they smoke!
V. 6 Flash forth the lightning, and scatter them,
send out your arrows and rout them!
V. 7 Stretch forth your hand from on high,
rescue me and deliver me from the mighty waters,
from the hands of aliens.

These two passages may be taken together. Both Ps. 18 and 144 are Royal Psalms and describe Yahweh's theophany which acts to deliver the king from the grasp of 'mighty waters', which are a way of describing the king's enemies. Hab. 3:13 may be compared, since here too Yahweh comes to the aid of his Anointed whilst he is engulfed by the chaos waters. Indeed, it is attractive to suppose that both these psalms, like Hab. 3, had their *Sitz im Leben* at the Feast of Tabernacles and that they allude to an experience of royal suffering and vindication within the Autumnal cultic celebration. The reasons are as follows:

(i) It is difficult to identify the events of Ps. 18 and 144 with any known historical event. Like the deliverance of Zion in Ps. 46, 48 and 76 they may reflect a corresponding deliverance of the king in the cult.[131] Ps. 2:6 is evidence that the king and Zion were associated in this context.

(ii) Hab. 3:13 has already been mentioned, with its allusion to the deliverance of the Lord's Anointed from the grasp of the chaos waters in the context of a psalm very probably having its *Sitz im Leben* at the Feast of Tabernacles. Similarly, it is noteworthy that Zech. 12–14 clearly represents the eschatologization of motifs originating in the Feast of Tabernacles – e.g. the conflict with the nations attacking Zion in Zech. 12:1ff. and 14:1ff. (cf. Ps. 46, 48, 76) and the worship of Yahweh as king, explicitly mentioned in connection with the Feast of Tabernacles (Zech. 14:16ff.; cf. the Enthronement Psalms) – so that it is therefore striking that it is in

131 Cf. A.R. Johnson, *Sacral Kingship in Ancient Israel* (2nd ed., Cardiff, 1967), pp. 116ff.; J.H. Eaton, *Kingship and the Psalms* (London, 1976), pp. 113–16, 127–9.

this very context that we find one or possibly two allusions to a suffering royal figure (Zech. 13:7, and possibly 12:10–13:1), suggesting that the motif of the suffering king may also have had its setting in the Autumn Festival. Zech. 13:1 appears to speak of the atoning effect of the royal suffering and this has often been compared with the description of the Suffering Servant in Is. 52:13–53:12. Quite apart from this there are good reasons for supposing that the description of the suffering and vindicated king of the psalms in part underlies the Suffering Servant. It is striking, therefore, that once again the context is that of the kingship of God – cf. Is. 52:7, 'Your God reigns' – suggesting that the suffering and vindicated figure of Is. 52:13–53:12 also has its background in the themes surrounding the kingship of God at the Autumn Festival. One may recall Ps. 22, where the suffering and vindication of a figure is explicitly associated with the coming of the kingdom of God (cf. vv. 28ff., ET 27ff.), a juxtaposition most easily understood if the figure is that of the king.

(iii) It is significant that at the end of Ps. 144 (vv. 12–15) the theme of the psalm suddenly changes to that of the hope for Yahweh's blessing to be manifested in the field of nature. On the view that Ps. 144 simply reflects a historical event this is rather surprising, so that some have seen vv. 12–15 as a later addition to the psalm.[132] The concluding verses of the psalm fit especially well, however, a *Sitz im Leben* in the Autumn Festival,[133] which was, in origin, a harvest festival (cf. Ps. 65:10ff., ET 9ff.) celebrated at the time when the rainy season was awaited, as alluded to in Zech. 14:17. In particular, Hab. 3 comes to mind again, since here again, the concluding verses (Hab. 3:17–19) contain an allusion to the fertility in nature following the divine victory over the sea, in which the king is involved, just as in Ps. 144. Cf. Ps. 65:8–14 (ET 7–13). It is therefore probable that Ps. 144 was celebrated at the Autumn Festival like Hab. 3.

The fact that a theophany in the storm against the sea is the mode of God's manifestation indicates that the imagery ultimately derives from Baal. However, it is interesting that Ps. 18:14 (ET 13) states in the midst of the theophany 'and the Most High (Elyon) uttered his voice'. The mention of Elyon, the name of the pre-Israelite Jebusite god of Jerusalem with whom Yahweh was

132 Cf. H. Gunkel, *Die Psalmen* (4th ed., Göttingen, 1926), p. 607.
133 Cf. J.H. Eaton, *op. cit.*, p. 128.

equated, gives us an indication of the medium through which this Baalistic imagery was probably transmitted to Israel, a subject to be taken up below[134] in the section on 'The origin of the "conflict with the notions" motif'.

I maintain strongly that the theophany is simply in the storm, involving lightning and thunder, and that we should not also see here allusions to volcanic phenomena.[135] That we do not have volcanic allusions here is supported by the fact that, so far as we know, nowhere else in the ancient near east are volcanic features attested in theophanies, the manifestations rather being in the storm and earthquake. Furthermore, it is noteworthy that Yahweh's theophany is explicitly stated to come down *from above*, which would not be true of a volcano: 'Bow your heavens, O Lord and come down! Touch the mountains that they smoke!', the reference to lightning being made explicit in the next verse, 'Flash forth your lightning, and scatter them, send out your arrows and rout them!' (Ps. 144:6–7). Cf. Ps. 18:9–10 (ET 8–9), where the smoke comes from Yahweh (v. 9, ET 8), who 'bowed the heavens and came down; thick darkness was under his feet' (v. 10, ET 9). Similarly in the passage where volcanic imagery is most commonly canvassed, in the Sinai theophany in Ex. 19:18, it is expressly stated that 'the Lord *descended* upon it in fire; and the smoke of it went up like the smoke of a kiln'. The fact that the fire descends from above, and does not emerge from the mountain itself, clearly indicates that it is lightning and not a volcano which is here in view, as in other theophanies in the Old Testament.

The origin of the 'conflict with the nations' motif

In various parts of the Old Testament we find the motif of nations coming up to conquer Zion and being miraculously defeated by Yahweh who intervenes in a storm theophany. The theme referred to here is variously called the inviolability of Zion or the conflict with the nations (*Völkerkampf*) motif. It is found, for example, in Ps. 46, 48 and 76. Although it was at one time thought that these psalms were alluding to a specific historical event, the deliverance of Jerusalem from the siege of Sennacherib in 701 B.C. described in

134 Cf. below, pp. 129ff.
135 Cf. the discussion in J. Jeremias, *Theophanie* (Neukirchen, 1965), pp. 73–90; F.M. Cross, *Canaanite Myth*, pp. 167–9.

2 Kings 18:17–19:37 (cf. Is. 36–7, 2 Chron. 32:1–21),[136] it is now generally accepted that this historical interpretation does not fit the details of the psalms very well, and it is widely thought that we have here rather a non-historical cultic motif. In the book of Isaiah, however, there are a number of passages where the motif is applied to the contemporary historical situation (Is. 8:9–10, 10:5–11, 27b–34, 14:24–7, 17:12–14. 28:14–22, 29:1–8, 30:27–33, 31:1–9, 33:20–4), and apart from the first and last of these allusions, it has been widely held that they represent the prophet Isaiah's application of the cultic motif to the events of 701 B.C., although this has recently been questioned by H. Barth and R.E. Clements,[137] who see rather evidence of redactional work from the time of Josiah. Is. 8:9–10 seems to apply the motif to the earlier threat to Zion posed by the Syro–Ephraimite crisis in 734–2 B.C., and this is also taken up in Is. 7, where the forthcoming deliverance of Zion from the Syro–Ephraimite siege is symbolized by Immanuel 'God is with us', a name surely reflecting the cry in Ps. 46:8, 12 (ET 7, 11) enunciating the inviolability of Zion, *Yahweh ṣᵉḇā'ōṯ ʿimmānū* 'the Lord of hosts is with us'. (Is. 8:5–8 also seems to reapply motifs from Ps. 46.) The conflict with the nations motif was also eschatologized, and besides the probable example of Is. 33:20–4, this is found in the proto-apocalyptic passages Ezek. 38–9, Zech. 12–14 and Joel 4 (ET 3), whilst Dan. 7 and 11–12 relate this theme to events and aspirations at the time of Antiochus IV Epiphanes.

What is the origin of this motif? A view which has been widely held, although it has been subject to certain criticism in recent years, is that it represents a historicization of the divine conflict with the sea. This was first enunciated by Gunkel, though defended in greater detail by Mowinckel and subsequent scholars such as Johnson and Hayes.[138] In support of this view may be noted a number of mythological features in the *Völkerkampf* psalms which find a ready explanation if the divine conflict with the nations

136 Cf. A.F. Kirkpatrick, *The Book of Psalms* (Cambridge, 1906), p. 253.

137 H. Barth, *Die Jesaja-Worte in der Josiazeit* (Neukirchen, 1977); R.E. Clements, *Isaiah and the Deliverance of Jerusalem* (Sheffield, 1980), *Isaiah 1–39* (London, 1980).

138 H. Gunkel, *Schöpfung und Chaos*, pp. 99f.; S. Mowinckel, *Psalmenstudien* 2 (Kristiania, 1922), pp. 57–65; H.-J. Kraus, *Psalmen* 1 (5th ed., Neukirchen, 1978), p. 106; J.H. Hayes, 'The tradition of Zion's inviolability', *JBL* 82 (1963), pp. 419–26; A.R. Johnson, *op. cit.*, pp. 92ff.; F. Stolz, *Strukturen und Figuren im Kult von Jerusalem* (*BZAW* 118, 1970), pp. 86ff.

attacking Zion described in them is a historicization of the mythological divine conflict with the waters attacking Zaphon. Thus, for example, the two verbs used to describe the nations in Ps. 46:7 (ET 6), *hmh* and *mwṭ*, 'the nations *rage*, the kingdoms *totter*', are precisely the ones used in vv. 3–4 (ET 2–3) of the chaos waters and their effects, cf. v. 4 (ET 3), 'though its waters *rage* . . .' and v. 3 (ET 2) 'though the mountains *totter* in the heart of the sea', suggesting that the one is a historicization of the other. If we do have a historicization of the cosmic sea here, this would account for the cosmic sweep of Yahweh's victory, cf. Ps. 46:10 (ET 9), 'He makes wars cease to the end of the earth', Ps. 76:13 (ET 12), 'who is terrible to the kings of the earth', Ps. 48:3 (ET 2), 'His holy mountain . . . the joy of all the earth'. Ps. 76:7 (ET 6) uses the root *gʿr* 'roar' of Yahweh's conflict with the nations, and there is no doubt that this is a sort of technical term for the divine conflict with the sea (cf. Job 26:11; Ps. 18:16, ET 15 = 2 Sam. 22:16, 104:7; Is. 17:13, 50:2; Nah. 1:4; also note Ps. 106:9). Furthermore, it is striking that in Ps. 48:3 (ET 2), Zion, the place of deliverance, is referred to as Zaphon, the name of Baal's sacred mountain dwelling place in Canaanite mythology, the very place where the victory over the dragon and the sea was localized (cf. *CTA* 3.IIID.44–IV.45 = *KTU* 1.3.III.47–IV.1, *ṭrd. bʿl bmrym. ṣpn* 'who has driven Baal from the heights of Zaphon'). Moreover, the divine victory comes by means of a theophany in the storm, just as was the case in the divine victory (of both Baal and Yahweh) over the dragon and the sea. This is indicated by Ps. 46:7 (ET 6), where we read 'he utters his voice, the earth melts' and Ps. 48:8 (ET 7), 'By the east wind you shatter the ships of Tarshish.'

Ps. 48:8 (ET 7), in fact, deserves further consideration. R.E. Clements[139] denies that this is a mythical element and contends that it may well refer to a specific historical event. That this is probably not the case, however, is indicated by the fact that the following verse suggests that the ships are defeated within sight of the city – 'As we have heard, so have we seen in the city of the Lord of hosts, in the city of our God, which God establishes for ever' – which cannot be literally true of Jerusalem. Rather, it is attractive to suppose that here too traditions have been taken over from the Syrian Mt Zaphon (cf. Ps. 48:3, ET 2), which was actually

139 R.E. Clements, *Isaiah and the Deliverance of Jerusalem*, pp. 77, 81.

on the coast and therefore in a position to be attacked by ships. It is interesting that in Esar-haddon's treaty with Baal king of Tyre, the god Baal Zaphon is specifically represented as one who shatters ships.[140] The view that the ships are poetically described as being shattered in the sight of Zion would be avoided if we were to read *k^{e}rūaḥ*[141] instead of *b^{e}rūaḥ* in this verse, with a few Hebrew manuscripts, or to take *b^{e}* as *beth essentiae*,[142] or to regard *k^{e}* as unnecessary before *b^{e}rūaḥ*,[143] so that vv. 7–8 (ET 6–7) would then read 'trembling took hold of them there, anguish as of a woman in travail, *like* the east wind which shatters the ships of Tarshish'. That this is to be rejected,[144] however, is strongly supported by Is. 33:21, part of a chapter taken up with the very same theme as Ps. 46, 48 and 76, with which it manifests certain similarities,[145] where in the eschatologized *Völkerkampf* Zion is actually stated to be inviolable to attack by ship, 'But the Lord will be mighty for us

140 Cf. R. Borger, *Die Inschriften Asarhaddons Königs von Assyrien* (*AfO* Beiheft 9, Graz, 1956), p. 109. Conveniently in *ANET*, p. 534, 'May Baal-sameme, Baal-malage and Baal-saphon raise an evil wind against your ships, to undo their moorings, tear out their mooring pole, may a strong wave sink them in the sea, a violent tide [. . .] against you.'

141 Those reading *k^{e}rūaḥ* include H. Gunkel, *Die Psalmen* (Göttingen, 1926), pp. 204, 207; W.O.E. Oesterley, *The Psalms* 1 (London, 1939), p. 262; E. Podechard, *Le Psautier* 1 (Lyon, 1949), p. 213; H.-J. Kraus, *Psalmen* 1 (Neukirchen, 1978), pp. 509–10; A. Weiser, *Die Psalmen* (5th ed., Göttingen, 1959), p. 256 (ET *The Psalms*, London, 1965, p. 379); *NAB*; *NEB*.

142 Thus, A.R. Johnson, *op. cit.*, p. 87, n. 2 takes *b^{e}* as *beth essentiae* (cf. *GK* §119*i*); J. Gray, *The Biblical Doctrine of the Reign of God* (Edinburgh, 1979), p. 61, n. 104.

143 M.J. Dahood, *Psalms* 1 (New York, 1966), pp. 288, 291, regards *k^{e}* as unnecessary to give this meaning on the principle of the double duty conjunction (preceding *kayyōlēḏāh* and following *ka'^{a}šer*).

144 Those retaining *b^{e}* include A.F. Kirkpatrick, *The Book of Psalms* (Cambridge, 1906), p. 265; R. Kittel, *Die Psalmen* (Leipzig, 1914), p. 191; J.H. Eaton, *Psalms* (London, 1967), p. 132; *RSV*.

145 Besides the common *Völkerkampf* motif, note the fact that deliverance comes in the morning (Is. 33:2, cf. Ps. 46:6, ET 5) by means of Yahweh's theophany in the thunder (Is. 33:3, cf. Ps. 46:7, ET 6), and there is a mythical river in Zion (Is. 33:21, cf. Ps. 46:5, ET 4). In addition, there are some striking verbal parallels, cf. *'āḥ^{a}zāh r^{e}'āḏāh* (Is. 33:14) and *r^{e}'āḏāh '^{a}ḥāzāṯam*, *sōp̱ēr 'eṯ hammiḡdālīm* (Is. 33:18) and *sip̱^{e}ru miḡdālehā* (Ps. 48:13), expressions which are unparalleled anywhere else in the entire Old Testament, although it must be admitted that the referents of these expressions are not the same in Is. 33 and Ps. 48. One may also compare Is. 33:2, which expresses the desire that Yahweh be 'our salvation in the time of trouble (*ṣārāh*)' with Ps. 46:2 (ET 1), where God is 'a very present help in trouble (*ṣārōṯ*)'.

there, a place of broad streams,[146] where no galley with oars can go, no stately ship can pass.' Furthermore, Is. 33:23a, which refers to shattered ships, is widely accepted to be out of place in its present context[147] as an allusion to Zion's defeat, for the context speaks rather of the inviolability of Zion. It is far better to suppose that Is. 33:23a with its ship allusion carries on the thought of Is. 33:21, following which it probably originally belonged, as is widely held: 'Its[148] tackle hangs loose (and) cannot hold the mast firm in its place, or keep the sail spread out.' We therefore have in Is. 33:21, 23a a good parallel to Ps. 48:8 (ET 7), and it is no longer plausible to deny that we have in this latter passage a mythological allusion.

A further mythological allusion is to be found in Ps. 46:5 (ET 4), 'There is a river whose streams make glad the city of God, the holy habitation of the Most High (Elyon)' (cf. Is. 33:21). Since El-Elyon (God Most High) is mentioned in Gen. 14:18 (cf. vv. 19, 20, 22) as the name of the pre-Israelite Jebusite god of Jerusalem, this appears to support the hypothesis that the *Völkerkampf* motif contained in Ps. 46 is not merely Canaanite but specifically a Jebusite tradition in origin[149] That Elyon was the name of an actual West Semitic deity is confirmed by the eighth century B.C. Aramaic Sefire treaty IA 11, where he is called Elyan,[150] and by Philo of Byblos in his account of Phoenician religion, where he is called Elioun. (Cf. Eusebius, *Praeparatio evangelica* i.10, 14–15.) Indeed, the very epithet of El-Elyon in Gen. 14:19, 22 'Creator of heaven and earth' (*qōnēh šāmayim wāʾāreṣ*) seems to be authenticated by Philo of Byblos, who refers to Elioun as father of Ouranos (Heaven) and Ge (Earth) (cf. Eusebius, *loc. cit.*). Although this is late, it is clearly independent

146 The MT has *m^{e}qōm n^{e}hārīm y^{e}ʾōrīm* 'a place of rivers, streams'. Probably *n^{e}hārīm* should be understood as a scribal gloss on the rarer word *y^{e}ʾōrīm*, which would account for the absence of the conjunction *w^{e}* 'and' between them.

147 Cf. A. Penna, *Isaia* (Turin and Rome, 1957), pp. 309–10; G. Fohrer, *Das Buch Jesaja* 2 (Zurich and Stuttgart, 1962), p. 133; W. Eichrodt, *Der Herr der Geschichte* (Stuttgart, 1967), p. 210; *Jerusalem Bible; NAB*.

148 Reading *ḥ^{a}ḇālāyw* 'its tackle' for MT *ḥ^{a}ḇālayiḵ* 'your tackle', since this conforms far better to the context. The *kaph* may have crept in as an inaccurate dittograph from the *bēth* at the beginning of the next word (*bal*).

149 Among the supporters of the Jebusite origin of this motif are S. Mowinckel, *Psalmenstudien* 2 (Kristiania, 1922), pp. 57–65; A.R. Johnson, *op. cit.*, pp. 92ff.; J.H. Hayes, 'The Tradition of Zion's inviolability', *JBL* 82 (1963), pp. 419–26.

150 See J.A. Fitzmyer, *The Aramaic Inscriptions of Sefîre* (Rome, 1967), pp. 12–13, 37–8; H. Donner and W. Röllig, *KAI*, no. 222 A 11.

of Gen. 14 in view of its overtly mythological nature and must reflect genuinely ancient tradition.[151] This suggests that Elioun was akin to El, who is also called *qn 'rṣ* 'creator of the earth'.[152] When therefore we find the name Elyon associated with El-like characteristics in the Old Testament we must similarly be dealing with genuine ancient tradition. This is the case in Ps. 82:6, where the gods are referred to as 'sons of Elyon', and this concept is clearly implicit in Deut. 32:8–9, just as in the Ugaritic texts the gods are sons of El. Another El-like characteristic is the fact that Is. 14:13–14 associates Elyon with the Mount of Assembly, just as El was so associated in the Ugaritic texts. Finally, Ps. 46:5 (ET 4), cited above, comes into this category, since its association of Elyon with the mythological river derives from the Canaanite tradition concerning the dwelling place of the god El, who lived 'at the source of the rivers, amid the springs of the two oceans' (cf. *CTA* 4.IV.21–2, 6.I.33–4 = *KTU* 1.4.IV.21–2, 1.6.I.33–4, etc.). Accordingly, the reference to God as Elyon in Ps. 46:5 (ET 4) is not *simply* an epithet of Yahweh meaning 'Most High' but reflects genuine mythological tradition about this deity appropriated from the Jebusites. Since Ps. 46 is centred on the theme of the inviolability of Zion it is reasonable to suppose that this motif derives from the same god Elyon.

This conclusion is further supported by the evidence of Ps. 110. Although it is a Royal Psalm, it is closely related to Ps. 46, containing as it does the theme of the conflict with the nations (Ps. 110:1–2, 5–6) comparable to Ps. 46, as well as an apparent reference to the

151 The evidence of Philo, confirming as it does the role of Elyon as creator of both heaven and earth, shows that the formula 'El Elyon, creator of heaven and earth' (Gen. 14:19, 22) does not involve a conflation of Elyon lord of heaven and El lord of earth as is supposed by G. Levi della Vida, 'El ʿElyon in Genesis 14 18–20', *JBL* 63 (1944), pp. 1–9; R. Lack, 'Les origines de *Elyon*, le très-haut, dans la tradition cultuelle d'Israël', *CBQ* 24 (1962), pp. 44–64; R. Rendtorff, 'El, Baʿal und Jahwe', *ZAW* 78 (1966), pp. 277–92. Lack and Rendtorff go further and equate Elyon with Baal Shamem. This too is unsatisfactory, since it is clear that Baal Shamem was simply the storm god Baal (Hadad), as is indicated by Esar-haddon's treaty with Baal king of Tyre, where Baal-sameme (Baal Shamem) is mentioned alongside Baal-malage and Baal-saphon (Baal Zaphon) as a god shattering ships with his wind. For the text, cf. above, n. 140. On the other hand, Hadad (of Aleppo) is already mentioned in the list of gods in the Sefire treaty I A 10 (this reconstruction is generally agreed), so that Elyan in line 11 cannot also be Baal-Hadad. In addition, as noted in the text, various features of Elyon suggest an El-like deity rather than Baal Shamem.

152 Cf. above, Ch. 1, n. 44.

king's birth (i.e. accession to power) at dawn in Ps. 110:3 ('From the womb of dawn you have the dew wherewith I have begotten you'),[153] paralleling the deliverance of Zion at dawn in Ps. 46:6 (ET 5). Now in Ps. 110:4 the Davidic king is promised, 'You are a priest for ever after the order of Melchizedek', Melchizedek, as we know from Gen. 14:18, being the pre-Israelite Jebusite king of Jerusalem (Salem) and priest of the god El-Elyon. It is very probable that these related passages indicate a fusion between the cult of Yahweh and Elyon or El-Elyon in the time of David and imply that the Davidic kings took over the religious and political status of the Jebusite kings of Jerusalem.[154] The rest of Ps. 110 is permeated with the theme of the conflict with the nations, comparable to Ps. 46. It would be surprising if there were no connection between the reference to Melchizedek in v. 4 and the theme of the conflict with the nations in the rest of the psalm, since otherwise one wonders why the allusion to Melchizedek was included. It is as Melchizedek's heir that the Davidic king defeats the nations and arises at dawn, suggesting that this theme derives from the cult of the Jebusite god Elyon, whose priest Melchizedek was (cf. Gen. 14:18). This confirms the conclusion already drawn from Ps. 46. It is perhaps not fortuitous that in Gen. 14:20 El-Elyon is specifically said to deliver Abraham's enemies into his hands, and it may further be noted that it is implied that it is Elyon who aids the king in his conflict with his enemies in Ps. 21:8 (ET 7), 57:3 (ET 2), 83:19 (ET 18), 91:1, 9, 92:2 (ET 1) (if we assume these are all Royal Psalms). Again, although it is late, it is interesting that in Dan. 7:18, 22, 25, 27, the little horn of the dragon is in conflict with the Most High (Elyon) and his holy ones, which may well reflect ancient tradition, as is the case with other elements.

153 Reading probably *šaḥar* for MT *mišḥar* (dittography from *m* of previous word), and *y^eliḏtīḵā* for MT *yalḏūṯeyḵā*, the latter with the support of LXX and Peshiṭta.

154 This view, which has been maintained by many scholars, is vindicated by J.A. Emerton's careful study, 'The riddle of Genesis xiv', *VT* 21 (1971), pp. 403–39. J. van Seters' view in *Abraham in History and Tradition* (New Haven, Conn., & London, 1975), pp. 306–8, that the expression 'High priest of God Most High', adopted by the Hasmoneans in the Maccabaean period (cf. Josephus, Ant. xvi. 163; Assumption of Moses 6:1), is late and originated with the post-exilic priesthood is to be rejected. It was important for the post-exilic priesthood to be Aaronite, which Melchizedek could not claim to be, and furthermore, the post-exilic high priests were not kings, whatever pre-exilic symbolism they may have appropriated. *Contra* van Seters, it is entirely natural that the Hasmoneans should have taken over this title from Gen. 14, since, taken with Ps. 110:4, this could be used to justify their non-Aaronite status.

In keeping with the Jebusite hypothesis of the origin of the *Völkerkampf* motif it is interesting to note that Ps. 76:3 (ET 2) applies the name Salem to Jerusalem, which is elsewhere in the Old Testament only found in Gen. 14:18, where it is used of Jubusite Jerusalem.[155] It may also be pointed out that the Jebusites did in fact have extreme confidence in the inviolability of their city prior to David's capture of it, for they said to David, '"You will not come in here, but the blind and the lame will ward you off" – thinking, "David cannot come in here"' (2 Sam. 5:6). This could, of course, be explained merely as overconfidence due to the city's strong defences and the fact that it had remained unconquered by the Israelites for so long, but it may nevertheless be a pointer to the Jebusite belief that Elyon protected their city.

Yet a further indicator of the origin of the theme of the inviolability of Zion in the cult of the Jebusite god Elyon is the fact that one of the psalms in which this motif occurs, Ps. 48:3 (ET 2) refers to Zion as Zaphon. The other clear allusion to this mythological expression in the Old Testament is in Is. 14:13, and the following verse makes it clear that this was the dwelling place of Elyon. Since Is. 14:12–15 is universally regarded as containing a fragment of Canaanite mythology, we have evidence that Ps. 48:3 (ET 2) has appropriated the name of the Jebusite god Elyon's dwelling to Zion. Here again, it is natural to conclude that the theme of the inviolability of Zion that permeates this psalm likewise derives from this source. We have had occasion to observe above, however, that in the Ugaritic texts Zaphon is the dwelling place of the god Baal. Again, in Ps. 46 it is by means of a theophany in the storm that God defeats the nations (v. 7, ET 6), a Baalistic feature, and God's enemies are associated with the chaos waters (v. 4, ET 3), the enemies of Baal in the Ugaritic texts. Furthermore, this picture is confirmed by Ps. 18:14 (ET 13) where we read that 'the Most High (Elyon) uttered his voice' against the chaos waters in order to deliver the king. Taken at their face value these allusions suggest that the god Elyon had Baalistic features in addition to the El-like features that have already clearly been established.[156] Against this,

155 That Salem in Gen. 14:18 really is Jerusalem and not some other city, as is sometimes thought, is indicated not only by Ps. 76:3 (ET 2), but also by Ps. 110:2, which makes it clear that 'the priest for ever after the order of Melchizedek' (v.4; cf. Gen. 14:18) rules from Zion.

156 Cf. F. Stolz, *Strukturen und Figuren im Kult von Jerusalem* (*BZAW* 118, 1970), pp. 152–7.

it might be supposed that this fusion of El and Baal features is more likely to be an Israelite construct than an authentic reflection of Canaanite religion. However, the following points should be taken into account when forming a decision on this question. First, we should not assume *a priori* that what was the case at Ugarit must automatically have been the case at Jebusite Jerusalem several centuries later. There is perhaps a danger of forcing all Canaanite religion into a Ugaritic straitjacket. The evidence of Phoenician religion indicates the divergence from the Ugaritic model that could obtain. Secondly, although Gen. 14:19, 20, 22 refer to El-Elyon, and Philo of Byblos confirms that Elyon was an El-like deity (even though he distinguishes the two deities), the eighth century B.C. Sefire treaty indicates that Elyon was not simply identical with El. The text refers to 'El and Elyan' in a series of paired deities, in which the pairs are consistently related but not identical gods. Accordingly, Elyon must be regarded as El-like rather than El *pure simple.*[157] It is only to be expected, therefore, that Elyon should possess certain attributes that distinguish him from El, and these may be preserved in the Old Testament. Thirdly, as we have seen, the Old Testament allusions to Elyon suggesting an El-like nature find some confirmation in Philo of Byblos, who refers to Elioun as father of Ouranos (Heaven) and Ge (Earth) (cf. Gen. 14:19, 22). The fact that the Old Testament may be shown to preserve authentic Canaanite traditions about Elyon suggests that when we find Elyon associated with Canaanite mythological motifs of a Baalistic variety, these also reflect reality. Fourthly, if the attribution of Baalistic features to Elyon in the Old Testament is an Israelite construct rather than an authentic reflection of the cult of Elyon, we are faced with the following problem: why was the name of one Canaanite god, Baal, replaced by that of another, Elyon? Would it not have been simpler and less confusing simply to have replaced the name of Baal by Yahweh?

In conclusion, therefore, it may be stated that, although Elyon was an El-like deity, there is reason to believe that he also possessed certain Baalistic features. Accordingly, there is no objection to supposing that the theme of the divine conflict with the chaos waters was mediated to the Israelites through the cult of the Jebu-

157 The analogy of the other paired deities tells against the view sometimes put forward that 'El and Elyan' is a composite divine name like Kothar-and-Ḫasis in the Ugaritic texts.

site god Elyon. Indeed, we have seen that there is good reason to believe that the motif of the divine conflict with the nations and the inviolability of Zion, which reflect a historicization of the deity fighting on Zaphon against the chaos waters, derives precisely from this god. (This is not to deny that the god Baal was also present in the syncretistic Jerusalem cultus as defeater of the dragon and presumably therefore in that of the Jebusites – cf. below, Ch. 4.)

In recent years a number of alternative suggestions to the Canaanite and specifically Jebusite mythological origin of the conflict with the nations motif have been put forward. Thus, according to G. Wanke,[158] the motif is not even a pre-exilic tradition but first appears in Ezek. 38–9, which develops the theme of 'the foe from the north' found in the early chapters of Jeremiah. However, several important arguments may be brought against such a late dating of the origin of the *Völkerkampf* motif. First of all, such a strong assertion of Zion's inviolability in the psalms seems much more natural before the destruction of the Temple than after it, and one may compare the confidence of the people in the Temple in Jer. 7:4. Again, it is very difficult to hold that none of the Isaianic passages illustrating the *Völkerkampf* motif listed above is authentic and therefore pre-exilic. Further, one of the Korahite psalms (to which group Ps. 46 and 48 belong) is certainly pre-exilic, namely Ps. 45, since it is a Royal Psalm. Finally, the term 'joy of all the earth' which is found in Lam. 2:15, written not long after the fall of Jerusalem, where passers-by mock, 'Is this the city which was called the perfection of beauty, the joy of all the earth?' is most naturally understood as referring back to the use of this expression with regard to Zion in Ps. 48:3 (ET 2), which must therefore be pre-exilic. (The phrase 'the perfection of beauty' is similarly a quotation from Ps. 50:2.)

Another scholar who rejects the view that the *Völkerkampf* motif derives from the theme of the conflict with the waters is H.-M. Lutz.[159] Nevertheless, he does hold that the motif is a Jebusite tradition in origin concerning the attack by the nations on Jerusalem (Zaphon) in which they are repelled by El-Elyon's theophany. However, it is surely simpler to suppose that there is just one

158 G. Wanke, *Die Zionstheologie der Korachiten* (*BZAW* 97, 1966). Cf. J. Vollmer, *Geschichtliche Rückblicke und Motive in der Prophetie des Amos, Hosea und Jesaja* (*BZAW* 119, 1971), pp. 158–60.

159 H.-M. Lutz, *Jahwe, Jerusalem und die Völker* (Neukirchen, 1968), esp. pp. 171ff.

Canaanite tradition here rather than to suppose that two different Canaanite traditions of an attack on Zaphon, both of which are repelled by a theophany, have here been brought together. Lutz also wants to distinguish the origins of the attack of the nations on Jerusalem which he sees as a Jebusite tradition, from the tradition of Yahweh's conflict with the nations, which he holds is a universalization of Holy War ideology. However, as against this latter Lutz himself has to admit that the theophany as a means of defeating the enemy is rare in Holy War ideology.

A further scholar who denies that the conflict with the nations attacking Zion was a historicization of the conflict with the chaos waters is J.J.M. Roberts.[160] He holds that the defeat of the Philistines by David in the Valley of Rephaim just outside Jerusalem (2 Sam. 5:17–25) provided the crystallization point around which the tradition of the unsuccessful attack of rebellious vassals grew. Roberts thus holds that the *Völkerkampf* psalms are directed at the vassals of the Davidic–Solomonic empire, warning them not to revolt. R.E. Clements[161] has also recently supported Roberts' view that Ps. 46, 48 and 76 were composed as warnings to the vassals of the Davidic–Solomonic empire not to revolt, rather than as a generalized doctrine of the inviolability of Zion inherited from the Jebusites. Roberts' arguments against the Jebusite hypothesis are not convincing. He emphasizes that the admittedly mythological motifs found in the Zion psalms derive partly from El (-Elyon) (the mythological river) and partly from Baal (the conflict with chaos) and holds that such a conflation is more credibly an Israelite than a Jebusite construct. However, detailed reasons have already been given above for rejecting this view. A second point which Roberts makes in attempting to counter the Jebusite hypothesis concerns the argument used from Ps. 110, where the Jebusite priest king is mentioned in v. 4 in the context of the conflict with the nations, suggesting that the latter too is Jebusite in origin. Roberts holds (i) that it is not certain that we should read Melchizedek in v. 4, and (ii) that even so, the connection between Melchizedek and the rest of the Psalm is loose. To this it may be replied (i) that there are no

160 J.J.M. Roberts, 'The Davidic origin of the Zion tradition', *JBL* 92 (1973), pp. 329–44.

161 R.E. Clements, *Isaiah and the Deliverance of Jerusalem* (Sheffield, 1980), pp. 73–81. Cf. *Prophecy and Tradition* (Oxford, 1975), pp. 67–8.

grounds for eliminating Melchizedek from the text,[162] and (ii) it would be difficult to suppose why v. 4 was included if there were no connection between the priesthood of the Jebusite Melchizedek and the conflict with the nations alluded to in the rest of the psalm. Furthermore, we have noted earlier that it is striking that in Gen. 14 it is Melchizedek's god El-Elyon who expressly delivers Abraham's enemies, the invading kings, into his hands (Gen. 14:20). As for Roberts' own construction, he himself notes that there is no known example of vassals of the Davidic–Solomonic empire seeking to attack Zion, which might have given rise to the motif of the Zion Psalms. His suggestion that the defeat of the non-vasssal Philistines near Jerusalem in 2 Sam. 5:17–25 gave rise to the tradition is clearly conjectural.

We turn now to Clements' recent study. He too maintains that Ps. 46, 48 and 76 do not reflect a generalized belief in the inviolability of Zion inherited from the Jebusites but rather contain a warning to the vassal states of the Davidic–Solomonic empire not to rebel. In this regard he strongly emphasizes their connection with the Royal Psalm 2, and even prefers to think of Ps. 46, 48 and 76 as Royal Psalms rather than as a separate genre of Zion Psalms, noting the reference in Ps. 48:3 (ET 2) to Zion as 'the city of the great king', i.e. the Davidic king.[163] The seemingly mythological reference to the shattering of the ships of Tarshish in Ps. 48:8 (ET 7) he maintains may reflect an actual historical event.[164] The more generalized belief in the inviolability of Zion which has usually been found in these psalms Clements refuses to see here, claiming that it emerged only as late as the time of Josiah, having arisen from theological reflection on the fact that Jerusalem was not destroyed like other cities of Judah in Sennacherib's invasion.[165] The narrative of Zion's deliverance from Assyria in 2 Kings 18:17–

162 On p. 337, n. 59 Roberts simply refers the reader to J.G. Gammie, 'Loci of the Melchizedek tradition of Genesis 14:18–20', *JBL* 90 (1971), p. 388, n. 23. Here Gammie writes, 'On the analogy of Ps. 89:36–37, where Yahweh promises David that his throne will endure forever because he has sworn on the basis of his holiness, so here he promises to one of David's house the priesthood forever on the basis of Yahweh's righteousness: "Yahweh has sworn and will not repent: 'Thou art a priest forever, because I have spoken righteously, my king'" (Ps. 110:4).' However, this rendering, which involves emendation of the Masoretic vocalization, can claim no support from the versions, which all see here a reference to Melchizedek, an allusion entirely appropriate to the context.

163 R.E. Clements, *Isaiah and the Deliverance of Jerusalem*, pp. 87–8.

164 R.E. Clements, *op. cit.*, p. 81. Cf. p. 77.

165 R.E. Clements, *op. cit.*, pp. 84–5.

19:37, reflecting this theology, is held to be the work of redactors in the time of Josiah,[166] and it does not reflect the historical Isaiah's own attitude, which envisaged only judgement for Judah and no message of special protection of Zion from the Assyrians. Clements also sees evidence of an extensive anti-Assyrian redaction from the time of Josiah in the oracles of Isaiah himself. Far from reflecting Isaiah's own belief in the inviolability of Zion in 701 B.C. these oracles, though attached to genuine prophecies of Isaiah, reveal a belief in the imminent downfall of Assyria during the period of increasing weakness in the time of Josiah.[167]

What are we to say to all this? Clements has certainly produced a study which is full of interest and stimulates to new thought. However, I do not think that his main theses should be accepted, First, with regard to Ps. 46, 48 and 76, although there clearly is some kind of connection with Ps. 2, it is striking that the former nowhere mention the Davidic king, but rather concentrate their thought on Zion, which makes it difficult to accept Clements' claim that they should be seen as basically Royal rather than Zion Psalms. In keeping with this the reference to Zion as 'the city of the great king' in Ps. 48:3 (ET 2) must surely be alluding to it as Yahweh's city, not the city of the Davidic king, since the former is a constant emphasis of this and the related Zion Psalms, including the adjacent verses (cf. Ps. 48:2, ET 1, 4, ET 3, 9, ET 8; 46:5 ET 4, 6, ET 5; 76:3, ET 2), whereas the latter is nowhere attested in these psalms. Furthermore, it is also noteworthy that Ps. 46, 48 and 76 nowhere describe the enemy kings as Israel's vassals, the impression they give being one rather of cosmic scope, e.g. Ps. 48:3 (ET 2), where Zion is 'the joy of *all* the earth', Ps. 48:11 (ET 10) where Yahweh's praise reaches 'to the *ends* of the earth', and Ps. 46:10 (ET 9), where Yahweh 'causes wars to cease to the *ends* of the earth'. Furthermore, attention has already been drawn above to the comparison between the shattering of the ships of Tarshish in Ps. 48:8 (ET 7) and the wreckage of the ships in Is. 33:21, 23a, which latter passage makes even clearer the mythical background of the allusion in the psalm, rendering any historical reference impossible, and again emphasizes the scope of the conflict as more cosmic than one simply involving petty vassal states. Ps. 2 may also be more cosmic than Clements thinks, since there too the king is

166 R.E. Clements, *op. cit.*, pp. 52–71.
167 R.E. Clements, *op. cit.*, pp. 28–51.

promised dominion 'to the *ends* of the earth' (cf. Ps. 72:8–11, where the king's dominion 'to the ends of the earth' is understood to include Tarshish and the isles, Arabia and Seba), and the vassals are depicted as rebelling against Yahweh as well as the king (Ps. 2:2), and this may be a more cosmic concept, since all nations were reckoned to be Yahweh's vassals in the Israelite ideology. Even if the enemies in Ps. 2 are only the vassal states of the Davidic–Solomonic empire, this does not mean that this is necessarily the case in Ps. 46, 48 and 76, for if these psalms are expressing a belief in the universal inviolability of Zion, then *ipso facto*, the Davidic monarch and Zion are inviolable to overthrow by the vassal states. Furthermore, the admitted relationship between these Zion Psalms and the Royal Psalms does not militate against the Jebusite hypothesis, as Clements seems to suppose, since the Coronation Psalm closely linked to Ps. 2 discussed above, *viz.* Ps. 110, which likewise contains the conflict with the nations motif, appropriates the role of the Jebusite priest-king Melchizedek to the Davidic king in v. 4. It would be most surprising if this were entirely unrelated to the theme of the conflict with the nations which dominates the rest of the psalm, for its presence in this context would then be hard to justify. On the other hand, that it should be as Melchizedek's successor that the Davidic king defeats his enemies is entirely understandable, since it was Melchizedek's god El-Elyon in Gen. 14:20 who is said to deliver David's forebear Abraham's enemies into his hands, enemies, moreover, who came from far beyond Syria-Palestine in Mesopotamia.

Accordingly, it may be argued that the Jebusite origin of the Zion tradition offers the best explanation of the evidence. This is not to deny, of course, that during the period of the Davidic–Solomonic empire the threat against the enemies of Zion would have had most relevance for Israel's vassal states. But the potential threat from the vassal states no more created the Zion tradition than did Sennacherib's abortive attempt to capture Jerusalem in 701 B.C., a thesis favoured by some older scholars. Rather, as I have attempted to show, it antedates both and is rooted in ancient Jebusite and Canaanite mythical traditions. In the light of this, the view of Clements that the doctrine of the inviolability of Zion did not arise until a relatively late time, amongst Josianic redactors of the book of Isaiah, is to be rejected.

Summary

In this chapter I have considered the historicization of the divine conflict with the dragon and the sea. The dragon, when historicized, was especially employed to symbolize Egypt or Pharaoh, a usage which seems to derive from the oppressive role that Egypt played *vis à vis* the Hebrews prior to the Exodus, as well as from the fact that a significant part of the deliverance took place at the sea (the Reed Sea). Accordingly, the imagery of the conflict was applied to the deliverance at the Reed Sea (Ps. 77:17–21, ET 16–20; Is. 51:10), whilst in Ex. 15 the conflict is no longer with the sea but simply at the sea. When historicized, the dragon and the sea also served to denote the dominant world power of the time, whether Assyria, Babylon or the Seleucids. The sea could also refer to hostile nations in general.

Conclusions were reached on a number of detailed points of interpretation. For example, it was concluded that the *tannīn* symbolizing Egypt in Ezek. 29 and 32 is the mythological chaos monster and not simply the crocodile; that the mythological *tannīn* 'dragon' and not MT *tannīm* 'jackals' is to be read in Ps. 44:20 (ET 19); that the correct vocalization of Is. 30:7 is *rahaḇ hammošbāṯ* 'the silenced Rahab'; and that Bashan in Ps. 68:23 (ET 22) is not a name for the chaos monster but the place of that name, probably denoting Mt Hermon as the mount of the gods. Similarly 'the beast of the reeds' in Ps. 68:30 (ET 29) is probably not a chaos monster but is an example of the use of an animal title to denote leaders or warriors. Other conclusions were that the swallowing up of Jonah by the great fish is not an allegory of the Babylonian exile based on Jer. 51:34, though there probably is a connection with the chaos monster, and with regard to Hab. 3, it was first pointed out by the present writer that the reference to Resheph in Hab. 3:5 in the context of *Chaoskampf* and the allusion to Yahweh's seven shafts of lightning in Hab. 3:9 have interesting parallels in Baal mythology. Original points were also made with regard to other passages but they will not be repeated here.

As for the theme of the inviolability of Zion and the conflict with the nations, support was given to the view that this represents a historicization of the divine conflict with the sea, and that it was derived from the Jebusites. Although a number of scholars have questioned this view in recent years, none of them has proved successful in establishing a more credible alternative. The considerable number of mythological allusions, the cosmic scope of the victory, the allusion to the priest-king of the Jebusite god El-Elyon, Melchizedek, in the context of the conflict with the nations in Ps. 110;4, etc., all cohere with this view.

4

The eschatologization of the divine conflict with the dragon and the sea

In the previous chapters we have considered the motif of the divine conflict with the dragon and the sea in the Old Testament from various points of view: the first chapter discussed its association with the creation of the world, the second chapter the alleged naturalization of the chaos monsters, and the third chapter the historicization of the conflict. In accordance with the principle *Urzeit wird Endzeit*, the conflict was also eschatologized, i.e. transposed into the future in association with the last things. From the New Testament, of course, we remember the Revelation of St John, where in Chapter 13 the oppressive Roman empire is symbolized by a seven-headed beast coming out of the sea, clearly deriving from Leviathan the seven-headed sea serpent, and 'the false prophet' is symbolized by a beast representing Behemoth, whilst the satanic power behind Rome is represented in Chapter 12 by a seven-headed dragon, which is overcome by the archangel Michael and thrown down from heaven.[1] A detailed consideration of these New Testament passages lies outside the scope of the present monograph, however, and we shall be concerned here with Is. 27:1 and related mythological passages in the proto-apocalyptic work Is. 24–7, and in particular with Dan. 7.

1 See H. Wallace, 'Leviathan and the beast in Revelation', *BA* 11 (1948), pp. 61–8. For a more recent and thorough study of this subject, see A.Y. Collins, *The Combat Myth in the Book of Revelation* (Missoula, Mt., 1976). For an older, thorough study of Rev. 12, written before the discovery of the Ugaritic texts, see H. Gunkel, *Schöpfung und Chaos*, pp. 171–398. On the second beast of Rev. 13 as Behemoth, see above, Ch. 2, n. 59.

The dragon-conflict in Isaiah 27:1 and related material in the 'Isaiah Apocalypse'

> Isaiah 27:1
>
> On that day the Lord with his hard and great and strong sword will punish Leviathan the twisting serpent, Leviathan the crooked serpent, and he will slay the dragon that is in the sea.

As has frequently been pointed out, these words from the proto-apocalyptic work in Is. 24–7 bear a very strong resemblance to those in the Ugaritic Baal myth, where Mot addresses Baal as follows: *ktmḫṣ. ltn. bṯn. brḥ tkly. bṯn. ʿqltn* 'Because you smote Leviathan the twisting serpent (and) made an end of the crooked serpent ...' (*CTA* 5.I.1–2 = *KTU* 1.5.I.1–2). Again, in *CTA* 3.IIID.37–9 (= *KTU* 1.3.III.40–42), Leviathan the crooked serpent is spoken of as a dragon as in Is. 27:1, *l'ištbm. tnn. 'ištm*[ ]*mḫšt. bṯn. ʿqltn šlyṭ. d. šbʿt. r'ašm* 'Surely I lifted up the dragon, I . . . (and) smote the crooked serpent, the tyrant with the seven heads.' The close similarity is all the more remarkable both in view of the time-scale involved and because the word *ʿaqallāṯōn* 'crooked' which is here paralleled in Ugaritic is found nowhere else in the Old Testament (though the plural of the verb *ʿql* [Hab. 1:4] and the adjective *ʿaqalqāl* [Judg. 5:6, Ps. 125:5] are so attested, and cf. Rahab which appears as *nāhāš bārīaḥ* 'twisting serpent' in Job 26:13). The striking parallelism between the relatively late text in Is. 27:1 and the Ugaritic texts almost a millennium earlier is a reminder that the closeness of the language of Old Testament texts to that of the Ugaritic texts is not necessarily an indication of an early date for the Old Testament passages in question. Quite often the parallels are in relatively late texts.

The Ugaritic texts cited above make it clear that Is. 27:1 is describing one monster, not three, as has sometimes been supposed. What is referred to in Is. 27:1 parallels the event referred to in Is. 24:21, 'On that day the Lord will punish the host of heaven, in heaven, and the kings of the earth, on the earth.' The reference to 'the host of heaven' in this parallel verse has sometimes been thought to indicate that the monster references in Is. 27:1 allude to three constellations, Serpens, Draco and Hydra.[2] However, whereas Is. 24:21 refers to the kings of the earth as a whole

2 So C.F. Burney, 'The three serpents of Isaiah XXVII 1', *JTS* 11 (1910), pp. 443–7, following R. Smend, 'Anmerkungen zu Jes. 24–27', *ZAW* 4 (1884), p. 213.

together with their angelic princes, it is probable that the reference to the defeat of Leviathan in Is. 27:1 alludes to the downfall of one particular hated power of the time, in view of the use of the sea monster imagery to refer to particular hostile nations elsewhere in the Old Testament, rather than to constellations. Moreover, the fact that it is here said to be in the sea, its normal habitat, suggests that we do not here have to do with constellations.

Which particular power is alluded to here? A vast number of different suggestions have been made. Qimḥi and Rashi saw three powers, Assyria, Egypt and Tyre. Some modern scholars have also seen an allusion to three powers, e.g. the Ptolemies, the Seleucids and the Parthians,[3] the Ptolemies, the Seleucids and Macedonia,[4] or Egypt, Babylon and Assyria,[5] though sometimes only two powers have been noted, the Ptolemies and the Seleucids.[6] All these combinations are to be rejected, however, since, as has been noted above, it is now clear that Is. 27:1 is describing only one dragon, not three (or two). Those who posit a single power have cited Babylon[7] or Egypt.[8] However, there are some scholars who think that no specific power is meant[9] but rather evil in general, but this seems improbable.

Part of the problem in identifying Leviathan in Is. 27:1 is the fact that there is no general agreement about the date of Is. 24–7. Often in the past these chapters have been dated very late and have been seen as having their background in the Hellenistic period, e.g. ca. 250 B.C. In keeping with this late date these chapters have frequently been called 'the Isaiah Apocalypse'. However, many of the features of the full-blown apocalypses are absent here, which leads one to question the necessity for such a late date. The writing is rather proto-apocalyptic or late prophecy. It belongs, however, 'to that phase in prophecy in which the sharp contours of the here and now begin to be lost in more spacious visions of a transform-

3 B. Duhm, *Das Buch Jesaia* (4th ed., Göttingen, 1922), p. 189; K. Marti, *Das Buch Jesaja* (Tübingen, 1900), p. 196.
4 O. Procksch, *Jesaia* 1 (Leipzig, 1930), p. 334.
5 F. Delitzsch, *Commentar über das Buch Jesaia* (4th ed., Leipzig, 1889), p. 305; F. Feldman, *Das Buch Isaias*, 1 (Münster, 1925), p. 312.
6 O. Eissfeldt, *Einleitung in das alte Testament* (3rd ed., Tübingen, 1964), p. 439 (ET *The Old Testament. An Introduction*, Oxford, 1966, p. 326).
7 W. Gesenius, *Der Prophet Jesaja* 2 (Leipzig, 1821), p. 810.
8 H. Wildberger, *Jesaja*, 2 (Neukirchen, 1978), p. 1004.
9 P. Auvray, *Isaïe 1–39* (Paris, 1972), p. 239; O. Kaiser, *Der Prophet Jesaja Kapitel 13–39* (Göttingen, 1973), p. 179 (ET, *Isaiah 13–39*, London, 1974, p. 223).

ation of all things'.[10] This indicates that the pre-exilic date suggested at the other extreme for these chapters[11] is also to be rejected.

In trying to date Is. 24–7, it would seem that whilst the exile is presupposed (cf. Is. 27:8, etc.), indicating a date after 586 B.C., the fact that the Asherim are still standing, symbols of the Canaanite goddess Asherah (Is. 27:9), suggests that the *terminus ante quem* cannot be too long after the return from exile, since every other allusion to the Asherim in the Old Testament relates to the pre-exilic or exilic period. A date therefore in the exilic, or more probably post-exilic period seems certain, but not as late as has sometimes been supposed. The dominant world power of the time would therefore be either Babylon[12] or more probably Persia, and it is therefore conceivable that Leviathan alludes to one of them. However, since the dragon when historicized can symbolize not only the dominant world power of the time (cf. Jer. 51:34; Dan. 7) but also Egypt (cf. Ps. 87:4; Is. 30:7, 51:9; Ezek. 29:3, 32:2), it is possible that Egypt is specifically in view. That Egypt in particular should be singled out for judgement at this time gains in credibility when we recall that this is the case in other proto-apocalyptic

10 G.W. Anderson, 'Isaiah XXIV–XXVII reconsidered', *SVT* 9 (1963), p. 126.

11 Cf. J. Mauchline, *Isaiah 1–39* (London, 1962), pp. 195–7; J.H. Eaton, 'The origin of the book of Isaiah', *VT* 9 (1959), pp. 150–1.

12 A number of references in Is. 24–7 speak of the destruction of a city (cf. Is. 24:10–12, 25:2, 26:5–6, 27:10–11) and this has often been identified with Babylon, e.g., J. Lindblom, *Die Jesaja-Apokalypse* (Lund, 1938), pp. 72–84; M.-L. Henry, *Glaubenskrise und Glaubensbewahrung in den Dichtungen der Jesajaapokalypse* (Stuttgart, 1967), pp. 17–34; B. Otzen, 'Traditions and structures of Isaiah XXIV–XXVII', *VT* 24 (1974), p. 206. If this were so, the case for the identification of Leviathan with Babylon might be strengthened. However, in spite of certain attractions, it should probably be rejected. Is. 26:6 speaks of the poor and needy (i.e. the Jews, cf. 25:4) trampling the city, which suggests that it was not far from Judah, the vantage point from which the work is written. According to Is. 25:10–12 the city is in Moab, which would be appropriate on that score (cf. Zeph. 2:9), but these verses are often supposed to be a later addition. However, it may be unwise to reject the one concrete allusion in the book, and Is. 24:17–18 similarly repeats the Moabite oracle in Jer. 48:43–4. The implication in Is. 24:7–12 that wine plays an important role in the city also fits Moab very well, as Is. 16:7–10 indicates. Is. 24–7 would then merit comparison with Is. 34–5, in that both proclaim judgement on a nation in the vicinity of Judah (in the one case Moab and in the other Edom), which extends into a world disaster, and this is contrasted with the state of Zion. Cf. O. Eissfeldt, *Einleitung in das alte Testament* (3rd ed., Tübingen, 1964), pp. 438–9 (ET *The Old Testament. An Introduction*, Oxford, 1966, pp. 326–7). There can, however, be no question of Leviathan representing Moab, since elsewhere in the Old Testament the dragon symbolizes either the dominant world power or Egypt.

works of about the same period, in Joel 4:19 (ET 3:19) and Zech. 14:18–19.

Finally, it is perhaps worthy of note, as J.M. Court[13] has pointed out, that Is. 27:1, as well as some of the preceding verses, may have influenced the imagery in Rev. 12. Thus, Is. 26:17f. with its imagery of a woman wailing in labour seems to be alluded to in Rev. 12:2; Is. 26:20 refers to hiding for a little while until the wrath is past, just as in Rev. 12 the woman is carried to safety into the wilderness for the period of the tribulation; whilst Leviathan, referred to in Is. 27:1, is known to lie behind the seven-headed dragon of Rev. 12.

Other related mythological motifs in Isaiah 24–7

The fact that Is. 27:1 bears such a strikingly close relationship to the Ugaritic Baal epic leads one to ask whether other motifs in Is. 24–7 derive from the same circle of ancient mythic ideas. This is in fact the case, although their full number and significance have not previously been noted.[14]

One instance is to be found in Is. 24:18b–19,[15] where we read

v. 18b For the windows on high are opened,
and the foundations of the earth tremble.
v. 19 The earth is utterly broken,
the earth is rent asunder,
the earth is violently shaken.

With this one should compare *CTA* 4.VII.25ff. (= *KTU* 1.4.VII.25ff.)

25 ypth̠. h̠(26)ln. bbhtm.	He opened a lattice in the mansion,
’urbt (27) bqrb. hk[lm.]	a window in the midst of the pal[ace),
[yp]th̠ (28) bʿl. bdqt [.ʿrp]t	Baal [ope]ned a rift (in) the clouds).

13 J.M. Court, *Myth and history in the book of Revelation* (London, 1979), p. 112.

14 J.C. de Moor, *Seasonal Pattern*, p. 244, n. 8, called for an examination of Is. 26:19–27:5 in the light of the Ugaritic Baal myth, and W.R. Millar, *Isaiah 24–27 and the Origin of Apocalyptic* (Missoula, Mt., 1976) finds that they share a common thematic pattern.

15 E.S. Mulder, *Die Teologie van die Jesaja-Apokalipse* (Groningen and Jakarta, 1954), pp. 16–17, notes this and the other Ugaritic references to *’urbt*, but fails to note the similar theophanic context of this particular reference and Is. 24:18b–19. Similarly, J. Gray, *The Biblical Doctrine of the Reign of God* (Edinburgh, 1979), p. 202.

29 qlh. qdš[.] b[ʿl. y]tn	Ba[al utt]ered his holy voice,
30 yṯny. bʿl. ṣ[ʾat.š]pth	Baal repeated the is[sue] of his lips;
31 qlh. q[dš. t]r. ʾarṣ	(he uttered) his h[oly] voice [(and)] the earth did q[uake],
32 [ṣʾat. špth.] ġrm	(he repeated) [the issue of his lips] (and) the rocks (did quake)

The striking thing is not merely the parallelism of the god's theophany and the quaking of the earth in response, but the fact that the Ugaritic text speaks of Baal's opening a window (*ʾurbt*) in his palace, corresponding to the clouds, just as Is. 24:18b says that the *windows* on high were opened (*ʾᵃrubbōṯ mimmārōm nip̱tāḥū*). It has generally been supposed that the allusion to the opening of the windows of heaven refers back to the P flood story, where this expresssion is found (cf. Gen. 7:11, 8:2), so that some speak of there being a second flood here.[16] I think this is correct, and further evidence for the dependence of Is. 24 on the story of Noah is provided by the reference in v. 5 to those who 'have . . . broken the everlasting covenant', the worldwide nature of the sin involved suggesting that this can only be the Noachic covenant of Gen. 9 (explicitly called 'the everlasting covenant' in v. 16, cf. v. 12). If so, it must be concluded that Is. 24 has made the unconditional promise of the covenant of Gen. 9 conditional, since the return of the flood because of the sin of man contradicts Gen. 9:15. However, it is striking that Is. 24:19 makes it clear that the primary emphasis here is on the theophany in the thunder, resulting in the shaking of the earth, rather than in the rain, just as in the Ugaritic passage, and similarly both the Ugaritic and Isaianic passages, unlike Genesis, have an asociation with the theme of the kingship of the deity. It thus seems likely that Is. 24 has combined motifs from the Noah story in Genesis with mythic themes concerning the theophany of the enthroned deity, ultimately deriving from Baal mythology.

Immediately following, in Is. 24:21–3, we have a description of Yahweh's punishment of the kings of the earth and their tutelary gods, the latter we know from later writings being seventy in number (cf. Targum Pseudo-Jonathan on Deut. 32:8; 1 Enoch

16 Cf. O. Kaiser, *Der Prophet Jesaja Kapitel 13–39* (Göttingen, 1973), p. 154 (ET *Isaiah 13–39*, London, 1974), p. 191.

89:59ff., 90:22ff.), deriving from the seventy sons of El and Asherah, the divine pantheon (cf. *CTA* 4.VI.46 = *KTU* 1.4.VI.46 *šbʿm. bn. ʾat̲rt*). In v. 23 we read, 'Then the moon will be confounded, and the sun ashamed; for the Lord of hosts will reign on Mount Zion and in Jerusalem his glory will be before his elders'. Clearly the sun and moon are thought of as disappearing, but how is this envisaged? Sawyer[17] thinks in terms of an eclipse, but against this stands the fact that in actual experience, when there is a total eclipse of the sun, some of the other luminaries are known to reappear, not disappear (as Sawyer himself informs us!), and furthermore, comparable language elsewhere in the Old Testament seems to be associated with Yahweh's theophany in the storm (e.g. Hab. 3:11; Ezek. 32:7, cf. 30:3, 18). Since the previous verses describe Yahweh's theophany in the storm, it is most natural to suppose that this is the cause of the fading of the sun and moon here too. It has never previously been noted that we find precisely the same thing happening in the Ugaritic Baal myth, following Baal's theophany in the storm:

CTA 4.VII. 52–60 (= *KTU* 1.4.VII.52–60)

52	gm. lǵ	Baal surely cried aloud
53	[lm]h. bʿl. kyṣḥ. ʿn	to his se[rvitors]: Look,
54	[gpn]. w'ugr. bǵlmt	[Gupn]-and-Ugar, in obscurity
55	[ʿmm.] ym. bn. ẓlmt. r	the daylight [is veiled], in darkness [the exalted princess] (is veiled),
56	[mt. prʿ]t[.] ʾibr mnt	the [blazing] pinions of . . .[18] (are veiled).
57	[ṣḥrrm. ḥblm. bʿ]rpt	[Flocks are circling round in the c]louds,
58	[tḥt. bšmm. ʿṣrm.] ḥt	[birds] are circling round [in the heavens]
59	[- - glt̲. ʾisr - - -]m	[I shall bind the snow]
60	[brq - - - - ymtm -]h	[the lightning]

We clearly have a reference to the veiling of the sun here, and the allusion to the clouds in line 57 confirms that this is because of a storm, which surely results from Baal's immediately preceding the-

17 J.F.A. Sawyer, 'Joshua 10:12–14 and the solar eclipse of 30 September 1131 B.C.', *PEQ* 104 (1972), p. 139.

18 This seems to be another term denoting the sun.

ophany.[19] This Ugaritic parallel supports the view that Is. 24:21–3 belong with vv. 17–20 and are not, as a number of scholars have thought, the work of a separate redactor.[20]

Finally, yet another passage in Is. 24–7 seems to have its ultimate origin in the same circle of mythic ideas in the Baal text. It has previously been noted by E.S. Mulder.[21] This is Is. 25:6–8, the description of the eschatological banquet when all nations would come to Zion: 'On this mountain the Lord of hosts will make for all peoples a feast of fat things, a feast of wine on the lees, of fat things full of marrow, of wine on the lees well refined. And he will destroy on this mountain the covering that is cast over all peoples, the veil that is spread over all nations. He will swallow up death for ever, and the Lord God will wipe away tears from all faces, and the reproach of his people he will take away from all the earth; for the Lord has spoken.' As a number of scholars point out,[22] the words 'on this mountain' in 25:6 refer back to 24:23, which speaks of Yahweh's reigning on Mt Zion. We have, therefore, in Is. 25:6–8 a reference to the banquet in celebration of Yahweh's enthronement. It is striking that the Baal text similarly describes a banquet in celebration of Baal's kingship, on the completion of his temple on Mt Zaphon:

CTA 4.VI.44–59 (= *KTU* 1.4.VI.44–59)

44 ṣḥ. ’aḫh. bbhth. ’a[r]yh	He did call his brothers into his mansion, his ki[ns]folk
45 bqrb hklh. ṣḥ	into the midst of his palace, he did call
46 šbʿm. bn. ’aṯrt	the seventy sons of Asherah;
47 špq ’ilm. krm. y[n]	he did supply the gods with rams (and) with wine,

19 This seems more natural than the view of J.C.L. Gibson, *Canaanite Myths and Legends* (Edinburgh, 1978), p. 66, n. 5, that 'The passage is prob. simply a poetic description of the setting sun and the coming of evening, though it is possible (see apparatus) to translate "the sons of obscurity, darkness have veiled etc." and find a reference to attacks by Mot's henchmen (so also by translating "seized" in *l.* 35).'

20 Those seeing separate redactions here include J. Lindblom, *op. cit.*, p. 66; O. Kaiser, *op. cit.*, p. 145 (ET, p. 178); J. Vermeylen, *Du Prophète Isaïe à l'Apocalyptique* 1 (Paris, 1977), pp. 360, 379, 381; H. Wildberger, *Jesaja* 2 (Neukirchen, 1978), pp. 904, 943.

21 E.S. Mulder, *op. cit.*, p. 30. H. Wildberger, *op. cit.*, p. 962 also notes it, though he thinks the passage cited from the Rephaim text a better parallel (see below).

22 Cf. H. Wildberger, *op. cit.*, pp. 900, 960.

48 špq. ’ilht. ḫprt [.yn]	he did supply the goddesses with ewes [(and) with wine],
49 špq. ’ilm. ’alpm. y[n]	he did supply the gods with oxen (and) with wine,
50 špq. ’ilht. ’arḫt [.yn]	he did supply the goddesses with cows [(and) with wine]
51 špq. ’ilm. kḥṯm. yn	he did supply the gods with seats (and) with wine,
52 špq. ’ilht. ks’at [.yn]	he did supply the goddesses with thrones [(and) with wine],
53 špq. ’ilm. rḥbt yn	he did supply the gods with tuns of wine,
54 špq. ’ilht. dkrt[.yn]	he did supply the goddesses with casks [of wine],
55 ʿd. lḥm. šty. ’ilm	while the gods did eat (and) drink,
56 wpq mrǵṯm. ṯd	and they were supplied with a suckling of the teat;
57 bḥrb. mlḥt. qs[.m]r	with a salted knife they did carve [a fat]ling;
58 ’i.tšty. krp[nm.y]n	they drank flag[ons of wi]ne,
59 [bk]s. ḫrṣ. d[m. ʿṣm]	the bl[ood of trees from cu]ps of gold.

It has hitherto remained unnoted that ‘the seventy sons of Asherah’ invited to the feast, corresponding to the totality of the divine pantheon, account for the universality of the banquet in Is. 25:6, where ‘*all* peoples’ come. The seventy sons of Asherah and El lie behind the seventy gods or angels of the nations (cf. Deut. 32:8 [LXX, 4Q Deut.], 1 Enoch 89:59ff., 90:22ff.) the same as are referred to in Is. 24:21–2, corresponding to the seventy nations thought to exist (cf. Gen. 10). Moreover, we have here another example of the application of traditions to Mt Zion which originally related to Mt Zaphon – besides Ps. 48:3 (ET 2; cf. Is. 14:13) note Ex. 15:17, where Yahweh’s enthronement (v. 18) takes place on Mt Zion, the language used being that which is applied to Mt Zaphon (following his victory over the sea; cf. Is. 27:1). Wildberger[23] also compares the Ugaritic Rephaim text (*CTA* 22.A.13ff. = *KTU* 1.22.II.13ff.) which speaks of banqueting, apparently in connection with Baal’s enthronement:

13 šmʿ. ’a!tm [rp’um. hn ’iln]	Hear you [*rp’um*, sons of divine] beings: on the pa[te of the victor Baal]

23 Cf. H. Wildberger, *op. cit.*, p. 962.

14 ym. lm. qd[qd. 'al'iyn bʿl]	oil of . . . [shall be poured] and he shall vow
15 šmn. prst [yṣq. wndr]	[vows]: lo [the victor Baal shall be k]ing
16 ydr. hm. ym [lk. 'al'iyn bʿl]	at (my) command (and) shall ta[ke the throne of his
17 ʿl 'amr. y'u[ḫd. ks'a. mlkh]	kingship],
18 nḫt. kḫṯ. d[rkth. bbty]	the resting place of the seat of [his dominion. Into my house]
19 'aṣḥ. rp'i [m. 'iqr'a. 'ilnym]	I have called the *rp'u*[*m*, I have called the divine beings]
20 bqrb. h[kly. 'aṯrh. . . . . . .]	into the midst of my pa[lace, its shrine.]

Wildberger further compares the festal meal held in connection with Marduk's enthronement (Enuma elish III, 134ff.), but, though comparable, this would not have been in the direct line of tradition lying behind Is. 25:6–8, which is rather to be sought in the Canaanite mythology alluded to above.

It is wholly in keeping with the view that the eschatological banquet in Judaism (to which Is. 25:6–8 is the first reference) had its origin in the banquet following Yahweh's and ultimately Baal's victory over the unruly sea and the chaos monsters that in 2 Esdras 6:52, 2 Baruch 29:4, 1 Enoch 60:24 and Baba bathra 74, it is specifically the chaos monsters Leviathan and Behemoth which are to be devoured at the Messianic banquet. We recall too the reference to the slaying of Leviathan in Is. 27:1.

A word may be said here about Is. 25:8a, where we read of Yahweh that 'He will swallow up death for ever . . .' Sometimes these words are regarded as a later gloss.[24] This, however, seems unnecessary, since not only is the thought of the resurrection of the dead – probably to be understood as a collective restoration of the nation rather than individual resurrection beyond the grave – found elsewhere in the work in Is. 26:19, but it is significant that Baal's kingship was specifically associated with his victory over Mot ('Death'), and that it closely followed on Baal's feast on Mt Zaphon. Thus it may be maintained that traditio-historically the thought of Yahweh's victory over Death is in place in the context of Is. 25:6–8. The parallel allusion to the resurrection of the dead in Is. 26:19 is likewise appropriately placed, since it precedes vir-

24 E.g. O. Kaiser, *op. cit.*, p. 162 (ET, p. 201).

tually immediately the allusion to Yahweh's defeat of Leviathan in Is. 27:1, the verse from which our discussion began. This is strikingly paralleled in the Ugaritic texts, for no sooner has Baal risen from the dead and defeated Mot than we find the dragon (i.e. Leviathan) posing a threat, at the very end of the Baal cycle (*CTA* 6.VI.50–2 = *KTU* 1.6.VI.51–3).

The exaltation of the one like a son of man over the dragons in Daniel 7

Dan. 7 is one of the most widely discussed chapters in the entire Old Testament. A vast literature has grown up around it, but there is no sign of scholarly agreement either as to the present meaning of the symbolism or as to its ultimate origin. In a dream, alleged to have occurred in the first year of Belshazzar, king of Babylon, Daniel sees the four winds of heaven stirring up the great sea. Out of the sea emerge, one after the other, a series of beasts, four in number, all of fabulous form. Attention is focused on the fourth beast, which is especially terrible and has ten horns. Then another horn emerges, speaking great things, and three of the other horns are plucked up before it. Next, one who is called the Ancient of Days sits on his throne with his court and the fourth beast is destroyed, and dominion is taken away from the other beasts, and one like a son of man comes with the clouds of heaven and is presented before the Ancient of Days and receives the dominion and kingdom for ever in succession to the beasts. Daniel then enquires of one of those seen in the vision what it all means. He is informed that the beasts represent kings or kingdoms, but that their rule will be succeeded by that of the holy ones of the Most High, who will rule for ever and ever. The ten horns are also explained as representing ten kings, and similarly the horn speaking great things is explained as a particularly terrible king who will oppress the holy ones of the Most High (or simply holy ones), speak words against the Most High, and change the times and the law, for a period of a time, two times, and half a time. But finally the people of the holy ones of the Most High will receive the kingdom.

The four beasts from the sea

There is no doubt amongst critical scholars that the four beasts represent in succession the Babylonian, Median, Persian and

Hellenistic empires, with the little horn symbolizing the Seleucid monarch Antiochus IV Epiphanes, who proscribed Judaism and persecuted those who remained faithful to their religion.[25] The idea of four world empires occurring here, found also in Dan. 2, appears to be based on an oriental tradition attested elsewhere.[26] The four hostile beasts emerge from the sea, which is noted for its turbulence (vv. 2–3). There can be no doubt, in the light of the material considered earlier in this monograph, that the motif of the turbulent sea hostile to God is of Canaanite origin, and it will emerge in the course of this chapter that the imagery of the one like a son of man enthroned by the Ancient of Days over the beasts of the sea is likewise ultimately Canaanite in origin, deriving from the enthronement of (Yahweh-)Baal by El over Yam and his accompanying dragons (Leviathan, etc.). Whilst the four beasts, and especially the last, appear to play the *role* ascribed to the dragon Leviathan in Canaanite mythology, the fact remains that the precise *form* of the beasts does not correspond to that of Leviathan and the other

25 See especially H.H. Rowley, *Darius the Mede and the Four World Empires in the Book of Daniel* (2nd ed., Cardiff, 1959). D.J. Wiseman, 'The last days of Babylon', *Christianity Today* 2, no. 4 (25 Nov. 1957), p. 10, in D.W. Thomas (ed.), *Documents from Old Testament Times* (London, 1958), p. 83, and in D.J. Wiseman, T.C. Mitchell, R. Joyce, W.J. Martin and K.A. Kitchen, *Notes on Some Problems in the Book of Daniel* (London, 1965), pp. 9–16, has attempted to dismiss the Median empire from the book of Daniel by reading explicative *waw* in Dan. 6:29 (ET 28) and so identifying Darius the Mede with Cyrus the Persian, reading 'So this Daniel prospered during the reign of Darius, *even* the reign of Cyrus the Persian.' He has been followed by other conservative scholars such as J.M. Bulman, 'The identification of Darius the Mede', *Westminster Theological Journal* 35 (1972–3), pp. 247–67, A.R. Millard, 'Daniel 1–6 and history', *EQ* 49 (1977), p. 73, J.G. Baldwin, *Daniel* (Leicester, 1978), pp. 26f., and D.W. Baker, 'Further examples of the *wāw explicativum*', *VT* 30 (1980), p. 134, though not all conservatives share this view, e.g. J.C. Whitcomb, *Darius the Mede* (Grand Rapids, Mich., 1959), who prefers rather to equate Darius the Mede with Gubaru. To Wiseman's view it may be objected *inter alia* that, apart from the inherent implausibility of one and the same person being called both Darius the Mede and Cyrus the Persian, it is impossible to spirit away the Median empire from the book of Daniel by such exegetical ingenuity, since it is required by the presence of the second beast in Dan. 7: the first beast clearly denotes Babylon, the fourth beast must represent the Hellenistic empires, since it is clear from elsewhere in the book (e.g. Dan. 11) that the dénouement comes in Seleucid times; this leaves two more beasts, the latter of which must represent Persia (cf. Dan. 10:1, 20, 11:2), so that the former beast must represent a further empire, that of the Medes, and specifically Darius the Mede, since no other Median ruler is cited between Belshazzar and Cyrus. The presupposition of a Median empire between those of Babylon and Persia likewise rules out Whitcomb's equation of Darius the Mede with Gubaru, quite apart from the

dragons attested in Ugaritic (cf. *CTA* 3.IIID.37–43 = *KTU* 1.3.III.40–46).[27]

Whence, then, is the precise form of the beasts derived? Various views have been put forward to account for them. These may be summarized as follows: (i) the view that the beasts are derived from Hos. 13:7–8; (ii) that they have been derived from ancient near eastern *Mischwesen*; (iii) that they have an astrological origin; (iv) that they derive from the language of treaty curses. Of these the last may be quickly dismissed. T. Wittstruck[28] has recently argued that the imagery of the beasts was derived from the treaty curses, citing

fact that the latter was not a king (he was governor of Babylon and the district west of the Euphrates) and there is no evidence that he was called Darius.

26 J.C. Swain, 'The theory of the four monarchies: opposition history under the Roman empire', *Classical Philology* 35 (1940), pp. 1–21, has drawn attention to the fact that the notion of four great empires followed by a more glorious fifth (Assyria, Media, Persia, Macedonia + Rome) appears in various classical texts, including Aemilius Sura (cited by Velleius Paterculus) who can be dated between 189 and 171 B.C., so that the notion pre-dates the Maccabaean period. The fact that Media is included in the series and Babylon omitted indicates a Persian origin, and the fourfold sequence of empires in Daniel may therefore derive from Persia, Assyria's place being taken by Babylon because of its association with the legendary Daniel. The four metal ages of Dan. 2, already attested in Hesiod, may likewise be derived from Persia, as they are also found in Zoroastrian sources (cf. D. Flusser, 'The four empires in the fourth Sibyl and in the book of Daniel', *Israel Oriental Studies* 2, 1972, pp. 148–75), but the dating of the Zoroastrian evidence is uncertain, cf. W.G. Lambert, *The Background of Jewish Apocalyptic* (London, 1978), pp. 7–9. G.F. Hasel, 'The four world empires of Daniel 2 against its near eastern environment', *JSOT* 12 (1979), pp. 17–30 has recently pointed out that the Babylonian Dynastic Prophecy also contains a series of four empires, Assyria, Babylon, Persia, Greece (on this text see A.K. Grayson, *Babylonian Historical-Literary Texts*, Toronto and Buffalo, N.Y., 1975, pp. 24–37) and claims that this sequence is closer than any of the texts traditionally associated with Dan 2. Whilst it is difficult to see why the omission of Media but addition of Babylon makes this any closer to Daniel than the other parallels so far as sequence is concerned, it is interesting as further evidence of the diffusion of the notion of four empires in the oriental world during the Hellenistic period and raises the possibility of a Babylonian origin of the concept in Daniel. The striking parallel between the detailed *vaticinia ex eventu* of Daniel and the Babylonian Dynastic Prophecy and other Mesopotamian texts, to which attention has been drawn by other scholars (cf. W.G. Lambert, *op. cit.*, pp. 9ff.), may lend support to this view.

27 In this Ugaritic passage we find Yam, the dragon (Leviathan), the calf Arš (cf. Behemoth) and Fire (Ishat), the bitch of the gods associated together. In Enuma elish the monster companions of Tiamat are described several times as 'the Viper, the Dragon, and the Sphinx, the Great-Lion, the Mad Dog, and the mighty Lion-demons, the Dragon-Fly, the Centaur'. Only the lion is in common with Dan. 7.

28 T. Wittstruck, 'The influence of treaty curse imagery on the beast imagery of Daniel 7', *JBL* 97 (1978), pp. 100–2.

the Sefire treaty 11 A 9, where we find the sequence lion, —, leopard, and conjectures on the basis of Sefire treaty I A 31, where apparently we have the sequence snake, scorpion, bear and leopard, that the animal missing from the broken text is the bear. However, it is doubtful whether Sefire treaty I A 31 can give one confidence in this, since the leopard is the only animal common to both lists as they stand, and even this is not certain, and J.A. Rimbach[29] thinks that one should read *dbrh* 'bee' and *nmlh* 'ant' rather than *dbhh* 'bear' and *nmrh* 'leopard' in Sefire treaty I A 31. Even if the sequence lion, bear, leopard were attested in the eighth-century B.C. Syrian Sefire treaty, it would be extremely hazardous to conclude that it must therefore be treaty usage which lies behind the beasts in the second century B.C. book of Daniel.

The theory of the astrological origin of the beasts is rather more difficult to evaluate, but it should probably be rejected. A. Caquot[30] proposed this view, noting that the mention of the four winds of heaven stirring up the sea from which the four beasts emerged (cf. Dan. 7:2–3) suggests a connection of each of the beasts with one of the four cardinal points. He then seeks to find the origin of the first three beasts in astrological symbols connected with those regions from which the empires sprang. Caquot thinks especially in terms of the system of Teucer, whose influence is sometimes found elsewhere in Daniel, *viz*. in Dan. 8, where the symbolism of the ram and the goat, denoting Persia and Syria, is claimed to be due to the fact that in the zodiacal system of Teucer the ram and the goat represent those very nations. However, although the ram in Dan. 8 does denote Persia (cf. v. 20), the goat is actually stated there to represent Greece, not Syria (cf. v. 21). The influence of Teucer's astrological symbolism on Dan. 8 is therefore questionable.

To return to Dan. 7, Caquot notes that, in addition to the zodiac, there was something which he calls the 'dodécaoros', a system of thirty-six 'décans' according to which three 'paranatellonta' were attached to each sign of the zodiac. It is the influence of these which Caquot endeavours to find in the animal symbolism of the first three beasts of Dan. 7. Now in Teucer's system we find that the cat is one of those in the 'dodécaoros'

29 J.A. Rimbach, 'Bears or bees? Sefire 1 A 31 and Daniel 7', *JBL* 97 (1978), pp. 565–6.

30 A. Caquot, 'Sur les quatre bêtes de Daniel VII', *Semitica* 5 (1955), pp. 5–13.

corresponding to the ram of the zodiac (= Persia). Though the cat is not mentioned in Dan. 7, v. 6 does allude to the leopard as symbolizing Persia, and Caquot thinks that it has taken the place of the cat on the grounds that the latter would not have been known to the Jews. However, the fact that the word *ḥāṯūl* denotes the cat in post-biblical Hebrew (cf. Targum to Is. 13:22, 34:14) shows that the cat was known to the Jews, and the Letter of Jeremiah 21 (ET 22) actually attests the cat at a date which cannot be far removed from that of the book of Daniel. There is therefore no reason why Dan. 7 should not have alluded to the cat if precise astrological symbolism was required.

There is, moreover, also a problem with the symbolism of Babylon by a lion (Dan. 7:4), since, as Caquot has to admit, it is not the lion but the dog which, in the 'dodécaoros', corresponds to Taurus of the zodiac, representing the south, with which one would expect Babylon to be associated. Here Caquot appeals to Ptolemy, where Mesopotamia, Babylonia and Assyria are ruled by Virgo, which corresponds to the lion of the 'dodécaoros'. The fact that he here has to appeal to a different astrological system weakens Caquot's case.

Noth[31] argued for the dependence of the beasts of Dan. 7 on ancient near eastern iconography. There is probably some limited influence from this, as the first beast, the winged lion, is a well-known *Mischwesen* in Mesopotamia, whilst the four wings and four heads of the leopard recall ancient near eastern portrayals of beasts with four wings and several heads. However, iconography cannot account for the sequence of bear and leopard amongst the beasts, since neither of these is attested frequently in the plastic arts of the ancient orient. Again, an Akkadian text, VAT 10057, discovered at Asshur and dating from the seventh century B.C., which has recently been claimed by H.S. Kvanvig[32] to be an important source underlying Dan. 7, reflects the same world of *Mischwesen*, in that it has a series of fifteen gods, mostly of monstrous form, e.g. several with lion and eagle features, one having two heads, and most

31 M. Noth, 'Das Geschichtsverständnis der alttestamentlichen Apokalyptik', *Gesammelte Studien zum Alten Testament* (Munich, 1966), pp. 267–9 (ET 'The understanding of history in Old Testament apocalyptic', *The Laws in the Pentateuch and other essays*, Edinburgh & London, 1966, pp. 210–11.)

32 H.S. Kvanvig, 'An Akkadian vision as background for Dan 7', *Studia Theologica* 35 (1981), pp. 85–9. Kvanvig's claims are made only in preliminary form and he intends to deal with the matter more thoroughly at some future stage.

having 'feet like a man'.[33] However, it should be noted that in keeping with their rarity in iconography, none of them have bear or leopard characteristics, two of the three named beasts of Dan. 7, and their number (fifteen) differs from that in Dan. 7 (four). Also there is no connection with the sea in the Akkadian text. Accordingly, whilst it may be agreed that Dan. 7 owes something to the general world of Mesopotamian *Mischwesen*, other features are also present. However, a more detailed refutation of Kvanvig's article, which claims other influence from the Akkadian text on Dan. 7, is reserved for discussion below in the section on the origin of the son of man imagery.

At this point it is also appropriate to note the view of S. Morenz,[34] followed by U. Staub,[35] that the horns of the fourth beast were suggested by the horned caps which are depicted on Seleucid coins, even though they are not attested of Antiochus IV Epiphanes himself, and indeed, do not occur at all after Antiochus I—Morenz believes that the old coins would have remained in circulation and the coins of Alexander, which also bear the horned cap, would have continued to be restruck. However, the fact that the kings of Media and Persia are also symbolized by a ram bearing two horns (Dan. 8:3, 20) indicates that horns are not a specific mark of the Seleucids for the writer. Since horns symbolized strength in the Old Testament and the ancient near east, they provided an appropriate element in the beastly symbolism of empires and require no special explanation such as Morenz's (cf. Zech. 1:18–21).

The most attractive view is that the four beasts of Dan. 7 owe their fundamental derivation to Hos. 13:7–8,[36] where God declares, 'Therefore I will be[37] like a lion to them, like a leopard on the road I will keep watch. I will attack them like a bear robbed

33 It was originally published by E. Ebeling, 'Höllenfahrt eines assyrischen Königs', in his book *Tod und Leben nach den Vorstellungen der Babylonier* 1 (Berlin and Leipzig, 1931), pp. 1–9, but a more up to date translation was published by W. von Soden, 'Die Unterweltsvision eines assyrischen Kronprinzen', *ZA* 43 n.F. 9 (1936), pp. 1–31.

34 S. Morenz, 'Das Tier mit den Hörnern. Ein Beitrag zu Dan. 7, 7f.', in his collected essays, E. Blumenthal and S. Herrmann (edd.), *Religion und Geschichte des alten Ägypten* (Weimar, 1975), pp. 429–32 (reprinted from *ZAW* 63, 1951, pp. 151–4).

35 U. Staub, 'Das Tier mit den Hörnern. Ein Beitrag zu Dan 7, 7f.', *Freiburger Zeitschrift für Philosophie und Theologie* 25 (1978), pp. 366–81.

36 Cf. A.M. Farrer, *A Study in Mark* (Westminster, 1951), pp. 255–8.

37 Reading *w^{e}'ehyeh* with LXX for MT *wā'^{e}hī*.

of its young, and tear their hearts from their breasts; and I will devour them like a lion, a beast of the field will rend them.' In both Hosea 13:7–8 and Dan. 7 we therefore find four beastlike allusions – 'like a lion', 'like a leopard', 'like a bear' and an unnamed wild beast – to describe the affliction that will overtake Israel from the exile till the time of renewed blessing. Furthermore, we know from the fact that the proto-apocalyptic work in Is. 26–7 was heavily dependent on Hos. 13–14, as I have shown elsewhere,[38] that Hos. 13 was a good quarry for an apocalyptic writer seeking to describe the period of affliction prior to the eschaton. Moreover, the fact that the last beast is unnamed, being simply dubbed 'a beast of the field', offers an excellent explanation why the fourth beast of Dan. 7 is left unnamed: the apocalyptist was thus able to exercise his own imagination to the full in his description. The suggestion of U. Staub[39] that the writer was describing an elephant is accordingly uncalled for: the apocalyptist deliberately left the fourth chaos monster uncompared with any actually existing creature.

In conclusion, therefore, it may be maintained that, though the element of the cosmic sea hostile to God has been taken up from Canaanite mythology, the fundamental basis for the four types of beast is drawn from Hos. 13:7–8, with some influence from ancient near eastern *Mischwesen.*

The origin of the figure of the one like a son of man

But what of the origin of the figure of the one like a son of man? This is a much controverted question and it is impossible to review every single view that has been put forward. So far as the *expression* 'one like a son of man' is concerned, it is probably derived from Ezek. 1:26, where the divine presence is said to have 'a likeness as it were of a human form' (*dᵉmūṯ kᵉmar'ēh 'āḏām*). Such a claim is supported not only by the general evidence of dependence of Daniel on the book of Ezekiel, including Dan. 7 – the fiery wheels of the divine throne in Dan. 7:9 clearly deriving from Ezekiel (e.g. Ch. 1) – but also by the particular fact that the description of the body of the similarly named 'one in the likeness of the sons of men' of Dan. 10:16 (cf. 18) in Dan. 10:6 is clearly taken

38 J. Day, 'A case of inner Scriptural interpretation. The dependence of Isaiah xxvi. 13–xxvii. 11 on Hosea xiii. 4–xiv. 10 (Eng. 9) and its relevance to some theories of the redaction of the "Isaiah apocalypse"', *JTS* 31 n.s. (1980), pp. 309–19.

39 U. Staub, *op. cit.*, pp. 389–96.

from Ezek. 1:27, thus suggesting that the expression 'one in the likeness of the sons of men' is taken from the similar expression in the preceding verse Ezek. 1:26, which ought therefore to be the case for the comparable term 'one like a son of man' in Dan. 7:13. The expression 'one like a son of man' thus derives from the description of the divine glory in Ezek. 1:26.[40]

Some scholars in the past, however, e.g. C.H. Kraeling[41] and S. Mowinckel[42] saw Anthropos or *Urmensch* speculation lying behind the figure, such as is attested in the Iranian and Hellenistic worlds. However, the evidence of this in the pre-Christian Semitic world is very slight, and there is now widespread agreement that this is not the source in which the origin of the figure of the one like a son of man should be sought.[43]

Other scholars, however, such as A. Bentzen[44] and F.H. Borsch[45] saw *Urmensch* speculation as having been combined with royal ideology in the Jerusalem cultus and the coming of the rule of the one like a son of man as representing an eschatologization of the king's conflict with the nations at the Autumn Festival, such as is reflected, for example, in Ps. 2. It is true, as we shall see, that the ideology of the Autumn Festival probably does lie behind Dan. 7, but, apart from the dubiety of holding that the king was equated with the *Urmensch*,[46] it is very peculiar to speak of the king coming with the clouds of heaven; this suggests rather a heavenly being, indeed, in origin, at least, a divine being, in the light of the universal occurrence of the clouds imagery elsewhere in the Old Testament. Indeed, there is no evidence in the book of Daniel at all that the writer was expecting the coming of a Messianic king: in view of the eschatological orientation of the book, such a belief would have been made clear had it existed. On the contrary, we find that the one occasion on which the term *māšîaḥ* 'Anointed' is employed (Dan. 9:26), it is used of the High Priest Onias III. We may accordingly reject all forms of the view that the one like a son of man in

40 Cf. A. Feuillet, 'Le fils de l'homme de Daniel et la tradition biblique', *RB* 60 (1953), pp. 180ff., which also notes other parallels between Daniel and Ezekiel.

41 C.H. Kraeling, *Anthropos and Son of Man* (New York, 1927).

42 S. Mowinckel, *He That Cometh* (ET, Oxford, 1959), pp. 420–37.

43 C. Colpe, 'ὁ υἱὸς τοῦ ἀνθρώπου', in G. Kittel and G. Friedrich (edd.), *Theological Dictionary of the New Testament* 8 (ET, Grand Rapids, Mich., 1972), pp. 408–15.

44 A. Bentzen, *King and Messiah* (ET, 2nd ed., Oxford, 1970), pp. 74–5.

45 F.H. Borsch, *The Son of Man in Myth and History* (London, 1967), pp. 89ff.

46 J.A. Emerton, 'The origin of the Son of Man imagery', *JTS* 9 n.s. (1958), p. 231.

Dan. 7 is a royal Messianic figure, whether this be the kind of view held by Bentzen and Borsch, the traditional Messianic view, or the view of H. Sahlin and G.W. Buchanan[47] that he represents Judas Maccabaeus.[48]

Recently, H.S. Kvanvig, to whom we have already referred above,[49] has suggested a novel explanation of the origin of the son of man imagery, as of other features in Dan. 7. He claims that the main source behind Dan. 7 is an Akkadian text, VAT 10057, which was discovered at Asshur and dates from the seventh century B.C. In this text a ruler has a night vision in which he sees a series of fifteen gods, mostly in the form of monstrous *Mischwesen*, then a human figure, next a throne vision of Nergal, out of whose arms comes lightning and who is surrounded by the Anunnaki, and this is followed by a scene in which Nergal proclaims judgement on the ruler seeing the vision and speaks of a future ruler who will receive eternal dominion over all nations from the king of the gods. Kvanvig wishes to equate the human figure seen in the vision with this future ruler.

However, although at first the parallelism between this vision and that of Dan. 7 might appear quite striking, it is less so on closer examination. Thus, the gods are fifteen in number in the Akkadian text, unlike the beasts of Dan. 7, which are four in number, none of the divine *Mischwesen* in the Akkadian text have bear or leopard characteristics, unlike two of the three named beasts of Dan. 7, and they are not associated with the sea. Moreover, the judgement that is proclaimed is not on the *Mischwesen*, as in Dan. 7, but on the ruler seeing the vision. Again, although Nergal in the Akkadian text and the Ancient of Days in Dan. 7 both have the role of divine judges, from whom fire emerges and who are surrounded by a host of attendants, the name of the Ancient of Days and his white hair cannot be derived from Nergal but resemble rather, as we shall see, the god El 'the Father of years'. Finally, it is doubtful whether the future ruler is to be equated with the human figure seen in the vision following the

47 H. Sahlin, 'Antiochus IV. Epiphanes und Judas Mackabäus', *Studia Theologica* 23 (1969), pp. 41–68; G.W. Buchanan, *To the Hebrews* (New York, 1972), p. 43.

48 P.M. Casey, 'Porphyry and the origin of the book of Daniel', *JTS* 27 n.s. (1976), pp. 20–3, has shown that the commonly accepted view that already Porphyry identified the one like a son of man in Dan. 7 with Judas Maccabaeus is due to a misunderstanding based on Jerome's Daniel commentary (PL 25:533).

49 See above, p. 155f. and n. 32.

fifteen gods. Ebeling[50] says that the human figure is probably to be equated with Išum, who appears as Nergal's adviser later in the vision. This would fit with the fact that the human figure is clearly represented as standing below Nergal, and that he is depicted as wearing a red garment, which is consonant with Išum's name, which means 'fire'. Accordingly, it may be concluded that there is only a superficial resemblance between the Akkadian text and Dan. 7, and that there is no reason to suppose that traditions taken up from it have influenced Dan. 7.

As noted above, the figure of the one like a son of man coming with the clouds of heaven is suggestive of a heavenly being, indeed, in origin at least, a god. One view which posits a god behind the figure is that of J. Morgenstern,[51] who seeks an ultimate Canaanite–Phoenician origin of the imagery. He holds that Dan. 7:13–14 reflects Antiochus IV Epiphanes' reform of the Tyrian solar religion: in this Tyrian solar religion the sun is divided into two parts, Baal Shamem and Melḳart, which represent respectively the winter and the summer suns, the latter, a young god, taking the place of the former. Morgenstern understands the one like a son of man's taking the place of the Ancient of Days as a reflection of this. However, against Morgenstern it has to be said that his whole reconstruction of Antiochus IV Epiphanes' alleged reform of the Tyrian religion is entirely conjectural and without supporting evidence. Furthermore, it may be noted that the one like a son of man does not take over the place of the Ancient of Days, but rather that of the beasts. Finally, it may be noted that Morgenstern curiously maintains that Dan. 7:13–14 is an interpolation, on the grounds that nothing corresponds to the one like a son of man in the interpretation of the vision, thereby overlooking the holy ones of the Most High.

There is, however, another view which seeks the ultimate origin of the one like a son of man in a Canaanite divine being and which has great plausibility. It was first enunciated in 1958 by J.A. Emerton,[52] and also in the same year in far less detail by L. Rost.[53]

50 E. Ebeling, *op. cit.*, p. 6, n. g.

51 J. Morgenstern, 'The "Son of Man" of Daniel 7:13f. A new interpretation', *JBL* 80 (1961), pp. 65–77.

52 J.A. Emerton, 'The origin of the Son of Man imagery', *JTS* 9 n.s. (1958), pp. 225–42.

53 L. Rost, 'Zur Deutung des Menschensohnes in Daniel 7', *Studien zum Alten Testament* (Stuttgart, 1974), pp. 72–5, originally published in *Festgabe für Erich Fascher zum 60. Geburtstag* (Berlin, 1958), pp. 41–3.

I shall now consider in detail the arguments adduced in support of this ultimately Canaanite origin of the Son of Man imagery in Dan. 7.

(i) God is represented as the Ancient of Days and posseses white hair (v. 9), i.e. he is depicted as an old man. This is unique in the entire Old Testament. It agrees admirably, however, with the supreme god of the Ugaritic pantheon, El, who is called *'ab šnm* 'Father of Years' (*CTA* 4:IV:24 = *KTU* 1.4.IV.24, etc.). Opponents of this correlation have pointed out, however, that the word for 'years' in Ugaritic is elsewhere *šnt*, not *šnm*, and other possible translations have been proposed, namely 'Father of exalted ones',[54] 'Father of mortals',[55] and 'Father of (the god) Šnm'.[56] But there is nothing compelling about these alternative renderings. However, that two forms of the word for 'years' should occur in Ugaritic is not at all surprising, since in Hebrew besides the normal plural *šānīm* there also exists a plural construct form *š^e^nōṯ* (in addition to *š^e^nē*).[57] Moreover, in Ugaritic itself, we find the word *r'iš* 'head' having three plurals *r'ašm, r'ašt* and *r'išt*. Two points strengthen one's conviction that 'Father of Years' is indeed the correct translation. First, *KTU* 1.108.26–7 (*Ugaritica V*. 2, *RS* 24.252, rev. 11–12) refers to *lymt. špš. wyrḫ wnʿmt. šnt. 'il* 'all the days of Shapash and Yarikh and the most lovely *years* of El'. Secondly, El is clearly to be regarded as old since there are allusions to his grey hair (*CTA* 4.V.66; 3.VE.10, 32–3 = *KTU* 1.4.V.4; 1.3.V.10, 32–3). Thus, even apart from the epithet *'ab šnm*, there is evidence that El was an aged god. A further point that may be noted is that El is now known to have been called 'judge' (cf. *KTU* 1.108.3a = *Ugaritica V*. 2, *RS* 24.252, line 3a *'il ṯpṭ*, 'El the judge'), just as the Ancient of Days plays the role of judge in Dan. 7.

(ii) Just as the one like a son of man comes with the clouds of heaven, so Baal's stock epithet is *rkb ʿrpt* 'Rider of the clouds'

54 Cf. M.H. Pope, *El in the Ugaritic Texts* (*SVT* 2, 1955), p. 33, connecting with one or other of the Arabic roots *snw, sny* 'shine, be exalted, eminent, old', or *sanima* 'be tall, prominent'.

55 O. Eissfeldt, *El im ugaritischen Pantheon* (Berlin, 1951), p. 30. n.4. Cf. Syriac *š^e^nā* 'to depart'.

56 So C.H. Gordon, *Ugaritic Textbook* (Rome, 1965), p. 492, and 'El, Father of Šnm', *JNES* 35 (1976), pp. 261–2. On the deities *ṯkmn* and *šnm* and the question of their identity with the Kassite deities Šuqamuna and Šumaliya, see O. Eissfeldt, 'Ugaritisches, 4. *ṯkmn wšnm*', *ZDMG* 99, n.F. 24 (1945–9), pp. 29–42, and *El im ugaritischen Pantheon* (Berlin, 1951), pp. 66ff.

57 Similarly with other expressions of time, *yōm* 'day' having construct plurals *y^e^mē* and *y^e^mōṯ* and *dōr* 'generation' having plurals *dōrīm* and *dōrōṯ*.

(*CTA* 2.IV.8, 29 = *KTU* 1.2.IV.8, 29, etc.). As Emerton has pointed out,[58] since elsewhere in the Old Testament it is *always* the deity who manifests himself in the clouds, it is probable that a divine being underlies the one like a son of man.

(iii) The rise to power of the one like a son of man follows the destruction of the sea monsters, especially the fourth one. Although not explicitly stated, we are probably to understand that the one like a son of man himself (under God) defeated the dragon, in view of the fact that the previously mentioned dragon-symbolized empires each in turn (under God) overthrew the one that preceded it. This recalls Baal, whose kingship was assured by defeating the god of the sea Yam (*CTA* 2.IV.32 = *KTU* 1.2.IV.32), and Baal is also credited with defeating the seven-headed sea monster Leviathan (*CTA* 5.I.1–3 = *KTU* 1.5.I.1–3), who appears to have been an associate of Yam (cf. *CTA* 3.IIID.35–9 = *KTU* 1.3.III.38–42). In this connection it is interesting to note that Rev. 12:3, 13:1 and 17:3 actually credit the ten-horned dragon and beast (both reflecting the fourth beast of Dan. 7) with seven heads. There are a number of passages in the Old Testament which allude to God's battle with the sea monster (e.g. Is. 27:1; Job 26:12–13; Ps. 74:13–14, 89:10f., ET 9f.) which have been considered above, and from a number of expressions used (Leviathan, twisting serpent, crooked serpent) it is clear that it is Canaanite mythology rather than, say, the Babylonian myth of Marduk and Tiamat (as Gunkel thought and as some scholars still erroneously suppose) which underlies these Old Testament references (cf. above, Chapter 1).[59] When in Dan. 7 we find God in opposition to sea monsters, we are therefore led to postulate an ultimate Canaanite myth there also.

(iv) No other view accounts so easily for the fact that we have seemingly two divine beings, the Ancient of Days who sits as heavenly judge upon his throne, and the one like a son of man who comes like a god with the clouds of heaven. The one like a son of man is appointed king by the Ancient of Days and acts as his vice-gerent. This accords very well with what we know of the relationship between El and Baal. Thus, *CTA* 6.VI.32ff. (= *KTU* 1.6.VI.32ff.) may actually refer to El's enthronement of Baal as king, but we cannot be certain, as the text is damaged, whilst *CTA* 3.V.43–4 (= *KTU* 1.3.V.43–4) and 4.IV.48 (= *KTU* 1.4.IV.48) *'il*

58 J.A. Emerton, *op. cit.*, p. 232.
59 See pp. 4–7.

mlk. dyknnh may also refer to El's appointment of Baal as king, but it is possible that *mlk* 'king' here alludes to El, not Baal.

Nevertheless, there is clear evidence of El's appointment of gods to their kingship elsewhere in the Ugaritic texts, e.g. in *CTA* 6.I.43ff. (= *KTU* 1.6.I.43ff.). El appoints Athtar as king following the death of Baal, and on another occasion Shapash threatens that El will deprive Athtar of his kingship (*CTA* 2.III.17f. = *KTU* 1.2.III.17f.) and in *CTA* 6.VI.27ff. (= *KTU* 1.6.VI.27ff.). Shapash threatens Mot that El will deprive Mot of his kingship if he continues fighting Baal. It is therefore likely that Baal's kingship similarly depended ultimately on that of El, as that of the one like a son of man depended on the Ancient of Days. The complementary nature of the kingship of El and Baal is suggested by *KTU* 1.108.2b–3a (*Ugaritica V*. 2, *RS* 24.252, lines 2b–3a), where we read *'il. yṯb. bʿṯtrt 'il ṯpṭ. bhd rʿy* 'El sits next to Astarte, El the judge next to Hadad the shepherd'.[60] This harmonious association of rulers bears comparison with the statement in Philo of Byblos that 'Astarte the great and Zeus Demarous who is Hadad, king of the gods, reigned over the place with the consent of Kronos' (Eusebius, *Praep. Ev.* 1.10.31). Such an understanding of the relationship between El and Baal is much more satisfactory than the view that they were in opposition to one another,[61] and has most recently been vigorously defended by C.E. L'Heureux.[62]

This view of the origin of the imagery of Dan. 7, argued most forcibly by Emerton, has met with a mixed reception. Thus, on the one hand, Cross[63] refers to Emerton's article as a 'superb paper',

60 Cf. A.J. Ferrara and S.B. Parker, 'Seating arrangements at divine banquets', *UF* 4 (1972), pp. 37–9 for a convincing refutation of the translation of this passage (including the previous word *yqr*) by B. Margulis (Margalit) in 'A Ugaritic Psalm (RŠ 24.252)', *JBL* 89 (1970), pp. 292–304 as 'While the Honor of El sits (enthroned) in Ashtoreth, El rules in Edrei' (cf. Josh. 12:4). In addition to the points made by Ferrara and Parker it should be noted that the fact that Edrei begins with ʾ but *hd rʿy* with *h* tells against Margulis' interpretation.

61 The view that Baal and El were in opposition to each other, held by such scholars as U. (M.D.) Cassuto, *The Goddess Anath* (E.T., Jerusalem, 1971), pp. 55–7, A.S. Kapelrud, *Baal in the Ras Shamra Texts* (Copenhagen, 1952), pp. 86–93, and M.H. Pope, *op. cit*., pp. 27–32, is presented in its most extreme form by U. Oldenburg, *The Conflict between El and Baal in Canaanite Religion* (Leiden, 1969).

62 C.E. L'Heureux, *Rank among the Canaanite Gods El, Baʿal, and the Repha'im* (Missoula, Mt., 1979), pp. 3–108. Similarly, much more briefly, J. Gray, *The Legacy of Canaan* (*SVT* 5, 2nd ed., Leiden, 1965), pp. 154–5.

63 F.M. Cross, *Canaanite Myth*, p. 345, n. 8.

and this view is fully supported by J.J. Collins,[64] A. Lacocque[65] and E.W. Nicholson.[66] On the other hand, a number of scholars, e.g. A.B. Rhodes,[67] emphasize that the theory is conjectural, and A.J. Ferch[68] has written an article raising questions against Emerton's viewpoint. His points are basically as follows: (i) he notes that the Ugaritic material is complex and ambiguous; (ii) he emphasizes that the resemblances between Dan. 7 and the Ugaritic texts are outweighed by the differences. Thus, (a) on the one hand there are things in the Canaanite myth which are not in Dan. 7 and (b) there are features in Dan. 7 which are not explained by Canaanite mythology. However, I would reply to this that (i) in spite of all uncertainties in the interpretation of the Ugaritic material, the relationship between El and Baal as presupposed by Emerton's article is clear enough. With regard to (ii) it may be argued: (a) it is not surprising that there are elements of the Canaanite myth that are not in Dan. 7, since over one thousand years separate them and the contexts are different, the Ugaritic texts being polytheistic and Dan. 7 monotheistic; (b) Ferch overlooks the fact that Emerton's theory does not claim to explain every detail of Dan. 7 from the Ugaritic myth, but only the most significant underlying theme, for which the parallel is clear enough.

C. Colpe,[69] whilst offering a number of criticisms, concludes that Emerton's theory accounts for the facts better than any other. However, he misunderstands the theory as it has been presented by Emerton (though not by Rost), for he writes: 'Yet either way, and on all the possible variations, the transfer of dominion from the Ancient of Days to the Son of Man would seem to go back to the wresting of power from an old god by a young one as this was handed down in Canaanite mythology, the rivalry between Baal and El in the Ras Shamra texts being thus far the closest par.'[70]

64 J.J. Collins, *The Apocalyptic Vision of the Book of Daniel* (Missoula, Mt., 1977), pp. 99–101.

65 A. Lacocque, *The Book of Daniel* (Atlanta, Ga., 1979), p. 129. This is part of a section not in the French, *Le livre de Daniel* (Neuchâtel and Paris, 1976), though on p. 108 of the latter (ET pp. 142–3) he notes the probable origin of the Ancient of Days in El.

66 E.W. Nicholson, in G.W. Anderson (ed.), *Tradition and Interpretation* (Oxford, 1979), p. 206.

67 A.B. Rhodes, 'The Kingdoms of Men and the Kingdom of God: A study of Daniel 7:1–14', *Interpretation* 15 (1961), p. 428.

68 A.J. Ferch, 'Daniel 7 and Ugarit: a reconsideration', *JBL* 99 (1980), pp. 75–86.

69 C. Colpe, *op. cit.*, pp. 415–19.

70 C. Colpe, *op. cit.*, p. 419.

This is clearly a misunderstanding, since in Dan. 7 the one like a son of man does not wrest power from the Ancient of Days. On the contrary, it is the Ancient of Days who appoints the one like a son of man king, and the kingship is transferred rather from the fourth beast to the one like a son of man. Similarly, as noted above, Baal does not wrest power from El, but would rather seem to have been appointed by him. Colpe also expresses doubts about the meaning of *'ab šnm* as 'Father of Years', but, as has been noted above, this remains the most likely translation, and, in any case, El is clearly represented as being an old man.

A frequently expressed doubt about the theory of an ultimately Canaanite origin of the Son of Man imagery is the long period of time separating the Ugaritic texts (ca. 1350 B.C.) from the time of the composition of the book of Daniel (ca. 165 B.C.). However, this theory does not postulate a direct Canaanite influence on the book of Daniel. Rather, the mythology was handed down in the Jerusalem cult at the Autumn Festival, as has been indicated in Chapter 1. It is commonly accepted by scholars that the theme of the divine conflict with the dragon, with which the kingship of Yahweh was associated, had its *Sitz im Leben* at this festival, even by those who prefer not to speak of it as an Enthronement Festival. Various Old Testament texts show that the myth of God's battle with the dragon was known in Israel as late as the exilic and post-exilic periods, a remarkable example being the passage from Is. 27:1 discussed earlier in this chapter. What is peculiar about the source underlying Dan. 7, unlike these Old Testament texts, is that it preserves a more primitive, Canaanitizing version of the myth in which a distinction is still made between the god who is supreme and the one who is enthroned over the dragon. How are we to account for this phenomenon in Dan. 7? Emerton has conjectured that, at any rate in some parts of the Jerusalem cultus, Yahweh was first identified with Baal, the god who fought the dragon, and subsequently, as Yahweh was identified with El-Elyon, Yahweh-Baal was demoted to the role of an angel, whence the figure of the one like a son of man in Dan. 7. That Yahweh was equated with Baal in certain circles is clear, for example, from Hos. 2:18 (ET 16), where the prophet refers to those who call Yahweh 'my Baal'. In such circles, Yahweh-Baal would presumably have remained inferior to El, like Baal in the Ugaritic texts. The gap in dating that has to be bridged is not therefore between the Ugaritic texts in ca. 1350 B.C. and the book of Daniel in 165 B.C., but the end of the kingdom of Judah in 586 B.C., when we know such syncretistic beliefs existed, and the writing of the book of Daniel in 165 B.C., i.e. just over four centuries.

It is possible that, just as the spread of Christianity has often not totally eliminated some pagan beliefs amongst certain peoples, so the exile did not totally eliminate some pagan beliefs amongst the Jews. An indication of the syncretism that was possible in the post-exilic period is indicated by the Elephantine papyri, where we find Yahweh, or Yahu as he is called, furnished with a consort Anat-Yahu (Anat being Baal's consort in the Ugaritic texts), and worshipped alongside a number of other deities, Ḥerem-Bethel, Ishum-Bethel, and Anat-Bethel.[71] The figure of Yahweh-Baal inferior to Yahweh-El might therefore have lived on as an angelic figure in popular belief amongst some people and this could have been taken up in Dan. 7. On the other hand, it is possible, as J.J. Collins[72] has argued, that the use of ultimately Canaanite mythological motifs in Dan. 7 is a result of a learned rather than a folk tradition. He points out that we know that Canaanite mythology similar to that of the Ugaritic texts, was available as late as the Roman period from Philo of Byblos, who about the end of the 1st century A.D. translated Sanchuniathon's 'Phoenician history', and that this interest in ancient traditions characterized the Hellenistic age more broadly (cf. Berossus) and was the product of learned scribes. In any case, however the mythological imagery reached the author of Daniel, it is clear that for him it had lost its original pagan associations and that it was considered safe to be employed as a vehicle of faith in the time of the crisis posed by Antiochus IV Epiphanes. M. Casey[73] misunderstands Emerton when he claims that the latter maintains that the one like a son of man in Dan. 7 is

71 See A. Cowley, *Aramaic Papyri of the Fifth Century B.C.* (Oxford, 1923), 44^3 (Anat-Yahu), 7^7 (Ḥerem-Bethel), 22^{124} (Ishum-Bethel), 22^{125} (Anat-Bethel).

72 J.J. Collins, *The Apocalyptic Vision of the Book of Daniel* (Missoula, Mt., 1977), p. 103.

73 M. Casey, *Son of Man. The Interpretation and Influence of Daniel 7* (London, 1979), p. 37. Admittedly, on p. 232, Emerton's words 'If Dan. vii. 13 does not refer to a divine being, then it is the only exception out of about seventy passages in the O.T.' could lead one to Casey's conclusion, but it is clear from p. 242 that at this late stage Emerton regards the Son of Man as an angel: 'At some stage, the old myth was reinterpreted in terms of the supremacy of Yahwe, who had been identified with both Elyon and Baal. Then the Son of Man was degraded to the status of an angel, even though he retained the imagery which was so closely attached to him in tradition.'

a second god: rather Emerton is alluding to the prehistory of Dan. 7.

The one like a son of man as the angel Michael

I now hope to show that the one like a son of man in Daniel 7 is to be equated with the angel Michael. If this is accepted, the case for the ultimately Canaanite origin of the one like a son of man will be considerably strengthened, for, as will be seen, the angel Michael is himself a figure having his ultimate origin in the same Canaanite mythology. What, then, is the evidence for this view? First, it may be noted that Dan. 7:13 does not actually speak of the Son of Man but rather of one like a son of man. This suggests that the figure is not actually human but rather resembles a human being. Whilst this language is admittedly partly used to set the figure over against the various preceding beasts ('. . . like a lion', '. . . like a bear'), the terminology definitely suggests that it is more than this and that an angelic being is in mind, since phrases comparable to this are found elsewhere in Daniel referring to angels, as was first pointed out by Nathaniel Schmidt[74] in 1900. Thus, in Dan. 8:15 Gabriel is described as 'one having the appearance of a man' and in Dan. 10:16 an angel (possibly Gabriel) is referred to as 'one in the likeness of the sons of men' and again in Dan. 10:18 as 'one having the appearance of a man'. Similarly elsewhere the manlike appearance of angels is alluded to (cf. Dan. 3:25, 9:21, 12:6–7; Gen. 18). In addition, it may be noted that the fact that the one like a son of man comes with the clouds of heaven suggests a heavenly being. Indeed, it suggests a god, but as the writer of Daniel was a monotheist the heavenly figure must be on a lower level, *viz.* an angel.

Before I come to the question of which particular angel is intended, I may note a further piece of evidence suggesting the angelic nature of the one like a son of man. In Dan. 7:18 and throughout the interpretation of the vision, the writer refers to the holy ones of the Most High, the holy ones, or the people of the holy ones of the Most High receiving the kingdom, whereas the vision speaks of the one like a son of man so doing. The one like a son of man must therefore in some way represent these holy ones. But who are they? Here I touch on a controversial matter. Traditionally they have been understood as the faithful Jews who suf-

74 N. Schmidt, 'The Son of Man in the book of Daniel', *JBL* 19 (1900), p. 26.

fered at the hands of Antiochus IV Epiphanes. Noth,[75] however, followed up a suggestion made by Procksch[76] and Sellin[77] and argued that the holy ones of the Most High are rather to be understood as angels. In this he has been followed by a number of other scholars including Dequeker,[78] Barr[79] and Collins.[80] I too subscribe to this view. Although at first sight the references might seem to refer to the Jews, careful examination suggests that this is not the case. To begin with, apart from Ps. 34:10 (ET 9), it is clear that the expression 'holy ones' in the plural always alludes to angels in the Old Testament, and this is its usual meaning at Qumran and in other intertestamental literature.[81] It is interesting to note that in one instance, the proto-apocalyptic Zech. 14:5, these angelic holy ones appear at the time of the eschatological divine judgement on the foreign enemy occupying Jerusalem, a context identical to that in which the holy ones appear in Dan. 7.

Furthermore, in Daniel, it may be noted that outside the disputed Dan. 7 (and 8:24), the substantive 'holy ones' clearly refers to the angels (cf. 4:14, ET 17), interestingly mentioned in close connection with 'the Most High'. On this basis, if the meaning

75 M. Noth, '"Die Heiligen des Höchsten"', in *Interpretationes ad Vetus Testamentum pertinentes Sigmundo Mowinckel septuagenario missae* (Oslo, 1955), pp. 146–61, reprinted in M. Noth, *Gesammelte Studien* (Munich, 1966), pp. 274–90 (ET 'The Holy Ones of the Most High', *The Laws of the Pentateuch and other essays*, Edinburgh, 1966, pp. 215–28.)

76 O. Procksch, 'Der Menschensohn als Gottessohn', in *Christentum und Wissenschaft* 3 (1927), pp. 425–43, 473–81.

77 E. Sellin, *Alttestamentliche Theologie auf religionsgeschichtlicher Grundlage* (Leipzig, 1933), 1, pp. 129–30; 2, p. 126.

78 J. Coppens and L. Dequeker, 'Le fils de l'homme et les Saints du Très-Haut en Daniel VII, dans les Apocryphes et dans le Nouveau Testament', *Analecta Lovaniensia Biblica et Orientalia* Ser. 3, Fasc. 23 (1961), pp. 15–54. More recently, Dequeker has defended his thesis against its attackers in 'The "Saints of the Most High" in Qumran and Daniel', *OTS* 18 (1973), pp. 108–87.

79 J. Barr, 'Daniel', in H.H. Rowley and M. Black (edd.), *Peake's Commentary on the Bible* (London, 1962), p. 598.

80 J.J. Collins, *The Apocalyptic Vision*, pp. 123–52.

81 Cf. Deut. 33:3; Job 5:1, 15:15; Ps. 16:3, 89:6, 8 (ET 5, 7); Zech. 14:5. C.H.W. Brekelmans, 'The Saints of the Most High and their Kingdom', *OTS* 14 (1965), pp. 305–29 and R. Hanhart, 'Die Heiligen des Höchsten', *Hebräische Wortforschung* (*SVT* 16, 1967), pp. 90–101, in particular have criticized Dequeker's view that the holy ones in the Qumran literature are normally angels, but Dequeker has more recently convincingly answered these objections and reaffirmed his position in *OTS* 18 (1973), pp. 133–73. G.F. Hasel, 'The identity of "The Saints of the Most High" in Daniel 7', *Biblica* 56 (1975), pp. 173–92 and V. Poythress, 'The Holy Ones of the Most High in Daniel VII', *VT* 26 (1976), pp. 208–13, who both argue against the angelic identity of the holy ones, fail to deal with the arguments adduced by Dequeker in his later article.

'angels' makes good sense in Dan. 7, then it ought to be accepted. Now it is often objected that the expressions used in v. 21 '... this horn made war with the holy ones, and prevailed over them', and v. 25 '... and he shall wear out the holy ones of the Most High' must refer to pious Israelites and not angels, since it is thought strange that angels should suffer.[82] Even Noth feels compelled to regard the former verse as an interpolation, as does Dequeker, whilst in the latter verse he takes the dubious view that we should translate rather '... and shall *offend* the holy ones of the Most High' as more befitting angels.[83] However, I see no grounds at all to consider v. 21 an interpolation or to depart from the natural meaning of v. 25. Both these verses make good sense if the 'holy ones (of the Most High)' refers to angels, for in the very next chapter, Dan. 8:10–13, we similarly find the little horn engaged in what could be termed persecution of, or making war with angels, who are there equated with stars. In v. 10 we read, 'It (i.e. the little horn) grew great, even to the host of heaven; and some of the host of the stars it cast down to the ground, and trampled upon them.' V. 12 reads, 'And the host was given over to it together with the continual burnt offering through transgression; and truth was cast down to the ground, and the horn acted and prospered'; moreover, v. 13 refers to two holy ones (clearly angels) speaking. In the vision in the first half of Dan. 8 there is no reference to human beings suffering; rather we hear of angels suffering. Clearly the suffering of the Jews has given rise to the language, but the seer rather takes us behind the scenes to see the repercussions of these events in the heavenly sphere, as he also does in the succeeding chapters, i.e. the war with the angels fighting on the side of the faithful Jews. It is possible that we also have the same idea in Dan. 11:36, where we read that Antiochus IV Epiphanes 'will exalt himself and magnify himself above every god (*'ēl*) and speak astonishing things against the God of gods', if, as Collins supposes,[84] this alludes to his

82 E.g., A. Feuillet, 'Le fils de l'homme de Daniel et la tradition biblique', *RB* 60 (1953), p. 194; G.F. Hasel, *op. cit.*, pp. 185–6, 188–9; A.A. di Lella, 'The one in human likeness and the holy ones of the Most High in Daniel 7' *CBQ* 39 (1977), p. 8.

83 Noth seems obliged to reject the traditional translation 'wear out', since this does not seem appropriate for angels. However, in view of the persecution of the host of heaven (angels) in Dan. 8:10–13, the traditional translation is entirely appropriate. Furthermore, it may be noted that Noth's linguistic arguments have been demolished by Hasel, *op. cit.*, pp. 185–6.

84 J.J. Collins, *The Apocalyptic Vision of the Book of Daniel* (Missoula, Mt., 1977), pp. 135–6.

exalting himself above Yahweh's heavenly host rather than pagan gods (contrast v. 37). At any rate, this is certainly the case in Dan. 8:10–13 and there is therefore no reason why this should not also be the case in Dan. 7. The only reference to the Jews in Chapter 7 would seem to be the allusion to '*the people* of the holy ones of the Most High' in v. 27. I take this to refer to the Jews, since the word 'people' is nowhere else found referring to angels, contrary to what Noth supposes,[85] but suggests rather an earthly nation, i.e. Israel. This is entirely natural, since if the angels on the side of Israel are to receive the kingdom, it is entirely appropriate for the faithful Jews to share in this too. Indeed, the book would offer no word of hope if this were not the case. (Cf. Dan. 12:3, which speaks of the pious Jews in the new age 'shining like the stars', i.e. becoming like angels.) The objection that we cannot have a reference to angels here, since an angelic kingdom is elsewhere unattested in Judaism, is invalid, since we do in fact find this in the Qumran War Scroll 17:7, where we read that God is going 'to raise up the rule (משרת) of Michael amongst the angels and the dominion (ממשלת) of Israel amongst all flesh'.[86] As will shortly emerge, this, in my opinion, is precisely the meaning of Dan. 7.

After this excursus on the holy ones of the Most High I now return to the question of the identity of the one like a son of man. The purpose of the excursus was to add yet further evidence for the view that the one like a son of man is angelic in nature: if the holy

85 Noth, *op. cit.*, pp. 150 and 160–1, n. 24 (= *Ges. St.*, pp. 280, 284–5, n. 24, ET pp. 220, 223–4, n. 26), however, maintains that *'am* can refer to the 'host' of the angels on the basis of 1QH III, 21–2, where we read להתיצב במעמד עם צבא קדושים ולבוא ביחד עם עדת בני שמים which he translates 'To join the garrison of the *host* of the army of the holy ones and to enter into the union of the *host* of the congregation of the heavenly ones (lit. sons of heaven)', but all other translations render עם as עִם 'with', and rightly so. This is clear from the close parallel in 1QH X1, 13, where we read ולהתיצב במעמד לפניכה עם צבא עד 'that he may stand in the garrison before you *with* the everlasting host', and where עם can only be עִם 'with'. This has been pointed out by various scholars, e.g. Brekelmans, *op. cit.*, p. 321.

86 C.H.W. Brekelmans, 'The Saints of the Most High and their Kingdom', *OTS* 14 (1965), pp. 326–9, maintains that the notion of an angelic kingdom is unknown in Judaism, claiming on p. 327 that 1QM 17, 6–8 'deals with the dominion of Michael only and his dominion extends to the gods, i.e. the other angels, whereas the kingdom of Israel extends "to all flesh"'. This, however, would appear to be a false antithesis: since, *ipso facto*, Michael and the angels are superior to Israel, Michael being Israel's guardian angel, it is difficult to see how it can be denied that the rule of Michael and the angels extends over the world.

ones of the Most High are angelic, then so should be the one who is represented as symbolizing them, the one like a son of man, though it should be noted that the evidence for the angelic identity of the one like a son of man can stand quite apart from the question of the identity of the holy ones. That a particular angel is intended by the one like a son of man, and that it is not merely a collective symbol of the angels as Coppens thought,[87] is supported by the fact that the preceding beasts are stated each to represent an individual king as well as a kingdom (Dan. 7:17). That this is in fact the case, and that MT 'kings' is not simply a scribal error for 'kingdoms',[88] is borne out by a study of the beasts in question. Thus, just as the first metal of Dan. 2 is specifically stated to denote Nebuchadrezzar (Dan. 2:37–8), so the reference to the first beast in Dan. 7:4 seems to contain an allusion to Nebuchadrezzar and his madness, as a comparison with Dan. 4:13, 30 (ET 16, 33) indicates. The second beast (Dan. 7:5) must have Darius the Mede specifically in mind, since he is the only Median ruler in the author's scheme of things, being immediately followed by Cyrus the Persian (Dan. 6:29, ET 28). Again, the fourth beast (Dan. 7:7–8) has in mind particularly Antiochus IV Epiphanes, indicated by the little horn on whom attention is especially focused. The third beast (Dan. 7:6) denoting Persia ought similarly to have a specific king in mind: although this is conceivably Cyrus, there is no way of being certain.

In the interests of consistency, therefore, the one like a son of man ought similarly to be not merely a collective symbol of the holy ones, as is often thought, but also their specific angelic representative or leader. If so, which particular angel is intended? Z. Zevit has proposed that he is the angel Gabriel, since in Dan. 9:21 there is a reference to 'the man Gabriel, whom I had seen in the vision at the first', i.e. the vision of Dan. 7. In his first article Zevit[89] simply maintained that the only heavenly man-like figure in Dan. 7 is the one like a son of man, so that he must therefore be

87 *Contra* J. Coppens, 'Le Fils d'Homme daniélique, vizir céleste?', *Miscellanées bibliques* 33, *Analecta Lovaniensia Biblica et Orientalia* ser. 4, fasc. 12 (1964), p. 79, who sees the one like a son of man as simply a symbol of the angels, with no particular angelic being in mind. Further arguments in favour of seeing a specific angel, i.e. Michael, as the one like a son of man, will be given below.

88 The LXX and Theodotion read *βασιλεῖαι* 'kingdoms', but this probably represents an attempt to bring consistency to the interpretation of the beasts.

89 Z. Zevit, 'The structure and individual elements of Daniel 7', *ZAW* 80 (1968), pp. 394–6.

the one to be identified with Gabriel. However, Zevit thereby overlooked the fact that in Dan. 7:16 we read of another angelic being appearing in the vision, one whom Daniel asked to explain its meaning. In a more recent article,[90] in an attempt, presumably, to take account of this oversight, Zevit has argued that, although we have a reference to another angelic figure in Dan. 7:16, this cannot be equated with 'the man Gabriel, whom I had seen in the vision at the first' (Dan. 9:21), since the vision of Dan. 7 only extends from vv. 2–15, whilst v. 16 refers to what happens after the vision. This, however, is completely erroneous, since Dan. 7:16 states that Daniel 'approached one of those who stood there', which can only mean one of the angelic beings standing before God in the vision in v. 10. Zevit is therefore incorrect in denying that the figure in v. 16 belongs to the vision and may be identified with Gabriel. Since, moreover, it is Gabriel who elsewhere explains the visions (cf. Dan. 8:15, 9:21), it is more natural to suppose that it is this figure who is to be identified with Gabriel rather than the 'one like a son of man'. Furthermore, as we shall presently see, a considerable body of evidence rather favours the identity of the one like a son of man with another angel.

Which particular angel is, then, intended by the figure of the one like a son of man? Since he serves as a symbol for the angels as a whole he ought to be their leader, and since he also represents the people of the holy ones of the Most High, i.e. the pious Jews, he ought also to be Israel's patron angel. In view of the important role which he plays we ought also to expect to find allusions to him elsewhere in the book of Daniel. On all these scores the evidence points in the direction of the angel Michael, a view first propounded by Nathaniel Schmidt[91] and more recently taken up by U.B. Müller,[92] J.J. Collins[93] and others.[94] Thus, first, in Jewish thought

90 Z. Zevit, 'The exegetical implications of Daniel viii 1, ix 21', *VT* 28 (1978), pp. 488–92.

91 N. Schmidt, 'The "Son of Man" in the book of Daniel', *JBL* 19 (1900), pp. 22–8. Rowley, *op. cit.*, p. 63, n. 2, notes a few other scholars early in the century who followed this view.

92 U.B. Müller, *Messias und Menschensohn im jüdischen Apokalypsen und in der Offenbarung des Johannes*, (Gütersloh, 1972), p. 28.

93 J.J. Collins, 'The mythology of Holy War in Daniel and the Qumran War Scroll: a point of transition in Jewish apocalyptic', *VT* 25 (1975), p. 602, n. 29, and in *The Apocalyptic Vision of the Book of Daniel* (Missoula, Mt., 1977), pp. 144–6.

94 A passing reference in J.A. Emerton, *op. cit.*, p. 242 suggests some kind of connection between Michael (and Metatron) and the one like a son of man.

Michael is not only Israel's guardian angel but also usually the chief angel. Similarly in Daniel itself we find him referred to as 'your prince' (Dan. 10:21) and 'the great prince who has charge of your people' (Dan. 12:1). Secondly, it is significant that, just as the one like a son of man appears at the time of the demise of Antiochus IV Epiphanes in Dan. 7, so in Dan. 12:1 the angel Michael is specifically mentioned as appearing and delivering the people at the time of the overthrow of Antiochus. It is certainly justified to correlate the figure of the one like a son of man of Dan. 7 with the angel Michael in Dan. 12:1, since, even if those are right who maintain that Dan. 2:4b–7:28 and 8–12 come from different authors, the writer of the latter having drawn on an earlier Aramaic source containing the former, the fact remains that the theology and style of the two sections seem identical, and Dan. 8–12 forms a kind of midrash on Dan. 7, so that it may be argued that the overall redactor of the book of Daniel wished to equate the one like a son of man with the angel Michael. Thirdly, it is significant that in Rev. 12 it is the angel Michael who defeats the seven-headed and ten-horned dragon, the ten horns clearly deriving from the fourth beast of Dan. 7. Since in Dan. 7 it is implicitly the one like a son of man who overcomes the fourth beast, and since it is very probable, as various scholars have argued,[95] that a Jewish source underlies Rev. 12 – it is striking, for example, that it is Michael and not Christ who is said to defeat the dragon – we appear to have here evidence of an underlying Jewish tradition which equated the one like a son of man with Michael. It is possible that further evidence for the equation of the one like a son of man with the angel Michael in sources underlying the Apocalypse is provided by Rev. 10:1ff. and 14:14. In the former passage, we have a description of what is clearly the most important of the seven archangels who appear in Rev. 8:2ff., and ought therefore to be the angel Michael, yet the description of him 'wrapped in a cloud . . . his face was like the sun, and his legs like pillars of fire' (Rev. 10:1) recalls the 'one like a son of man . . . his feet were like

Further, it may be noted that B. Lindars, 'Re-enter the apocalyptic Son of Man', *NTS* 22 (1975–6), p. 56, regards the equation of the one like a son of man and Michael as possible, and J.H. Hayes, *An Introduction to Old Testament Study* (Nashville, Tenn., 1979), p. 380, regards it as probable.

95 H. Gunkel, *Schöpfung und Chaos*, pp. 391–7; R.H. Charles, *A Critical and Exegetical Commentary on the Revelation of St. John* 1 (Edinbugh, 1920), pp. 303ff.; A.Y. Collins, *The Combat Myth in the Book of Revelation* (Missoula, Mt., 1976), pp. 104–7.

burnished bronze . . . and his face was like the sun shining in full strength' (Rev. 1:13–16), and who customarily comes with the clouds of heaven (cf. Rev. 14:14). This suggests an equation of the angel Michael with the one like a son of man, but since the one like a son of man in Rev. is Christ, it may be argued that the equation pertains to a source underlying the book. Similarly, in Rev. 14:14f. the one like a son of man is alluded to in terms which suggest he is simply another angel (cf. vv. 17–18), and since six other angels appear, the addition of the one like a son of man would make seven, the number of the archangels. Since, however, in the book as it stands, the one like a son of man must be Christ (cf. Rev. 1:13), it is arguable that, as in Rev. 10:1ff., we have here further attestation of the archangelological identification of the one like a son of man with the angel Michael in a source underlying the work.

I therefore hold that an extremely strong case can be made for identifying the one like a son of man in Dan. 7 with the angel Michael. To the objection that, if this be so, he should have been directly mentioned by name in Dan. 7,[96] it may be pointed out that it is in the nature of apocalyptic to be allusive, and that neither Antiochus IV Epiphanes nor any of the other kings or kingdoms alluded to in the chapter is directly mentioned by name either.

I come now to that part of the argument which presents new evidence for the ultimate origin of Michael in the figure of the Canaanite god Baal, though more immediately in the figure of Yahweh, with whom in certain circles he was identified, and which consequently strengthens the case for the ultimately Canaanite origin of the one like a son of man argued by Emerton and others, since, if the two figures have an identical origin, it is likely that they are to be equated. Michael, it will be remembered, is Israel's guardian angel. In Dan. 10:13 and 21 he is depicted fighting the angelic princes of Persia and Greece. Jewish apocalyptic in fact affirmed that there were seventy angelic princes, corresponding to the seventy nations of the world such as are attested in Gen. 10 (cf. Targum Pseudo-Jonathan on Deut. 32:8; 1 Enoch 89:59ff., 90:22ff.). Now this concept is derived from the theology which we find in Deut. 32:8, 'When the Most High gave to the nations their inheritance, when he separated the sons of men, he fixed the bounds of the peoples according to the number of the sons of God.' As is commonly accepted, this involves reading *bᵉnē 'ēl* 'sons of

96 So M. Casey, *Son of Man* (London, 1979), p. 32; N.W. Porteous, *Daniel* (2nd ed., London, 1979), p. 192.

God/El' with the support of the Qumran fragment 4Q Deut.,[97] the LXX, Symmachus, Old Latin and the Syro-Hexaplaric manuscript Cambr. Or. 929,[98] rather than *bᵉnē yiśrāʾēl* 'sons of Israel' with the MT. That the MT is clearly a deliberate alteration of the original Hebrew text by a scribe who did not like the polytheistic overtones of the expression 'sons of El/God' and not a simple scribal error, as some have supposed,[99] is shown by the fact that the reference to 'the gods' in Deut. 32:43 has similarly been eliminated from the MT.[100] Now, according to the Ugaritic texts El (or more precisely his consort Asherah) did in fact have seventy sons (cf. *CTA* 4.VI.46 = *KTU* 1.4.VI.46 *šbʿm. bn. ʾaṯrt* the seventy sons of Asherah), thus proving that the ultimate origin of the angelic princes of the nations of Jewish apocalyptic, including those of the book of Daniel, is to be sought in the seventy sons of the Canaanite god El. As for Michael, the chief of the guardian angels of the nations, he too should be derived from one of the sons of El, indeed he should be El's supreme son. This points in the direction of Baal, the chief and most active of the gods under El, who, as well as being termed 'son of Dagon' (cf. *CTA* 2.I.19, 5.IV.23–4 = *KTU* 1.2.I.19, 1.5.VI.23–4), is also represented as the son of El in the Ugaritic texts (cf. 3.VE.43, 4.IV.47 = *KTU* 1.3.V.35, 1.4.IV.47).[101]

97 Cf. P.W. Skehan, 'A fragment of the "Song of Moses" (Deut. 32) from Qumran', *BASOR* 136 (1954), pp. 12–15. The fragmentary text has *bny ʾl . . .*, which could represent *bᵉnē ʾēl*, *bᵉnē ʾēlīm*, or *bᵉnē ʾᵉlōhīm*.

98 On the Cambr. Or. 929 reading (*mlʾkwh dʾlh*), see M.H. Gottstein, 'Eine Cambridger Syrohexaplahandschrift', *Le Muséon* 67 (1954), p. 293; J. Hempel, 'Zu IVQ Deut 32 8', *ZAW* 74 (1962), p. 70.

99 Thus, J.B. Lightfoot, *The Apostolic Fathers, part 1. St. Clement of Rome*,[2] (London, 1890), p. 94, followed by *NAB* (cf. *BH3* and *BHS*), held that 'Israel' in Deut. 32:8 has accidentally crept in from the end of the following verse (v. 9), where it is attested in the LXX and Samaritan versions. H.L. Ginsberg, 'A strand in the cord of Hebraic hymnody', *Eretz-Israel* 9 (W.F. Albright volume, Jerusalem, 1969), p. 45, n. 4, held that MT's *yiśrāʾēl* arose through a conflation of *bᵉnē ʾēl* and an explanatory gloss *śārē*.

100 A.D.H. Mayes, *Deuteronomy* (London, 1979), p. 385, fails to take account of Deut. 32:43 when he states that in Deut. 32:8 we do not have deliberate alteration of a text whose polytheistic implications were found unacceptable, maintaining that similar allusions elsewhere were not tampered with. Moreover, just because a scribe tampered with Deut. 32:8 and 43 does not require him to have systematically done the same to all the other passages, some of which, e.g. Ps. 82, were more readily capable of being interpreted in other ways (in the case of Ps. 82, of judges).

101 That Baal should be represented as the son of both El and Dagon is capable of being interpreted in two possible ways: either (i) these represent variant traditions, or (ii) Baal was the son of Dagon in the strict sense, but a son of El in the sense of being a member of the pantheon which had its ultimate origin in El. I prefer the latter suggestion. Perhaps he was son of Dagon and grandson of El (suggestion of Prof. D. Pardee).

The angel Michael therefore has his ultimate origin in Baal, but more immediately we should think in terms of Yahweh-Baal and indeed Yahweh, since the writer of Dan. 7 would not have been conscious of the Baalistic origin of the imagery. This is an important new confirmation of Emerton's theory of the ultimately Baalistic, more immediately Yahweh-Baalistic and Yahwistic origin of the Son of Man imagery, since Michael, who appears to be equated with the one like a son of man in the book of Daniel, has been shown to have precisely the same origin as Emerton postulates for the one like a son of man. At the same time, it may be argued, the fact that Michael and the one like a son of man appear to have an identical origin serves to support the view of their equation in the book of Daniel. A further previously unnoted point supporting the ultimately Baalistic origin of the angel Michael may now be pointed out: this is the fact that in Jewish sources Michael is held to be the lord of the winter season and is especially connected with water and snow.[102] This agrees very well with Baal, who likewise was lord of the winter season and brought the rain, and even the snow.[103]

Accordingly, we reject the view of W.C. Graham and H.G. May,[104] followed by M. Hengel[105] and H.O. Thompson,[106] that Michael derives from the Canaanite god Mekal (who was equated with the plague god Resheph), a view which in any case had little to commend it. The name Michael, which means 'Who is like God?', is formed on the same analogy as the other angelic names ending in -el, e.g. Gabriel, Raphael, Uriel, etc., and there is no need to seek some other name behind it. However, the name Michael, meaning 'Who is like God?', an expression of the incomparability of the deity[107] (cf. *mī ḵāmōḵāh bā'ēlīm yahweh* 'Who is like you, O Lord, among the gods?' in Ex. 15:11), is consonant with the view maintained here that the figure has its origin in a god, indeed it

102 E.g., Midrash rabba on Job 25:2. On Michael, cf. W. Lueken, *Michael* (Göttingen, 1898).

103 That Baal brought the rain needs no documentation. His bringing of the snow is attested in *CTA* 4.V.69 = *KTU* 1.4.V.7, where we read that he should appoint *'dn. ṯkt. bglṯ* 'a time for the ship with snow'.

104 W.C. Graham and H.G. May, *Culture and Conscience* (Chicago, 1936), p. 108.

105 M. Hengel, *Judentum und Hellenismus* (Tübingen, 1969), p. 344 (ET *Judaism and Hellenism* 1, London, 1974, p. 188).

106 H.O. Thompson, *Mekal, the God of Beth-Shan* (Leiden, 1970), p. 178.

107 Cf. C.J. Labuschagne, *The Incomparability of Yahweh in the Old Testament* (Leiden, 1966).

suggests Yahweh. Such an origin suggests itself likewise for the figure of Metatron, the exalted angel who acts as God's vice-gerent in 3 Enoch and who resembles Michael, for in 3 Enoch 12:5 he is actually called 'the lesser Yahweh'.[108]

Summary

In this chapter I have considered the eschatologization of the divine conflict with the dragon and the sea. First of all Is. 27:1 was discussed, and it was concluded that Leviathan is there a term used most probably to denote Egypt, though it might refer to Babylon or Persia. The fact that this passage has such a remarkable parallel in the Ugaritic texts led to an investigation of whether related mythological motifs are attested elsewhere in Is. 24–7. It was concluded that this is indeed the case: the description of the theophany in Is. 24:18b–19, the fading of the luminaries in the face of it in Is. 24:23, the universal banquet of the deity on the sacred mountain in Is. 25:6, and the swallowing up of death in Is. 25:8, all ultimately derive from Baal mythology, as does Is. 27:1.

Detailed attention was then devoted to Dan. 7. Various views of the origin of its imagery were surveyed, and it was concluded that the best theory is that of J.A. Emerton, since it can explain it as an organic whole. This postulates an ultimately Canaanite origin, the Ancient of Days deriving from El, the one like a son of man from Yahweh-Baal, and the sea monsters, especially the fourth one, from Leviathan or Yam. However, this does not explain everything in Dan. 7. The expression 'one like a son of man' is taken over from the description of the divine glory in Ezek. 1:26 as 'a likeness as it were of a human form', whilst the types of the four beasts are derived from Hos. 13:7–8, with some influence from ancient near eastern *Mischwesen*.

With regard to the present meaning of the imagery, it was argued that the one like a son of man is to be equated with the angel Michael, Israel's guardian angel. This was suggested by the use of comparable expressions elsewhere in Daniel to denote angels and by the evidence supporting the equation of the holy ones (symbolized by the one like a son of man) with angels. That a particular angel is intended is supported by the fact that the beasts

108 Cf. J.A. Emerton, *op. cit.*, p. 242. Interestingly, Metatron is equated with Enoch in 3 Enoch, just as 1 Enoch 71:14 equates Enoch with the Son of Man.

are similarly interpreted individually as well as corporately in Dan. 7:17, and that the angel is specifically Michael is indicated by the comparable allusion to him in Dan. 12:1. Evidence for the identification of the one like a son of man with Michael amongst the Jews was also deduced from the book of Revelation.

Summary and conclusions

In the first chapter I began by elucidating a number of controverted questions relating to the subject of the divine conflict with the dragon and the sea in its association with the creation of the world. It was established, for example, that there are passages in the Old Testament which allude to a conflict between Yahweh and a dragon (variously termed Leviathan, Rahab, twisting serpent or simply dragon) or the sea at the time of creation, a point which is still not universally conceded. The context renders this the most probable interpretation in the following passages: Ps. 65:7–8 (ET 6–7), 74:12–17, 89:10–15 (ET 9–14), 93:1–4, 104:1–9, Job 9:5–14, 26:5–14, 38:8–11, and it is probably implicit in Ps. 24. Again, although nothing in the context explicitly demands it, the analogy of these passages and the absence of any more credible explanation, renders this the most probable understanding of the time of the conflict alluded to or implicit in the following passages: Job 7:12, 40:15–41:26 (ET 34). In addition, Job 3:8 seems to allude to a reversal of the original process of *Chaoskampf* and creation. Although not referring to Yahweh's original act of creation, Ps. 29:3, 10 and Nah. 1:4 allude to Yahweh's power over the cosmic sea in connection with his present lordship over the created order.

It was also shown that the Old Testament's use of the imagery of the divine conflict with the dragon and the sea is appropriated from Canaanite mythology, deriving from the myth of Baal's conflict with the sea-god Yam and his dragon associates Leviathan, El's calf Atik, etc. (*CTA* 2; 3.IIID.35ff.; 5.I.1–3 = *KTU* 1.2; 1.3.III.38ff.; 1.5.I.1–3), and not from the Babylonian myth of Marduk's conflict with Tiamat recounted in Enuma elish, as some scholars still mistakenly suppose. Yam and Leviathan, it should be noted, are not to be equated, even though they are closely related, whilst the Old Testament Rahab is probably an alternative name for Leviathan. It is probable that the Canaanites envisaged a pre-creation conflict between Baal and Yam and his associates, even though our extant Baal–Yam text (*CTA* 2 = *KTU* 1.2) from Ugarit is not specifically connected with the creation.

In Israel the imagery was taken up and used in the celebrations of the Autumn Festival, where it was associated with the notion of Yahweh's enthronement as king. It is against this background that the allusions in the psalms noted above should be understood or at any rate had their origin. Furthermore, the passages in the book of Job also are indebted to creation hymns which doubtless had their setting in the Autumn Festival, the author of the book of Job finding the theme of the conflict between the dragon and God an apt parallel to the motif of the conflict between Job and God portrayed in the book. One point of detail in the book of Job to which attention was drawn is Job 3:8, where it was concluded that the common emendation of MT *yōm* 'day' to *yām* 'sea' should be rejected, and that Job is longing for Leviathan to be roused with his pre-creation darkness, and a parallel was noted in the Ugaritic texts where the dragon (= Leviathan) appears to be an enemy of the sun at the very end of the Baal myth, probably the time of the end of the year, and also corresponding to the time immediately before the creation (*CTA* 6.VI.44–52 = *KTU* 1.6.VI.45–53).

In the course of time the divine conflict with the dragon and the sea underwent a process of demythologization, so that the control of the sea simply became regarded as a job of work. We find this, for example, in Gen. 1, and also in Ps. 33:7–8, Prov. 8:24, 27–9, Jer. 5:22 and 31:35. Contrary to a widespread view, Gen. 1 is neither dependent on nor polemicizing against the Babylonian Enuma elish. Rather, as elsewhere, the underlying mythology is ultimately Canaanite, but Gen. 1's immediate dependence seems to be on Ps. 104, where the order of the survey of creation is identical with the order of creation in Gen. 1, the presence of the poetic form *ḥayᵉṯō* in the latter and overtly mythological features in the former supporting the priority of Ps. 104 over against Gen. 1.

In the second chapter I concentrated attention on the sections of the second divine speech in the book of Job dealing with Behemoth and Leviathan (Job 40:15–41:26, ET 34). The widespread view that Behemoth is the hippopotamus and Leviathan the crocodile was rejected, as were other views equating these beasts with actually occurring creatures, i.e. Behemoth with the buffalo or crocodile, and Leviathan with the whale, tunny fish or (in part) the hippopotamus. The descriptions do not properly fit any known natural creature and it is clear that Behemoth and Leviathan cannot be captured by man but only by God, (cf. Job 40:9ff., 19, 24, 25ff., ET 41:1ff.), since otherwise God's argument falls to the ground. Moreover, as Gunkel first recognized, both these creatures have mythological features: e.g. there is the very name Leviathan, elsewhere in the Old Testament (and in Ugaritic) a mythical creature, and in Job 41 he breathes out fire and smoke, the angels being afraid when he raises himself, and he is termed 'king over all the sons of pride', whilst Behemoth is 'the first of God's works'.

It is accordingly more appropriate to regard Leviathan and Behemoth as mythological creatures. Leviathan would then be the mythical sea serpent or dragon referred to elsewhere in the Old Testament, although it would appear that he now has only one head instead of seven. Such a conclusion is reinforced by the fact that the book of Job elsewhere contains allusions to the mythological Leviathan, dragon and Rahab, so that it is most natural to assume that this is the case in Job 40:25–41:26 (ET 34) also, especially if, as I maintain, the second divine speech is an authentic part of the book. The grounds which have frequently been alleged against its authenticity are inadequate. That the second divine speech is authentic I support *inter alia* on the original ground that the allusion to Leviathan inherently belongs at the climax of the list of the various works of the universe contained in Job 38–39, since we find the same phenomenon elsewhere: in Ps. 104, Leviathan is mentioned in v. 26 virtually at the climax of a list of various creatures and phenomena comparable to Job 38–9, and elsewhere in the book of Job, in 9:2–14, we find a comparable account of God's works coming to a conclusion in v. 13 with a reference to the bowing low of the helpers of Rahab (= Leviathan). This significantly leads to Job's declaration, 'How much less can I answer him or find words to dispute with him?', thus providing in addition a remarkable parallel to Job 41–2, where Job's inability to answer Yahweh (42:1–6) follows the account of Leviathan. Accordingly, Leviathan is surely here the chaos monster referred to elsewhere in Job.

I argue that the figure of Behemoth, as is natural, also has its origins in Baal mythology, in the figure of Arš or *ʿgl ʾil ʿtk* 'El's calf Atik', who is twice mentioned in the Ugaritic texts alongside Leviathan (*CTA* 3.IIID.37–41; 6.VI.50–2 = *KTU* 1.3.III.40–44,

1.6.VI.51–3), just as Behemoth is described alongside Leviathan in Job 40:15ff. Moreover, in the second Ugaritic reference Arš is depicted as living in the sea, just as Behemoth is depicted as dwelling in the river in Job 40:23. We thus have in both cases an ox-like creature capable of living in water mentioned alongside Leviathan. No other view of the origin of Behemoth can claim such striking support. As for Wakeman's theory of the presence of an earth monster in the Old Testament, who is to be equated with Behemoth, this has been found to be without valid supporting evidence.

In the third chapter I considered those passages in the Old Testament in which the divine conflict with the dragon and the sea is historicized, the dragon denoting a particular nation and the sea or waters commonly referring to an enemy nation or hostile nations in general. It was noted that, in particular, the dragon could serve to denote Egypt (so Rahab, Is. 30:7, 51:10; Ps. 87:4) or Pharaoh (Exek. 29:3–5, 32:2–8, reading *tannīn* 'dragon' for MT *tannīm* 'jackals'). Amongst detailed controverted points, it was argued that in Is. 30:7 the meaningless MT *rahab̲ hēm šāb̲et̲* should be read as *rahab̲ hammošbāt̲* 'the silenced Rahab', and that in the Ezekiel passages the dragon is the chaos monster and not simply the crocodile, as is often thought. The Old Testament allusions to Egypt and Pharaoh as Rahab or the dragon probably arose as a result of the oppressive role that Egypt played towards Israel before the Exodus, and the use of this imagery was also conditioned by the fact that the heart of the Exodus deliverance actually took place at the sea (Ex. 14). In keeping with this, the imagery of the *Chaoskampf* is taken up and applied to the deliverance at Yam Suph: in addition to Is. 51:10, this is the case in Ps. 77:17–21 (ET 16–20) and Ex. 15. In Ex. 15, although the imagery is taken up, the conflict is at the sea and not with the sea, and the passage is not as early as some (especially American) scholars maintain, presupposing as it does the Solomonic Temple (Ex. 15:17, cf. v. 13), which is spoken of in terms appropriated from Baal's dwelling on Zaphon. Since the latter was built as a direct consequence of Baal's victory over the Sea, this proves that v. 17 is not part of a poem originally separate from vv. 1b–12 (*contra* Hyatt).

The theme of the chaos waters is also taken up to denote the oppressive Assyrians (Is. 17:12–14, cf. Is. 8:5–8) and the waters and the dragon are both used to denote the oppressive Babylonians (Hab. 3; Jer. 51:34). The night threat posed by the powers of chaos in Is. 17:14 is paralleled in the Ugaritic texts in *CTA* 6.VI.44–52

(= *KTU* 1.6.VI.45–53). The reference to Resheph in the context of the conflict with chaos in Hab. 3:5 and Yahweh's seven shafts of lightning in Hab. 3:9 also have interesting parallels in Baal mythology first pointed out by the present writer. The swallowing of Jonah by the great fish, however, is neither dependent on Jer. 51:34 nor an allegory of the Babylonian exile, but the fish probably does ultimately derive from the mythological chaos monster, since Jonah's place of embarkation, Joppa, was strongly associated with Perseus' deliverance of Andromeda from the sea monster. With regard to the disputed passages Ps. 44:19–20 (ET 18–19) and Ps. 68:23 (ET 22), it was concluded that the former probably refers to the dragon (if we read *tannīn* 'dragon' for MT *tannīm* 'jackals'), although the nation thereby alluded to cannot be identified with certainty, whereas in Ps. 68:23 (ET 22) the MT is to be retained, and the widespread view that Bashan denotes the mythological chaos monster is to be rejected. Rather, as in Ps. 68:16f. (ET 15f.), it denotes the geographical area of that name, probably specifically Mt Hermon understood as the mount of the gods (*har 'ᵉlōhīm*, v. 16, ET 15). The reference to 'the beast of the reeds' a few verses later in Ps. 68:30 (ET 29) is likewise in all probability not a chaos monster (e.g. Behemoth) but rather an example of the use of an animal title to denote a leader or warrior as elsewhere in the Old Testament.

The imagery of the waters was also applied to hostile nations generally (cf. Ps. 18:5ff., ET 4ff., 46:3–4, ET 2–3, cf. v. 7, ET 6, 144:5–7). On specific points it was argued that in Ps. 46:6 (ET 5) (cf. too Is. 17:14), the deliverance of Zion comes at dawn because the victory over the waters was associated with the emergence of light at dawn, and in Ps. 18 and 144 it was maintained that the engulfing of the king in the waters and his subsequent deliverance has its *Sitz im Leben* in the Autumn Festival, and that there is no volcanic, but only storm, imagery in the theophany which delivers the king.

More significantly, it was argued against certain recent criticisms, that the *Völkerkampf* or conflict with the nations motif and the notion of the inviolability of Zion to attack by foreign nations (cf. Ps. 46, 48, 76, etc.), represent a historicization of the theme of the divine conflict with the chaos waters as argued by such scholars as Mowinckel and Johnson. Many features combine to suggest such a mythological origin, e.g. the parallelism of verbs with respect to the waters and nations in Ps. 46:3, 7 (ET 2, 6), the cosmic sweep of the victory, the equation of Zion with Zaphon in Ps. 48:3 (ET 2), the name of Baal's sacred mountain where the conflict between Baal and the chaos waters was localized, the use of the verb *gʿr* 'to roar' employed in Ps. 76:7 (ET 6) regarding Yahweh's conflict with the nations, which is a sort of technical term for the divine conflict with the sea, and the allusion to the shattering of the ships of Tarshish (Ps. 48:8, ET 7) in sight of Zion (Ps. 48:9, ET 8, cf. Is. 33:21, 23a), which looks like the appropriation of a motif more at home in a seaport such as the Syrian Zaphon (cf. Ps. 48:3, ET 2).

Furthermore, it seemed possible to posit not merely a Canaanite but a specifically Jebusite mediation of the material. This is suggested by the mention of the name of the Jebusite god Elyon (cf. Gen. 14:18–20, 22) in association with the notion of the mythological river in Ps. 46:5 (ET 4), by the fact that the related Royal Ps. 110:4 alludes to Melchizedek, the Jebusite priest of El-Elyon, in the context of the theme of the conflict with the nations, which pervades the rest of the Psalm, by the mention of Salem in Ps. 76:3 (ET 2), used elsewhere in the Old Testament only as the name of Jebusite Jerusalem in Gen. 14:18, as well as by a number of other suggestive factors.

None of the attempts to dispute the Canaanite/Jebusite hypothesis in recent years seems satisfactory. G. Wanke's view that the *Völkerkampf* motif is not a pre-exilic tradition at all is open to many objections, not least the fact that belief in the inviolability of Zion is more natural before the fall of Jerusalem in 586 B.C. than after it. H.-M. Lutz's view that the motif was derived from a Jebusite tradition concerning an attack by nations on Jerusalem (Zaphon) in which they are repelled by El-Elyon's theophany, but is to be distinguished in origin from the onslaught of the waters on Zaphon, which has secondarily been associated with it, involves an unnecessary multiplication of hypotheses. Finally, the view of J.J.M. Roberts and R.E. Clements, that Ps. 46, 48 and 76 are simply addressed to the vassals of the Davidic–Solomonic empire warning them not to revolt, fails to take into account the cosmic scope of the victory depicted in them ('to the ends of the earth'), as well as the full weight of evidence for a mythological background and Canaanite/Jebusite influence (e.g. the Melchizedek reference in Ps. 110:4).

In the fourth chapter I considered two places in the Old Testament where the divine conflict with the dragon and the sea has been eschatologized, *viz*. Is. 27:1 and Dan. 7. It was argued that the reference to Leviathan in Is. 27:1 denotes either the current world power (Babylon or Persia) or perhaps more likely Egypt and probably dates from the early post-exilic period. The fact that the expressions there used, 'Leviathan the twisting serpent, Leviathan the crooked serpent', have a remarkable parallel in the Ugaritic texts almost a thousand years earlier (*CTA* 5.I.1–2 = *KTU* 1.5.I.1–2), led to a consideration of whether Is. 24–7 contain other allusions to the same circle of ancient mythic ideas. These were indeed found. Thus, Yahweh's theophany and the quaking of the earth in response (Is. 24:18b–19), reflecting his assumption of kingship (cf. v. 23), are closely paralleled in the Baal myth in *CTA* 4.VII.25ff. (= *KTU* 1.4.VII.25ff.), where Baal manifests himself in the storm and the earth quakes in response, following the building of his Temple after he had assumed sovereignty in defeating Yam. In both we find a reference to the opening of the windows of heaven (Is. 24:19) *CTA* 4.VII.25–6 = *KTU* 1.4.VII.25–6), the Ugaritic parallel being closer in certain respects than the passage in the Genesis flood story (P) in Gen. 9:15 often cited, in that the emphasis is on thunder rather than rain and there is an association with the deity's kingship. Is. 24:23 follows with an allusion to the darkening of the luminaries, and similarly this is paralleled in *CTA* 4.VII.52–60 (= *KTU* 1.4.VII.52–60), which suggests that vv. 21–23 are not a later addition to vv. 17–20 as is sometimes supposed. In Is. 25:6–8 Yahweh's kingship (cf. Is. 24:23) is celebrated by an eschatological banquet on Mt Zion to which all nations come, and it leads to the declaration that Yahweh 'will swallow up death for ever'. Similarly, on the completion of Baal's Temple, following his assumption of kingship, Baal held a banquet on Mt Zaphon to which all the gods were invited (*CTA* 4.VI.44–59 = *KTU* 1.4.VI.44–59), and this is immediately followed by the story of Baal's conflict with Mot (Death), the god who swallows up men. Following Baal's resurrection from the dead and the defeat of Mot we read of the threat posed by the dragon (Leviathan) (*CTA* 6.VI.50–2 = *KTU* 1.6.VI.51–3). This pattern seems to be reflected in Is. 26:19, where the resurrection from the dead immediately precedes Yahweh's defeat of Leviathan in Is. 27:1.

In Chapter 4 I also discussed the origin and meaning of the imagery in Dan. 7, where the one like a son of man is enthroned in place of the dragons (especially the fourth one) of the cosmic sea. I argued that the most satisfactory theory of the origin of the imagery is that which derives the central notions from what is ultimately Canaanite Baal mythology, as maintained by J.A. Emerton. No other theory succeeds in explaining the imagery as an organic whole: just as the one like a son of man coming with the clouds of heaven was enthroned by the Ancient of Days in place of the cosmic sea and dragons, so in Canaanite mythology, Baal, the Rider of the clouds, was enthroned by the aged god El over the cosmic sea and dragons. The imagery was probably mediated through the Autumn Festival in the syncretistic Jerusalem cult of the pre-exilic period. In the post-exilic period it may have lived on in popular tradition, though more probably the writer of Dan. 7 had access to earlier Israelite sources.

However, not every feature of Dan. 7 is explicable in terms of Canaanite mythology. Apocalyptic is a complex phenomenon, and Dan. 7 is no exception. For example, although the chaos monster lies behind the imagery of the sea and the dragons, especially the fourth one, of Dan. 7, the specific types of the four individual beasts do not, which rather seem to be drawn from Hos. 13:7–8, with some influence from ancient near eastern *Mischwesen*. Again, the actual *expression* 'one like a son of man' seems to be drawn from Ezek. 1:26, just as the imagery of the fiery wheels of the throne-chariot of Dan. 7:9 appears to be derived from Ezekiel, like various other features of the book of Daniel.

Moving on to the present meaning of the imagery of Dan. 7, I argue that the one like a son of man is not merely a collective symbol of Israel, but specifically Israel's guardian angel, who is also the chief of the angels, Michael. Very similar expressions are used elsewhere in the book of Daniel of angels, and the view that specifically Michael is in mind is supported by the mention of his appearance elsewhere at the time of the demise of Antiochus IV Epiphanes in Dan. 12:1, by the fact that the angelic figure should be a particular angel and not just a general symbol (and therefore most probably the chief one), since the preceding beasts are said to denote individual kings as well as kingdoms, and also by the fact that Rev. 12 seems to rest on a Jewish tradition identifying the one like a son of man of Dan. 7 with the angel Michael (cf. too Rev. 14:14). Further, the holy ones of the Most High, represented by the one like a son of man in Dan. 7, are also angels, in keeping with the usual meaning of 'holy ones' in the Old Testament, though the people of the holy ones of the Most High are the pious Israelites.

Some concluding reflections

Now that the main body of this monograph has been summarized I shall turn to discuss some more general questions which the subject raises. First, there is the question of the date of the passages in which the imagery is found. It is clearly found in both pre-exilic and post-exilic texts, contrary to the statement of T.H. Gaster, for example, who claims that, 'Without exception, the passages are of exilic or post-exilic date.[1] In the pre-exilic period the imagery is especially found in the Psalms, e.g. in Ps. 18:5–18 (ET 4–17), 89:10–11 (ET 9–10), 144:5–7, whose pre-exilic date is indicated by their allusions to the king, Ps. 46:3–4 (ET 2–3), which assumes the inviolability of Zion, and a pre-exilic origin is also probable for Ps. 29:3, 10, 44:20 (ET 19), 93:3–4, and 104:6–9, 26. The pre-exilic date of Is. 17:12–14 (cf. 8:5–8), 30:7, is also generally conceded, although the pre-exilic date of Nah. 1:4 is uncertain. Ex. 15:1–18 is similarly of pre-exilic date, although the imagery has undergone a process of transmutation in this passage, since the conflict is at the sea rather than with it, and Jer. 5:22b is also pre-exilic, although here the control of the waters has simply become a job of work. Also it may be noted that the way in which the exilic passages Ps. 74:13–15 and Is. 51:9–11 appeal to the divine victory over the dragon (Leviathan, Rahab) in the past as a ground of confidence in the present, suggests that the symbolism was already deeply rooted in the consciousness of the people at that time, and therefore pre-dated the exile.

Although the imagery was already known in pre-exilic Israel, when it was especially associated with the Autumn Festival, it did become particularly prominent in the exilic period, as is evidenced by Ps. 74:13–14, Hab. 3:8–10, 15, Ezek. 29:3–5, 32:2–8, Jer. 51:34, and Is. 51:9–11; in addition possibly also Ps. 77:17–21 (ET 16–20) and Jer. 31:35, though in this last the control of the waters has become simply a job of work. Why should the imagery gain prominence at this time? With the exception of the references in Ezekiel, where the dragon alludes to Pharaoh, it is clear that it was the experience of exile itself which led to the fondness for the imagery, for Israel was now totally subject to a foreign power in a way which had not been the case in pre-exilic times. Thus it was that the dragon and sea were apt terms to be applied to Babylon, for it appeared that the powers of chaos defeated at creation and in the

1 Cf. Ch, 3, n. 9.

Exodus had reasserted themselves, but, as on the earlier occasions, they were to be overcome yet again.

Coming to the post-exilic period, we find further examples of the imagery. Its employment in the proto-apocalyptic passage Is. 27:1 and the apocalyptic work of Dan. 7 is a development of its exilic usage: the dragon symbolizes a kingdom whose destruction presages the end, the employment of this imagery giving vivid expression to the dualistic feeling inherent in apocalyptic. In the post-exilic period, however, it is in the book of Job that the imagery supremely finds expression (3:8, 7:12, 9:8, 13, 26:12–13, 38:8–11, 40:15–41:34, ET 41:26). Its prominence here may be attributed both to the fact that the writer found the conflict with the dragon and sea an apt parallel to the conflict between Job and God, and also to the fact that the theme of God's creative power is important to the work.

Finally, it is necessary to deal with the question of how living the mythological imagery of the divine conflict with the dragon and the sea was in ancient Israel and in the Old Testament. Was it taken literally or did it simply have the nature of poetic symbolism, as is often suggested, comparable to the citations from classical mythology in the work of Milton?[2] This is a question to which it is difficult to give a uniform and categorical answer. One argument that may favour its having the nature of poetic symbolism is the diverse way in which the imagery is used, the fact that the imagery of the dragon and the sea is not only applied in connection with the creation of the world, but is also historicized, i.e., used to symbolize various hostile nations.[3] In any case, when employed to denote foreign nations it has clearly attained the status of poetic metaphor. It is also clear that for those who accepted the demythologized picture of Gen. 1 in which the divine control of the waters at creation was simply a job of work, the notion of a primordial battle with a dragon and the sea would also be poetic

2 Neither of the two major works on myth in the Old Testament, B.S. Childs, *Myth and Reality in the Old Testament* (2nd ed., London, 1962) and J.W. Rogerson, *Myth in Old Testament Interpretation* (*BZAW* 134, Berlin, 1974) has a discussion bearing directly on this question. Indeed, surprisingly little is said about the myth of the dragon and sea at all, even though it is arguably the most pervasive myth in the Old Testament.

3 Cf. R. de Vaux, 'Les combats singuliers dans l'Ancien Testament', *Bible et Orient* (Paris, 1967), p. 229 (ET, 'Single combat in the Old Testament', *The Bible and the Ancient Near East*, New York, 1971, p. 134); D.J. McCarthy, '"Creation" motifs in ancient Hebrew poetry', *CBQ* 29 (1967), p. 406.

metaphor. However, it cannot be doubted that there were those in ancient Israel who practised a syncretistic form of Yahwism, equating Yahweh with Baal, for example (cf. Hos. 2:18, ET 16), and worshipping all the host of heaven (cf. Zeph. 1:5), and for them the mythology of the divine conflict with the dragon and the sea would surely have been living. The Old Testament itself, of course, does not tolerate syncretism, and its monotheism, first implicit, later explicit, must have exerted a transforming influence on the myth, shattering its polytheistic context. However, it should be noted that monotheism of itself does not imply that the myth could not have been taken literally,[4] since, whilst incompatible with the belief that the dragon and the sea were gods, it is compatible with the view that they were demonic forces, which we often find portrayed in animal form in the ancient world. If belief in snake-like angels seems to have been compatible with monotheism (cf. the seraphim of Is. 6), might not the same have been true of comparable demons? In the case of one book, the book of Job, this supposition seems to be demanded, since, if our conclusions are justified,[5] it is impossible to separate Leviathan and Behemoth, living creatures of the present (Job 40:21–3, 40:29, ET 41:5, cf. Ps. 104:26; Amos 9:3) from the chaos monsters overcome at creation (Job 3:8, 7:12, 9:13, 26:12–13). In conclusion, then, it would appear that for some in ancient Israel the mythology was living and for others it was not, and even for some of those for whom it was living Israelite monotheism had transformed it out of all recognition.

4 *Contra* de Vaux, *loc. cit.*
5 Cf. above, Ch. 2.

Bibliography

Ackroyd, P.R., *Exile and Restoration* (London, 1968)

Ahlström, G.W., *Psalm 89: eine Liturgie aus dem Ritual des leidenden Königs* (Lund, 1959)

Aistleitner, J., *Wörterbuch der Ugaritischen Sprache*. Ed. O. Eissfeldt (3rd ed., Berlin, 1967)

Albertson, J., 'Genesis 1 and the Babylonian Creation Myth', *Thought* 37 (1962), pp. 226–44

Albertz, R., *Welt- und Menschenschöpfung* (Stuttgart, 1974)

Albright, W.F., 'New light on early Canaanite language and literature', *BASOR* 46 (1932), pp. 15–20

'The North-Canaanite Epic of 'Al'êyân Baʿal and Môt', *JPOS* 12 (1932), pp. 185–208

'Zabûl Yam and Thâpiṭ Nahar in the Combat between Baʿal and the Sea', *JPOS* 16 (1936), pp. 17–21

Review of G. Hölscher, *Das Buch Hiob*, *JBL* 57 (1938), pp. 227–8

'What were the Cherubim?' *BA* 1 (1938), pp. 1–3

'Are the Ephod and the Teraphim mentioned in Ugaritic literature?', *BASOR* 83 (1941), pp. 39–42

'Anath and the dragon', *BASOR* 84 (1941), pp. 14–17

'The furniture of El in Canaanite mythology', *BASOR* 91 (1943), pp. 39–44

'The Psalm of Habakkuk', in H.H. Rowley (ed.), *Studies in Old Testament Prophecy* (Edinburgh, 1950), pp. 1–18

'Baalzephon', in W. Baumgartner, O. Eissfeldt, K. Elliger, L. Rost (edd.), *Festschrift Alfred Bertholet* (Tübingen, 1950), pp. 1–14

'A Catalogue of early Hebrew lyric poems (Psalm LXVIII)', *HUCA* 23, Part 1 (1950–1), pp. 1–39

From the Stone Age to Christianity (2nd ed., New York, 1957)

'Some remarks on the Song of Moses in Deuteronomy XXXII', *VT* 9 (1959), pp. 339–46

The Archaeology of Palestine (Rev. ed., Harmondsworth, 1960)
Archaeology and the Religion of Israel (5th ed., Baltimore, Md., 1968)
Yahweh and the Gods of Canaan (London, 1968)
Ammianus Marcellinus (Loeb Classical Library, 3 vols., London and Cambridge, Mass., 1971–2)
Anderson, A.A., *The Book of Psalms* (2 vols., London, 1972)
Anderson, B.W., 'Exodus Typology in Second Isaiah', in B.W. Anderson and W. Harrelson (edd.), *Israel's Prophetic Heritage* (London, 1962), pp. 177–95
Creation versus Chaos. The Reinterpretation of Mythical Symbolism in the Bible (New York, 1967)
Anderson, G.W., 'Isaiah XXIV–XXVII reconsidered', *SVT* 9 (1963), pp. 118–26
Apollodorus, *The Library* (Loeb Classical Library, 2 vols., London and Cambridge, Mass., 1921)
Auvray, P., *Isaïe 1–39* (Paris, 1972)
Avigad, N., 'Excavations in the Jewish quarter of the old city of Jerusalem, 1971', *IEJ* 22 (1972), pp. 193–200
Avi-Yonah, M., פרסאוס ואנדרומדיה ביפו, *Yediot* 31 (1967), pp. 203–10
Baker, D.W., 'Further examples of the *wāw explicativum*', *VT* 30 (1980), pp. 129–36
Baldwin, J.G., *Daniel* (Leicester, 1978)
Barr, J., 'Daniel', in H.H. Rowley and M. Black (edd.), *Peake's Commentary on the Bible* (London, 1962), pp. 591–602
'Ugaritic and Hebrew "šbm"?', *JSS* 18 (1973), pp. 17–39
'Philology and Exegesis', in C. Brekelmans (ed.), *Questions disputées d'Ancien Testament* (Louvain, 1974), pp. 39–61
Barth, H., *Die Jesaja-Worte in der Josiazeit* (Neukirchen, 1977)
Barton, G.A., 'Tiamat', *JAOS* 15 (1893), pp. 1–27
Bauer, T., 'Ein viertes altbabylonisches Fragment des Gilgameš-Epos', *JNES* 16 (1957), pp. 254–62
Baumgartner, E., *Zum Alten Testament und seiner Umwelt* (Leiden, 1959)
Beasley-Murray, G.R., *The Book of Revelation* (London, 1974)
Beer, G., *Exodus* (Tübingen, 1939)
Bentzen, A., *Messias–Moses redivivus–Menschensohn* (Zurich, 1948), ET *King and Messiah* (2nd ed., Oxford, 1970)
Daniel (2nd ed., Tübingen, 1952)
Bertholet, A., 'Der Schutzengel Persiens', in J.D.C. Pavry (ed.), *Oriental Studies in honour of Cursetji Erachji Pavry* (London, 1933), pp. 34–40
Beyerlin, W., (ed.) *Religionsgeschichtliches Textbuch zum Alten Testament* (Göttingen, 1975), ET *Near Eastern Religious Texts relating to the Old Testtament* (London, 1978)
Boadt, L., *Ezekiel's oracles against Egypt. A Literary and Philological Study of Ezekiel 29–32* (Rome, 1980)
Bochart, S. *Hierozoicon.* (2 vols., London, 1663)

Borger, R., *Die Inschriften Asarhaddons Königs von Assyrien* (*AfO* Beiheft 9, 1956)
Borsch, F.H., *The Son of Man in Myth and History* (London, 1967)
Botterweck, G.J., בהמות, in G.J. Botterweck and H. Ringgren (edd.), *Theologisches Wörterbuch zum Alten Testament* 1 (Stuttgart, 1973), cols. 533–6, ET *Theological Dictionary of the Old Testament* 2 (1975), pp. 17–20
Brandon, S.G.F., *Creation Legends of the Ancient Near East* (London, 1963)
Brekelmans, C.H.W., 'The Saints of the Most High and their Kingdom', *OTS* 14 (1965), pp. 305–29
Bright, J., *Jeremiah* (New York, 1965)
Brock, S.P., '*Νεφεληγερέτα = rkb ʿrpt*', *VT* 18 (1968), pp. 395–7
Brockington, L.H., *The Hebrew Text of the Old Testament* (Oxford and Cambridge, 1973)
Brown, J.P., *The Lebanon and Phoenicia. Ancient Texts Illustrating their Physical Geography and Native Industries* 1 (Beirut, 1969)
Bruce, F.F., *This is That. The New Testament Development of Some Old Testament Themes* (Exeter, 1968)
Buchanan, G.W., *To the Hebrews* (New York, 1972)
Budde, K., *Das Buch Hiob* (Göttingen, 1896)
'Jes 8 6b', *ZAW* 44 (1926), pp. 65–7
Bulman, J.M., 'The identification of Darius the Mede', *Westminster Theological Journal* 35 (1972–3), pp. 247–67
Burney, C.F., 'The three serpents of Isaiah XXVII 1', *JTS* 11 (1910), pp. 443–7
Burrows, M., 'The conduit of the upper pool', *ZAW* 70 (1958), pp. 221–7
Cantineau, J. 'Tadmorea (*suite*)', *Syria* 19 (1938), pp. 72–82
Caquot, A., 'Sur les quatre bêtes de Daniel VII', *Semitica* 5 (1955), pp. 5–13
'Les quatre bêtes et le "fils d'homme" (Daniel 7)', *Semitica* 17 (1967), pp. 37–71
'Léviathan et Behémoth dans la troisième "Parabole" d'Hénoch', *Semitica* 25 (1975), pp. 111–22
Caquot, A., Sznycer, M. and Herdner, A., *Textes ougaritiques* 1, *Mythes et légendes* (Paris, 1974)
Casey, (P.) M., 'Porphyry and the origin of the book of Daniel', *JTS* 27 n.s. (1976), pp. 15–33
Son of Man (London, 1979)
Cassuto, U. (M.D.), 'Il capitolo 3 di Habaquq e i testi di Ras Shamra', *Annuraio di Studi Ebraici* 2, 1935–7 (1938), pp. 7–22. ET 'Chapter iii of Habakkuk and the Ras Shamra texts', *Biblical and Oriental Studies* 2 (Jerusalem, 1975), pp. 3–15
תהלים ס"ח, *Tarbiz* 12 (1940), pp. 1–27. ET 'Psalm LXVIII', *Biblical and Oriental Studies* 1 (Jerusalem, 1973), pp. 241–84

שירת העלילה בישראל , *Keneset* 8 Part 3 (1943), pp. 121–42. ET 'The Israelite Epic', *Biblical and Oriental Studies* 2 (Jerusalem, 1975), pp. 69–109

האלה ענת (Jerusalem, 1951). ET *The Goddess Anath* (Jerusalem, 1971)

Cathcart, K.J., *Nahum in the Light of Northwest Semitic* (Rome, 1973)

Charles, R.H., *The Apocrypha and Pseudepigrapha of the Old Testament* (2 vols., Oxford, 1913)

A Critical and Exegetical Commentary on the Revelation of St. John (2 vols., Edinburgh, 1920)

The Book of Daniel (Oxford, 1929)

Cheyne, T.K., Review of H. Gunkel, *Schöpfung und Chaos*, *Critical Review* 5 (1895), pp. 256–66

'Behemoth and Leviathan', *Encyclopaedia Biblica* 1 (London, 1899), cols. 519–23

Childs, B.S., *A Study of Myth in Genesis I–XI* (Ph.D Dissertation, Basel University, Plymouth, Wisconsin, 1955)

'The Enemy from the North and the Chaos Tradition', *JBL* 78 (1959), pp. 187–98

Myth and Reality in the Old Testament (2nd ed., London, 1962)

Exodus (London, 1974)

Clay, A.T., *Amurru, the Home of the Northern Semites* (Philadelphia, Pa., 1909)

The Origin of Biblical Traditions (New Haven, Conn., 1923)

Clements, R.E., *God and Temple* (Oxford, 1965)

Prophecy and Tradition (Oxford, 1975)

Isaiah and the Deliverance of Jerusalem (Sheffield, 1980)

Isaiah 1–39 (London, 1980)

Clermont-Ganneau, C., 'Horus et Saint Georges', *Revue Archéologique* 32 n.s. (1876), pp. 196–204 and 372–99

Clifford, R.J., *The Cosmic Mountain in Canaan and the Old Testament* (Cambridge, Mass., 1972)

Clines, D., 'The evidence for an autumnal new year in pre-exilic Israel reconsidered', *JBL* 93 (1974), pp. 22–40

Colenso, J.W., *The Pentateuch and Book of Joshua Critically Examined* (7 parts, London, 1862–79)

Collins, A.Y., *The Combat Myth in the Book of Revelation* (Missoula, Mt., 1976)

Collins, J.J., 'The Son of Man and the Saints of the Most High in the Book of Daniel', *JBL* 93 (1974), pp. 50–66

'The Mythology of Holy War in Daniel and the Qumran War Scroll: a point of transition in Jewish Apocalyptic', *VT* 25 (1975), pp. 596–612

The Apocalyptic Vision of the Book of Daniel (Missoula, Mt., 1977)

Colpe, C., '*ὁ υἱὸς τοῦ ἀνθρώπου*', in G. Kittel and G. Friedrich (edd.), *Theologisches Wörterbuch zum Neuen Testament* 8 (Stuttgart, 1969), pp. 403–81, ET *Theological Dictionary of the New Testament* 8 (Grand

Rapids, Mich., 1972), pp. 400–77
Coogan, M.D., *Stories from Ancient Canaan* (Philadelphia, Pa., 1978)
Coppens, J., 'Le Fils d'Homme danielique, vizir céleste?', *Miscellanées bibliques* 33, *Analecta Lovaniensia Biblica et Orientalia* ser. 4, fasc. 12 (1964), pp. 72–80
'La vision danielique du Fils d'Homme', *VT* 19 (1969), pp. 171–82
'Daniel VII, un rituel d'intronisation?', *Miscellanées bibliques* 57, *Eph. Theol. Lovan.* 46 (1970), pp. 112–16
Coppens, J. and Dequeker, L., 'Le Fils de l'Homme et les Saints du Très-Haut en Daniel VII, dans les Apocryphes et dans le Nouveau Testament', *Analecta Lovaniensia Biblica et Orientalia* ser. 3, fasc. 23 (1961), pp. 15–72
Couroyer, B., 'Qui est Béhémoth?', *RB* 82 (1975), pp. 418–43
'Le "glaive" de Béhémoth: Job XL, 19–20', *RB* 84 (1977), pp. 59–79
Court, J.M., *Myth and History in the Book of Revelation* (London, 1979)
Cowley, A., *Aramaic Papyri of the Fifth Century B.C.* (Oxford, 1923)
Cox, D., 'The desire for oblivion in Job 3', *Studii Biblici Franciscani, liber annuus* 23 (1973), pp. 37–49
Craigie, P.C., 'The comparison of Hebrew poetry: Psalm 104 in the light of Egyptian and Ugaritic poetry', *Semitics* 4 (1974), pp. 10–21
Cross, F.M., 'Notes on a Canaanite Psalm in the Old Testament', *BASOR* 117 (1950), pp. 19–21
'The Divine Warrior in Israel's early Cult', in A. Altmann (ed.), *Biblical Motifs* (Cambridge, Mass., 1966), pp. 11–30
'The Song of the Sea and Canaanite Myth', *JThC* 5 (1968), pp. 1–25
Canaanite Myth and Hebrew Epic (Cambridge, Mass., 1973)
Cross, F.M. and Freedman, D.N., 'The blessing of Moses', *JBL* 67 (1948), pp. 191–210
'A Royal Song of Thanksgiving: II Samuel 22 = Psalm 18', *JBL* 72 (1953), pp. 15–34
'The Song of Miriam', *JNES* 14 (1955), pp. 237–50
Cunchillos, J.L., *Estudio del Salmo 29. Canto al Dios de la fertilidad–fecundidad. Aportación al conocimiento de la Fe de Israel a su entrada en Canaan* (Valencia, 1976)
Curtis, A.H.W., 'The "subjugation of the waters" motif in the Psalms; imagery or polemic?', *JSS* 23 (1978), pp. 245–56
Cyril of Alexandria, *Commentarius in Jonam*, J.P. Migne, *PG* 71 (Paris, 1864), cols. 597–638
Dahood, M.J., 'Ancient Semitic deities in Syria and Palestine', in S. Moscati (ed.), *Le antiche divinità semitiche* (Rome, 1958), pp. 65–94
'Mišmar "muzzle" in Job 7:12', *JBL* 80 (1961), pp. 270–1
Proverbs and Northwest Semitic Philology (Rome, 1963)
Psalms 1–3 (New York, 1966–70)
'Northwest Semitic texts and textual criticism of the Hebrew Bible', in C. Brekelmans (ed.), *Questions disputées d'Ancien Testament* (Louvain, 1974), pp. 11–37

Day, J., 'Echoes of Baal's seven thunders and lightnings in Psalm xxix and Habakkuk iii 9 and the identity of the Seraphim in Isaiah vi', *VT* 29 (1979), pp. 143–51

'New light on the mythological background of the allusion to Resheph in Habakkuk iii 5', *VT* 29 (1979), pp. 353–5

'A case of inner Scriptural interpretation. The dependence of Isaiah xxvi. 13–xxvii. 11 on Hosea xiii. 4–xiv. 10 (Eng. 9) and its relevance to some theories of the redaction of the "Isaiah apocalypse"', *JTS* 31 n.s. (1980), pp. 309–19

Delcor, M., 'Les sources de chapitre VII de Daniel', *VT* 18 (1968), pp. 290–312. Reprinted in M. Delcor, *Études bibliques et orientales de religions comparées* (Leiden, 1979), pp. 154–76

Le Livre de Daniel (Paris, 1971)

'Mythologie et Apocalyptique', in *Apocalypses et Théologie de l'Espérance, Congrès de Toulouse 1975* (Paris, 1977), pp. 143–77. Reprinted in M. Delcor, *Études bibliques et orientales de religions comparées* (Leiden, 1979), pp. 228–62

'Le mythe de la chute des anges et de l'origine des géants comme explication du mal dans le monde dans l'apocalyptique juive. Histoire des traditions' *RHR* 190 (1976), pp. 3–53. Reprinted in M. Delcor, *Études bibliques et orientales de religions comparées* (Leiden, 1979), pp. 263–313

'La festin d'immortalité sur la montagne de Sion à l'ère eschatologique en Is. 25. 6–9, à la lumière de la littérature ugaritique', in *Messianismo y escatologia. Estudios en memoria del Prof. Dr. Luis Arnalditch Perot* (*Bibliotheca Salmanticensis 21, Estudios 14*, 1976), pp. 89–98. Reprinted in *Études bibliques et orientales de religions comparées* (Leiden, 1979), pp. 122–31

Delitzsch, F., *Commentar über das Buch Jesaia* (4th ed., Leipzeig, 1889). ET *Biblical Commentary on the Prophecies of Isaiah* (2 vols., Edinburgh, 1890)

Dequeker, L., 'The "Saints of the Most High" in Qumran and Daniel', *OTS* 18 (1973), pp. 108–87 (See also J. Coppens)

Dhorme, É., *Le Livre de Job* (Paris, 1926). ET *A Commentary on the Book of Job* (London, 1967)

Dietrich, M., Loretz, O. and Sanmartín, J., *Die keilalphabetischen Texte aus Ugarit. Teil 1: Transkription* (*AOAT* 24, Neukirchen, 1976)

Dijkstra, M., 'Ba'lu and his antagonists: Some remarks on CTA 6:V.1–6', *Journal of the Ancient Near Eastern Society of Columbia University* 6 (1974), pp. 59–68

Diodorus Siculus (Loeb Classical Library, 12 vols., London and New York, 1933–67)

Donner, H., *Israel unter den Völkern*, *SVT* 11 (1964)

'Ugaritismen in der Psalmenforschung', *ZAW* 79 (1967), pp. 322–50

Donner, H. and Röllig, W., *Kanaanäische und aramäische Inschriften* (3 vols., Wiesbaden, 1962–4)

Driver, G.R., 'Studies in the vocabulary of the Old Testament. II', *JTS* 32 (1930–1), pp. 250–7

'L'interprétation du texte masorétique à la lumière de la lexicographie hébraïque', *Eph. Theol. Lovan.* 26 (1950), pp. 337–53

'Difficult words in the Hebrew prophets', in H.H. Rowley (ed.), *Studies in Old Testament Prophecy* (Edinburgh, 1950), pp. 52–72

'Problems in the Hebrew text of Job', *SVT* 3 (1955), pp. 72–93

'Mythical monsters in the Old Testament', in *Studi Orientalistici in onore di Giorgio Levi della Vida* 1 (Rome, 1956), pp. 234–49

Canaanite Myths and Legends (Edinburgh, 1956)

Review of H.H. Rowley, *Job*, *JTS* 22 n.s. (1971), pp. 176–9

Driver, S.R. and Gray, G.B., *A Critical and Exegetical Commentary on the Book of Job* (Edinburgh, 1921)

Duchesne-Guillemin, J., 'Genèse I, 2c, Ugarit et l'Égypte', *Comptes Rendus de l'Académie des Inscriptions et Belles-Lettres* (Paris, 1982), pp. 512–23 (including comments of A. Caquot on pp. 523–4)

Duhm, B., *Das Buch Hiob* (Freiburg, 1897)

Das Buch Jesaia (4th ed., Göttingen, 1922)

Eakin, F., 'The Reed Sea and Baalism', *JBL* 86 (1967), pp. 378–84

Eaton, J.H., 'The origin of the book of Isaiah', *VT* 9 (1959), pp. 138–57

'The origin and meaning of Habakkuk 3', *ZAW* 76 (1964), pp. 144–71

Psalms (London, 1967)

Kingship and the Psalms (London, 1976)

Festal Drama in Deutero–Isaiah (London, 1979)

Ebeling, E. 'Höllenfahrt eines assyrischen Königs', *Tod und Leben nach den Vorstellungen der Babylonier* 1 (Berlin and Leipzig, 1931), pp. 1–9

Eerdmans, B.D., 'Psalm lxviii', *Exp. Times* 46 (1934–5), pp. 169–72

Studies in Job (Leiden, 1939)

Eichrodt, W., *Der Prophet Hesekiel* (2 vols. Göttingen, 1959–66). ET *Ezekiel* (London, 1970)

Der Herr der Geschichte (Stuttgart, 1967)

Eissfeldt, O., *Baal Zaphon, Zeus Kasios und der Durchzug der Israeliten durchs Meer* (Halle, 1932)

Ras Shamra und Sanchunjaton (Halle, 1939)

'Das Chaos in der biblischen und in der phönizischen Kosmogonie', *Forschungen und Fortschritte* 16 (1940), pp. 1–3. Reprinted in *Kleine Schriften 2* (Tübingen, 1963), pp. 258–62

'Ugaritisches, 4. *ṯkmn wšnm*', *ZDMG* 99, n.F. 24 (1945–9), pp. 29–42. Reprinted in *Kleine Schriften 2* (Tübingen, 1963), pp. 528–41

El im ugaritischen Pantheon (Berlin, 1951)

Taautos und Sanchunjaton (Berlin, 1952)

Sanchunjaton von Berut und Ilumilku von Ugarit (Halle, 1952)

'Gott und das Meer', *Studia Orientalia Ioanni Pedersen septuagenario dicata* (Copenhagen, 1953), pp. 76–84. Reprinted in *Kleine Schriften* 3 (Tübingen, 1966), *p.* 256–64

'El and Yahweh', *JSS* 1 (1956), pp. 25–37

Das Lied Moses, Deuteronomium 32, 1–43 und das Lehrgedicht Asaphs, Psalm 78, samt einer Analyse der Umgebung des Mose-Liedes (Berlin, 1958)

'The Promises of Grace to David in Isaiah 55:1–5', in B.W. Anderson and W. Harrelson (edd.), *Israel's Prophetic Heritage* (London, 1962), pp. 196–207

'Genesis', *IDB* 2 (Nashville, Ten., 1962), pp. 366–80

Einleitung in das alte Testament (3rd ed., Tübingen, 1964). ET *The Old Testament. An Introduction* (Oxford, 1966)

Eitan, I., *A Contribution to Biblical Lexicography* (New York, 1924)

Elbogen, I., *Der jüdische Gottesdienst in seiner geschichtlichen Entwicklung* (Frankfurt a. Main, 1931)

Emerton, J.A., 'The Origin of the Son of Man Imagery', *JTS* 9 n.s. (1958), pp. 225–42

'"Spring and Torrent" in Psalm LXXIV 15', *SVT* 15 (1966), pp. 122–33

'The Riddle of Genesis xiv', *VT* 21 (1971), pp. 403–39

'A difficult part of Mot's message to Baal in the Ugaritic texts', *Australian Journal of Biblical Archaeology* 2, no. 1 (1972), pp. 50–71

'A further note on *CTA* 5 I 4–6', *UF* 10 (1978), pp. 73–7

'Leviathan and *ltn*: the vocalization of the Ugaritic word for the dragon', *VT* 32 (1982), pp. 327–31

Eusebius, *Praeparatio Evangelica* (See K. Mras)

Fantar, Mh., *Le dieu de la mer chez les Phéniciens et les Puniques* (Rome, 1977)

Farrer, A.M., *A Study in Mark* (Westminster, 1951)

Fawcett, T., *Hebrew Myth and Christian Gospel* (London, 1973)

Feigin, S.I., **מסתרי העבר** (New York, 1943)

Feldman, F., *Das Buch Isaias* (2 Vols., Münster, 1925)

Fensham, F.C., 'Ps. 68:23 in the light of the recently discovered Ugaritic tablets', *JNES* 19 (1960), pp. 292–3

'The burning of the golden calf and Ugarit', *IEJ* 16 (1966), pp. 191–3

Ferch, A.J., 'Daniel 7 and Ugarit: a reconsideration', *JBL* 99 (1980), pp. 75–86

Ferrara, A.J. and Parker, S.B., 'Seating arrangements at divine banquets', *UF* 4 (1972), pp. 37–9

Feuillet, A., 'Le Fils de l'Homme de Daniel et la tradition biblique', *RB* 60 (1953), pp. 170–202 and 321–46

Fischer, J., 'Das Problem des neuen Exodus in Isaias c. 40–55', *Theologische Quartalschrift* 110 (1929), pp. 111–30

Fishbane, M., 'Jeremiah IV 23–26 and Job III 3–13: a recovered use of the creation pattern', *VT* 21 (1971), pp. 151–67

Fisher, L.R., 'Creation at Ugarit and in the Old Testament', *VT* 15 (1965), pp. 313–24

(ed.) *Ras Shamra Parallels* 1–2 (Rome, 1972 and 1975)

Fitzgerald, A. 'A Note on Psalm 29', *BASOR* 215 (1974), pp. 61–3
Fitzmyer, J.A., *The Aramaic Inscription of Sefîre* (Rome, 1967)
Flusser, D., 'The four empires in the fourth Sibyl and in the book of Daniel', in *Israel Oriental Studies* 2 (1972), pp. 148–75
Fohrer, G., *Ezechiel* (Tübingen, 1955)
Das Buch Hiob (Gütersloh, 1963)
Überlieferung und Geschichte des Exodus (*BZAW* 91, 1964)
Das Buch Jesaja (3 vols., Zurich and Stuttgart, 1960–4
Freedman, D.N. (See F.M. Cross)
Gammie, J.G., 'Loci of the Melchizedek tradition of Genesis 14:18–20', *JBL* 90 (1971), pp. 385–96
'Behemoth and Leviathan: on the didactic and theological significance of Job 40:15–41:26', in J.G. Gammie, W.A. Brueggemann, W.L. Humphreys and J.M. Ward (edd.), *Israelite Wisdom: Theological and Literary Essays in Honor of Samuel Terrien* (New York, 1978), pp. 217–31
Gardiner, A.H., 'The Astarte Papyrus', *Studies Presented to F.Ll. Griffith* (London, 1932), pp. 74–85
Gaster, T.H., 'The battle of the rain and the sea', *Iraq* 4 (1937), pp. 21–32
'A Canaanite Magical Text', *Orientalia* 1 n.s. (1942), pp. 41–79
'Folklore motifs in Canaanite Myth', *JRAS* (1944), pp. 30–51
'Psalm 29', *JQR* 37 (1946–7), pp. 55–65
Thespis (1st ed., New York, 1950; 2nd ed., 1966)
'The Egyptian "Story of Astarte" and the Ugaritic Poem of Baal', *Bibliotheca Orientalis* 9 (1952), pp. 82–5
'Psalm lxxiv. 14', *Exp. Times* 68 (1956–7), p. 382
Myth, Legend and Custom in the Old Testament (London, 1969)
Gese, H., Höfner, M. and Rudolph, K., (edd.), *Die Religionen Altsyriens, Altarabiens und der Mandäer* (Stuttgart, 1970)
Gesenius, W., *Der Prophet Jesaja* (2 vols., Leipzig, 1820–1)
Gibson, J.C.L., *Syrian Semitic Inscriptions* (Oxford, 1971–82)
Canaanite Myths and Legends (Edinburgh, 1978)
Ginsberg, H.L., 'A Phoenician hymn in the Psalter', in *Atti del XIX Congresso Internazionale degli Orientalisti, 1935* (Rome, 1938), pp. 472–6
כתבי אגרית (Jerusalem, 1936)
'Did Anath fight the dragon?', *BASOR* 84 (1941), pp. 12–14
'The Ugaritic texts and textual criticism', *JBL* 62 (1943), pp. 109–15
'The arm of YHWH in Isaiah 51–63 and the text of Isa 53 10–11', *JBL* 77 (1958), pp. 152–6
'A strand in the cord of Hebraic hymnody', *Eretz-Israel 9* (1969), pp. 45–50
'Ugaritic Myths, Epics, and Legends', in J.B. Pritchard (ed.), *Ancient Near Eastern Texts relating to the Old Testament* (3rd ed. with suppl., Princeton, N.J., 1969), pp. 129–55

Ginsberger, M. (ed.), *Pseudo-Jonathan (Thargum Jonathan ben Usiël zum Pentateuch)* (Berlin, 1903)
Ginzberg, L., *The Legends of the Jews* (7 vols., Philadelphia, Pa., 1909–38)
Goetze, A., 'Hittite Myths, Epics, and Legends', in J.B. Pritchard (ed.), *Ancient Near Eastern Texts relating to the Old Testament* (3rd ed. with suppl., Princeton, N.J., 1969), pp. 120–8
Gordis, R., 'Job XL 29 – an additional note', *VT* 14 (1964), pp. 491–4
The Book of God and Man (Chicago and London, 1965)
The Book of Job (New York, 1978)
Gordon, C.H., *Ugaritic Literature* (Rome, 1949)
Ugaritic Textbook (Rome, 1965)
'Leviathan: symbol of evil', in A. Altmann (ed.), *Biblical Motifs* (Cambridge, Mass., 1966), pp. 1–9
'El, Father of Šnm', *JNES* 35 (1976), pp. 261–2
Gottlieb, H. (See B. Otzen)
Gottstein, M.H., '*Eine Cambridger Syrohexaplahandschrift*', *Le Muséon* 67 (1954), pp. 291–6
Gottwald, N.K., *A Light to the Nations* (New York, 1959)
Goulder, M.D., *The Psalms of the Sons of Korah* (Sheffield, 1982)
Grabbe, L.L., 'The seasonal pattern and the "Baal cycle"', *UF* 8 (1976), pp. 57–63
Comparative Philology and the Text of Job (Missoula, Mt., 1977)
Graham, W.C. and May, H.G., *Culture and Conscience* (Chicago, 1936)
Gray, G.B. (See S.R. Driver)
Gray, J., 'Canaanite Mythology and Hebrew Tradition', *TGUOS* 14 (1950–2), pp. 47–57
'The Hebrew conception of the Kingship of God: its origin and development', *VT* 5 (1956), pp. 268–85
'The Kingship of God in the Prophets and Psalms', *VT* 11 (1961), pp. 1–29
The Legacy of Canaan (*SVT* 5, 2nd ed., 1965)
Near Eastern Mythology (London, 1969)
'A Cantata of the Autumn Festival: Psalm lxviii', *JSS* 22 (1977), pp. 2–26
The Biblical Doctrine of the Reign of God (Edinburgh, 1979)
Grayson, A.K., *Babylonian Historical-Literary Texts* (Toronto and Buffalo, N.Y., 1975)
Greenfield, J.C., 'Ugaritic *mdl* and its cognates', *Biblica* 45 (1964), pp. 527–34
Griffiths, J.G., *Plutarch's De Iside et Osiride* (Cardiff, 1970)
Gruppe, O., 'Aithiopenmythen. 1. Der phönikische Urtext der Kassiepeialegende. Zusammenhang derselben mit anderen Aithiopenmythen', *Philogus* 47 (1889), pp. 92–107
Guillaume, A., *Studies in the Book of Job* (Leiden, 1968)
Gunkel, H., *Schöpfung und Chaos in Urzeit und Endzeit* (Göttingen, 1895)

Genesis (3rd ed., Göttingen, 1910)
'Jesaja 33, eine prophetische Liturgie', *ZAW* 42 (1924), pp. 177–208
Die Psalmen (4th ed., Göttingen, 1925–6)
Gunn, D.M., 'Deutero-Isaiah and the Flood', *JBL* 94 (1975), pp. 493–508
Güterbock, H., *Kumarbi* (Zurich and New York, 1946)
'The Song of Ullikummi. Revised text of the Hittite version of a Hurrian myth', *JCS* 5 (1951), pp. 135–61 and *JCS* 6 (1952), pp. 8–42
Gutman, J., 'Leviathan, Behemoth and Ziz: Jewish Messianic symbols in art', *HUCA* 39 (1968), pp. 219–30
Haas, G., 'On the occurrence of hippopotamus in the Iron Age of the coastal area of Israel (Tell Qasîleh)', *BASOR* 132 (1953), pp. 30–4
Habel, N.C., *Yahweh versus Baal: a Conflict of Religious Cultures* (New York, 1964)
The Book of Job (Cambridge, 1975)
Hanhart, R., 'Die Heiligen des Höchsten', *Hebräische Wortforschung* (*SVT* 16, 1967), pp. 90–101
Hanson, P.D., *The Dawn of Apocalyptic* (Philadelphia, Pa., 1975)
Haran, M., 'The graded numerical sequence and the phenomenon of 'automatism' in biblical poetry', *SVT* 22 (1972), pp. 238–67
Hartman, L.F. and di Lella, A.A., *The Book of Daniel* (New York, 1978)
Hasel, G.F., 'The polemic nature of the Genesis cosmology', *EQ* 46 (1974), pp. 81–102
'The identity of "The Saints of the Most High" in Daniel 7', *Biblica* 56 (1975), pp. 173–92
'The four world empires of Daniel 2 against its near eastern environment', *JSOT* 12 (1979), pp. 17–30
Haussig, H.W. (ed.), *Wörterbuch der Mythologie* 1 *Götter und Mythen im vorderen Orient* (Stuttgart, 1965)
Hayes, J., 'The Tradition of Zion's inviolability', *JBL* 82 (1963), pp. 419–26
An Introduction to Old Testament Study (Nashville, Tenn., 1979)
Heaton, E.W., *The Book of Daniel* (London, 1956)
Heidel, A., *The Babylonian Genesis* (2nd ed., Chicago and London, 1951)
Held, M., '*mḫṣ*/**mḫš* in Ugaritic and other Semitic Languages (A Study in Comparative Lexicography)', *JAOS* 79 (1959), pp. 169–76
Hempel, J., 'Zu IVQ Deut 32 8', *ZAW* 74 (1962), p. 70
Hengel, M., *Judentum und Hellenismus* (Tübingen, 1969). ET *Judaism and Hellenism* (2 vols., London, 1974)
Henry, M.-L., *Glaubenskrise und Gaubensbewahrung in den Dichtungen der Jesajaapokalypse* (Stuttgart, 1967)
Herdner, A., *Corpus des tablettes en cunéiformes alphabétiques* (2 vols., Paris, 1963) (See also A. Caquot)
Herodotus (Loeb Classical Library, 4 vols., London, 1920–5)
Hertlein, E., 'Rahab', *ZAW* 38 (1919–20), pp. 113–54
Hillmann, R., *Wasser und Berg* (Inaugural-Dissertation, Halle, 1965)

Höfner, M., (See H. Gese)
Hölscher, G., *Das Buch Hiob* (Tübingen, 1952)
Horst, F., *Hiob* (Neukirchen, 1968)
Hruška, B., *Der Mythenadler Anzu in Literatur und Vorstellung des alten Mesopotamien* (Budapest, 1975)
Humbert, P., 'La relation de Genèse 1 et du Psaume 104 avec la liturgie du Nouvel-An israëlite', *RHPR* 15 (1935), pp. 1–27
Hvidberg, F.F., *Graad og Latter i det Gamle Testamente* (Copenhagen, 1938). ET *Weeping and Laughter in the Old Testament* (Copenhagen, 1962)
'The Canaanitic background of Gen. I–III', *VT* 10 (1960), pp. 285–94
Hvidberg-Hansen, O., 'Die Vernichtung des goldenen Kalbes und der ugaritische Ernteritus', *Acta Orientalia* 33 (Copenhagen, 1971), pp. 5–46
Hyatt, J.P., *Exodus* (London, 1971)
Irwin, W.A., 'The Psalm of Habakkuk', *JNES* 1 (1942), pp. 10–40
'The mythological background of Habakkuk, chapter 3', *JNES* 15 (1956), pp. 47–50
Irwin, W.H., *Isaiah 28–33: Translation with Philological Notes* (Rome, 1977)
Jacobs, I., 'Elements of Near-Eastern Mythology in Rabbinic Haggadah', *JJS* 28 (1977), pp. 1–11
Jacobsen, T., 'The battle between Marduk and Tiamat', *JAOS* 88 (1968), pp. 104–8
Jeppesen, K. (See B. Otzen)
Jeremias, Jörg, *Theophanie* (Neukirchen, 1965)
'Lade und Zion: zur Entstehung der Ziontradition', in H.W. Wolff (ed.), *Probleme biblischer Theologie* (Munich, 1971), pp. 183–98
Jerome, *Commentaria in Danielem*, J.P. Migne, *PL* 25 (Paris, 1845), cols. 491–584
Commentaria in Jonam, J.P. Migne, *PL* 25 (Paris, 1845), cols. 1117–52
Jirku, A., *Der Mythus der Kanaanäer* (Bonn, 1966)
Jöcken, P., *Das Buch Habakuk* (Cologne and Bonn, 1977)
Johnson, A.R., *Sacral Kingship in Ancient Israel* (2nd ed., Cardiff, 1967)
The Cultic Prophet and Israel's Psalmody (Cardiff, 1979)
Joines, K.R., 'Winged serpents in Isaiah's inaugural vision', *JBL* 86 (1967), pp. 410–15
Serpent Symbolism in the Old Testament (Haddonfield, 1974)
Jones, E., *The Triumph of Job* (London, 1966)
Josephus (Loeb Classical Library, 9 vols., London and Cambridge, Mass., 1926–65)
Joüon, P., 'Notes de lexicographie hébraïque', *Biblica* 6 (1925), pp. 311–21
Kaiser, O., *Die mythische Bedeutung des Meeres* (*BZAW* 78, 1st ed., 1959, 2nd ed., 1962)
Der Prophet Jesaja 1–12 (2nd ed., Göttingen, 1973, 5th ed., Göttingen,

1981) ET *Isaiah 1–12* (London, 1972; new edition, London, 1983)
Der Prophet Jesaja Kapitel 13–39 (Göttingen, 1973), ET *Isaiah 13–39* (London, 1974)
Kapelrud, A.S., *Baal in the Ras Shamra Texts* (Copenhagen, 1952)
Ras Sjamra-funnene og det Gamle Testament (Oslo, 1953). ET *The Ras Shamra discoveries and the Old Testament* (Oxford, 1965)
'Baʿals kamp met havets fyrste i Ras Sjamra-tekstene', *NTT* 61 (1960), pp. 241–51
The Violent Goddess (Oslo, 1969)
'The mythological features in Genesis Chapter 1 and the author's intentions', *VT* 24 (1974), pp. 178–86
'Baʿal, Schöpfung und Chaos', *UF* 11 (1979), pp. 407–12
'Creation in the Ras Shamra Texts', *Studia Theologica* 34 (1980), pp. 1–11
Keel, O., *Jahwes Entgegnung an Ijob* (Göttingen, 1978)
Kiessling, N.K., 'Antecedents of the medieval dragon in sacred history', *JBL* 89 (1970), pp. 167–77
Kirk, G.S., *Myth, its Meaning and Functions in Ancient and Other Cultures* (Cambridge, 1971)
Kirkpatrick, A.F., *The Book of Psalms* (Cambridge, 1906)
Kissane, E.J., *The Book of Psalms* (2 vols., Dublin, 1953–4)
Kittel, R., *Die Psalmen* (Leipzig, 1914)
Klatt, W., *Hermann Gunkel. Zu seiner Theologie der Religionsgeschichte und zur Entstehung der formgeschichtlichen Methode* (Göttingen, 1969)
Knight, G.A.F., *Ruth and Jonah* (London, 1950)
Knudtzon, J.A., *Die El-Amarna-Tafeln* (2 vols., Aalen, 1915)
Koch, K., *Das Buch Daniel* (Darmstadt, 1980)
Koehler, L., 'Syntactica III. IV. *Jahwäh mālāk*', *VT* 3 (1953), pp. 188–9
König, E., *Die Psalmen* (Gütersloh, 1927)
Kraeling, C.H., *Anthropos and Son of Man* (New York, 1927)
Kraeling, E.G.H., 'Some Babylonian and Iranian Mythology in the seventh chapter of Daniel', in J.D.C. Pavry (ed.), *Oriental Studies in honour of Cursetji Erachji Pavry* (London, 1933), pp. 228–31
Kramer, S.N. (ed.), Mythologies of the Ancient World (New York, 1961)
Kraus, H.-J., *Psalmen* (2 vols., 5th ed., Neukirchen, 1978)
Kruse, H., 'Compositio Libri Danielis et idea Filii Hominis–II.–De Filio Hominis', *Verbum Domini* 37 (1959),, pp. 193–211
Kubina, V., *Die Gottesreden im Buche Hiob* (Freiburg, 1979)
Kutsch, E., '"... am Ende des Jahres"', *ZAW* 83 (1971), pp. 15–21
Kutscher, E.Y., *The Language and Linguistic Background of the Isaiah Scroll* (*IQIsa*[a]) (Leiden, 1974)
Kvanvig, H.S., 'An Akkadian vision as background for Dan 7', *Studia Theologica* 35 (1981), pp. 85–9
Labuschagne, C.J., *The Incomparability of Yahweh in the Old Testament* (Leiden, 1966)

Łach, S., 'Versuch einer neuen Interpretation der Zionshymnen', *SVT* 29 (1978), pp. 149–64

Lack, R., 'Les origines de *Elyon*, le Très-Haut, dans la tradition cultuelle d'Israël', *CBQ* 24 (1962), pp. 44–64

Lacocque, A., *Le Livre de Daniel* (Neuchâtel and Paris, 1976). ET *The Book of Daniel* (Atlanta, Ga., 1979)

Lambert, W.G., 'The great battle of the Mesopotamian religious year. The conflict in the Akītu House', *Iraq* 25 (1963), pp. 189–90

'The Reign of Nebuchadnezzar I: a turning point in the history of ancient Mesopotamian Religion', in W.S. McCullough (ed.), *The Seed of Wisdom. Essays in honour of T.J. Meek* (Toronto, 1964), pp. 3–13

'A new look at the Babylonian background of Genesis', *JTS* 16 n.s. (1965), pp. 287–300

'Myth and Ritual as conceived by the Babylonians', *JSS* 13 (1968), pp. 104–12

'Zum Forschungsstand der sumerisch-babylonischen Literatur-Geschichte', *ZDMG* Suppl. 3, 1 (1977), pp. 64–73

The Background of Jewish Apocalyptic (London, 1978)

Landsberger, B., 'Einige unerkannt gebliebene oder verkannte Nomina des Akkadischen', *WZKM* 57 (1961), pp. 1–23

Landsberger, B. and J.V. Kinnier Wilson, 'The fifth tablet of *Enuma Eliš*', *JNES* 20 (1961), pp. 154–79

Lang, B., 'Job xl 18 and the "bones of Seth"', *VT* 30 (1980), pp. 360–1

de Langhe, R., *Les Textes de Ras Shamra-Ugarit et leurs rapports avec le milieu Biblique de l'Ancien Testament* (2 vols., Gembloux and Paris, 1945)

Laroche, E., (See J. Nougayrol)

Legrand, L., 'La Création, tríomphe cosmique de Yahvé', *Nouvelle Revue Théologique* 83 (1961), pp. 449–70

Leivestad, R., 'Der apokalyptische Menschensohn ein theologisches Phantom', *ASTI* 6 (1968), pp. 49–105

Lelièvre, A., 'YHWH et la mer dans les Psaumes', *RHPR* 56 (1976), pp. 253–75

di Lella, A.A., 'The One in Human Likeness and the Holy Ones of the Most High in Daniel 7', *CBQ* 39 (1977), pp. 1–19 (See also L.F. Hartman)

Levi della Vida, G., 'El 'Elyon in Genesis 14 18–20', *JBL* 63 (1944), pp. 1–9

L'Heureux, C., *Rank among the Canaanite Gods El, Ba'al, and the Repha'im* (Missoula, Mt., 1979)

Lightfoot, J. B., *The Apostolic Fathers, part 1. St. Clement of Rome* 2 (London, 1890)

Lindars, B., 'Re-enter the Apocalyptic Son of Man', *NTS* 22 (1975–6), pp. 52–72

Lindblom, J., *Die Jesaja-Apokalypse* (Lund, 1938)

Lipiński, É., *La Royauté de Yahwé dans la Poésie et la Culte de l'Ancien Israel* (Brussels, 1965)
'El's abode. Mythological Traditions related to Mount Hermon and to the Mountains of Armenia', *Orientalia Lovaniensia Periodica* 2 (1971), pp. 13–69
Lods, A., 'La Victoire sur Léviatan', *Comptes Rendus de l'Académie des Inscriptions et Belles-Lettres* (Paris, 1943), pp. 283–97
Loewenstamm, S.E., 'The Ugaritic Fertility Myth – the result of a mistranslation', *IEJ* 12 (1962), pp. 87–8. Reprinted in *Comparative Studies in Biblical and Ancient Oriental Literatures* (Neukirchen, 1980), pp. 160–1
'The Ugaritic Fertility Myth – a Reply', *IEJ* 13 (1963), pp. 130–2. Reprinted in *Comparative Studies* . . . (Neukirchen, 1980), pp. 162–5
'The Making and Destruction of the Golden Calf', *Biblica* 48 (1967), pp. 481–90. Reprinted in *Comparative Studies* . . . (Neukirchen, 1980), pp. 236–45
מיתוס הים בכתבי אוגרית וזיקתו אל מיתוס הים במקרא, *Eretz-Israel* 9 (1969), pp. 96–101. ET 'The Ugaritic Myth of the Sea and its Biblical Counterparts', *Comparative Studies* . . . (Neukirchen, 1980), pp. 346–61
'The Muzzling of the Tannin in Ugaritic Myth', *IEJ* 9 (1959), pp. 260–1. Reprinted in *Comparative Studies* . . . (Neukirchen, 1980), pp. 91–2
'The Making and Destruction of the Golden Calf – a Rejoinder', *Biblica* 56 (1975), pp. 330–43. Reprinted in *Comparative Studies* . . . (Neukirchen, 1980), pp. 503–16
'Anat's Victory over the Tunnanu', *JSS* 20 (1975), pp. 22–7
Loretz, O., *Schöpfung und Mythos* (Stuttgart, 1968)
'Ugaritisch-Hebräisch in Job 3, 3–26: zum Disput zwischen M. Dahood und J. Barr', *UF* 8 (1976), pp. 123–7 (See also M. Dietrich)
Ludwig, T.M., 'The Traditions of the Establishing of the Earth in Deutero-Isaiah', *JBL* 92 (1973), pp. 345–57
Lueken, W., *Michael* (Göttingen, 1898)
Lutz, H.-M., *Jahwe, Jerusalem und die Völker* (Neukirchen, 1968)
Maag, V., 'Malkût Jhwh' *SVT* 7 (1960), pp. 129–53
McCarthy, D.J., '"Creation" Motifs in ancient Hebrew Poetry', *CBQ* 29 (1967), pp. 393–406
Macintosh, A.A., 'A Consideration of Hebrew גער', *VT* 19 (1969), pp. 471–9
McClellan, W.H., 'The meaning of Ruaḥ 'Elohim in Genesis 1, 2', *Biblica* 15 (1934), pp. 517–27
Mansoor, M., 'The Thanksgiving Hymns and the Massoretic Text (part II)', *Revue de Qumrân* 3 (1961–2), pp. 387–94
Margalit, B. (Margulis), 'A Ugaritic Psalm (RŠ 24.252)', *JBL* 89 (1970), pp. 292–304
A Matter of 'Life' and 'Death' (*AOAT* 206, Neukirchen, 1980)
'The Ugaritic Creation Myth: fact or fiction?', *UF* 13 (1981), pp. 137–45

Marti, K., *Das Buch Jesaja* (Tübingen, 1900)
Martin, A.D., *The Prophet Jonah: the Book and the Sign* (London, 1926)
Mauchline, J., *Isaiah 1–39* (*London, 1962*)
May, H.G., 'Some Cosmic Connotations of *Mayim rabbîm* "many waters"', *JBL* 74 (1955), pp. 9–21 (See also W.C. Graham)
Mayes, A.D.H., *Deuteronomy* (London, 1979)
Mettinger, T.N.D., *The Dethronement of Sabaoth* (Lund, 1982)
Meyer, R., 'Die Bedeutung von Deuteronomium 32, 8f. 43 (4D) für die Auslegung des Moseliedes', in A. Kuschke (ed.), *Verbannung und Heimkehr* (*Wilhelm Rudolph zum 70. Geburtstage*) (Tübingen, 1961), pp. 197–209
Michel, D., 'Studien zu den sogenannten Thronbesteigungspsalmen', *VT* 6 (1956), pp. 40–68
Millar, W.R., *Isaiah 24–27 and the Origin of Apocalyptic* (Missoula, Mt., 1976)
Millard, A.R., 'Daniel 1–6 and history', *EQ* 49 (1977), pp. 67–73
Miller, P.D., 'Two critical notes on Psalm 68 and Deuteronomy 33', *HTR* 57 (1964), pp. 240–3
'Fire in the Mythology of Canaan and Israel', *CBQ* 27 (1965), pp. 256–61
'Ugaritic *ǴZR* and Hebrew *'ZR* II', *UF* 2 (1970), pp. 159–75
'Animal names as designations in Ugaritic and Hebrew', *UF* 2 (1970), pp. 177–86
The Divine Warrior in Early Israel (Cambridge, Mass., 1973)
Genesis 1–11. Studies in Theme and Structure (Sheffield, 1978)
Mittmann, S., 'Komposition und Redaktion von Psalm XXIX', *VT* 28 (1978), pp. 172–94
Montgomery, J.A., *Aramaic Incantation Texts from Nippur* (Philadelphia, Pa., 1913)
A Critical and Exegetical Commentary on the Book of Daniel (Edinburgh, 1927)
'Ras Shamra Notes IV: the Conflict of Baal and the Waters', *JAOS* 55 (1935), pp. 268–77
de Moor, J.C., 'Der *mdl* Baals im Ugaritischen', *ZAW* 78 (1966), pp. 69–71
'Studies in the new alphabetic texts from Ras Shamra', *UF* 1 (1969), pp. 167–88
'The Semitic Pantheon of Ugarit', *UF* 2 (1970), pp. 187–228
The Seasonal Pattern in the Ugaritic Myth of Baʿlu (*AOAT* 16, Neukirchen, 1971)
New Year with Canaanites and Israelites (2 vols., Kampen, 1972)
'Cloud', *IDBS* (Nashville, Tenn., 1976), pp. 168–9
'El, the Creator', in G. Rendsburg, R. Adler, M. Arfa, N.H. Winter (edd.), *The Bible World. Essays in honor of Cyrus H. Gordon* (New York, 1980), pp. 171–87
Morenz, S., 'Das Tier mit den Hörnern. Ein Beitrag zu Dan 7, 7f.', *ZAW*

63 (1951), pp. 151–4. Reprinted in E. Blumenthal and S. Herrmann (edd.), *Religion und Geschichte des alten Ägypten* (Weimar, 1975), pp. 429–32

'Die orientalische Herkunft der Perseus-Andromeda-Sage. Ein Rekonstruktionsversuch', *Forschungen und Fortschritte* 36/10 (1962), pp. 307–9. Reprinted in E. Blumenthal and S. Herrmann (edd.), *Religion und Geschichte des alten Ägypten* (Weimar, 1975), pp. 441–7

Morgenstern, J., 'The sources of the Creation story – Genesis 1:1–2:4', *AJSL* 36 (1920), pp. 169–212

'Psalm 48', *HUCA* 16 (1941), pp. 1–95

'Jerusalem – 485 B.C.', *HUCA* 27 (1956), pp. 101–79

'The "Son of Man" of Daniel 7:13f. A new interpretation', *JBL 80* (1961), pp. 65–77

Moscati, S., 'The wind in Biblical and Phoenician Cosmogony', *JBL* 66 (1947), pp. 305–10

Mowan, O., 'Quatuor montes sacri in Ps 89, 13?', *Verbum Domini* 41 (1963), pp. 11–20

Mowinckel, S., *Psalmenstudien* (6 vols., Kristiania, 1921–4)

Det Gamle Testamentes Salmebok. Første del: Salmene i oversettelse (Kristiania, 1923)

Han som kommer (Copenhagen, 1951). ET *He that Cometh* (Oxford, 1959)

Offersang og Sangoffer (Oslo, 1951). ET *The Psalms in Israel's Worship* (2 vols., Oxford, 1962)

Salmene i oversettelse (Kristiania, 1923)

Der achtundsechzigste Psalm (Oslo, 1953)

'Psalm Criticism between 1900 and 1935', *VT* 5 (1955), pp. 13–33

'Drive and/or Ride in O.T.', *VT* 12 (1962), pp. 278–99

שחל, in D.W. Thomas and W.D. McHardy (edd.), *Hebrew and Semitic Studies presented to Godfrey Rolles Driver* (Oxford, 1963), pp. 95–103

Mras, K., *Die Praeparatio Evangelica* (Berlin, 1954)

Muilenburg, J., 'The Son of Man in Daniel and the Ethiopic Apocalypse of Enoch', *JBL* 89 (1960), pp. 197–209

'A Liturgy on the Triumphs of Yahweh', *Studia Biblica et Semitica Theodoro Christiano Vriezen . . . dedicata* (Wageningen, 1966), pp. 233–51

Mulder, E.S., *Die Teologie van die Jesaja-Apokalipse* (Groningen and Jakarta, 1954)

Mulder, M.J., *Kanaänitische Goden in het Oude Testament* (The Hague, 1965)

'Hat man in Ugarit die Sonnenwende begangen?', *UF* 4 (1972), pp. 70–96

Müller, C., *Geographi Graeci Minores 1* (Paris, 1855)

Müller, U.B., *Messias und Menschensohn in jüdischen Apokalypsen und in der Offenbarung des Johannes* (Gütersloh, 1972)

Murray, R., 'Prophecy and the Cult', in R. Coggins, A. Phillips, M. Knibb (edd.), *Israel's Prophetic Tradition. Essays in Honour of Peter R. Ackroyd* (*Cambridge, 1982*), pp. 200–16

Nagel, G., 'À propos des rapports du Psaume 104 avec les textes égyptiens', in W. Baumgartner, O. Eissfeldt, K. Elliger, L. Rost (edd.), *Festschrift Alfred Bertholet* (Tübingen, 1950), pp. 395–403

Neve, L., 'The common use of traditions by the author of Psalm 46 and Isaiah', *Exp. Times* 86 (1974–5), pp. 243–6

Nicholson, E.W., 'Apocalyptic', in G.W. Anderson (ed.), *Tradition and Interpretation* (Oxford, 1979), pp. 189–213

de Nicola, A., 'Il monte Hermon', *Bibbia e Oriente* 15 (1973), pp. 109–22

'L'Hermon, monte sacro', *Bibbia e Oriente* 15 (1973), pp. 239–51

Norin, S.I.L., *Er spaltete das Meer* (Lund, 1977)

North, C.R., *The Second Isaiah* (Oxford, 1964)

Noth, M., '"Die Heiligen des Höchsten"', in *Interpretationes ad Vetus Testamentum pertinentes Sigmundo Mowinckel septuagenario missae* (Oslo, 1955), pp. 146–61. Reprinted in M. Noth, *Gesammelte Studien zum Alten Testament* (Munich, 1966), pp. 274–90. ET 'The Holy Ones of the Most High', *The Laws in the Pentateuch and other essays* (Edinburgh, 1966), pp. 215–28

Das zweite Buch Mose, Exodus (Göttingen, 1959). ET *Exodus* (London, 1966)

'Das Geschichtsverständnis der alttestamentlichen Apokalyptik', *Gesammelte Studien zum Alten Testament* (Munich, 1966), pp. 248–73. ET 'The understanding of history in Old Testament Apocalyptic', *The Laws in the Pentateuch and other essays* (Edinburgh, 1966), pp. 194–214

Nougayrol, J., Laroche, E., Virolleaud, C., Schaeffer, C.F.A., *Ugaritica V* (Paris, 1968)

O'Brien, J. and Major, W., *In the Beginning. Creation Myths from Ancient Mesopotamia, Israel and Greece* (Chico, Cal., 1982)

Oesterley, W.O.E., *The Psalms* (2 vols., London, 1939)

Ohler, A., *Mythologische Elemente im alten Testament* (Düsseldorf, 1969)

Oldenburg, U., *The Conflict between El and Baal in Canaanite Religion* (Leiden, 1969)

Olmstead, A.T., *A History of Assyria* (Chicago, 1923)

Oppian, Colluthus, Tryphiodorus (Loeb Classical Library, London and New York, 1928)

Orlinsky, H.M., 'Studies in the St. Mark's Isaiah Scroll, IV', *JQR* 43 n.s. (1952–3), pp. 329–40

'*Madhebah* in Isaiah XIV 4', *VT* 7 (1957), pp. 202–3

'the plain meaning of ruaḥ in Gen. 1.2', *JQR* 48 (1957–8), pp. 174–82

'The new Jewish version of the Torah', *JBL* 82 (1963), pp. 249–64

Otten, H., 'Ein kanaanäischer Mythus aus Boğazköy', *Mitteilungen des Instituts für Orientforschung 1* (1953), pp. 125–50

Otzen, B., 'Traditions and structures of Isaiah XXIV–XXVII', *VT* 24 (1974), pp. 196–206

Otzen, B., Gottlieb, H. and Jeppesen, K., *Myter i Det gamle Testamente* (Copenhagen, 1976). ET *Myths in the Old Testament* (London, 1980)

Pallis, S.A., *The Babylonian Akîtu Festival* (Copenhagen, 1926)

Parker, S.B. (See A.J. Ferrara)

Pausanias, *Description of Greece* (Loeb Classical Library, 2 vols., London and New York, 1926–8)

Pedersen, J., 'Passahfest und Passahlegende', *ZAW* 52 (1934), pp. 161–75

Israel: its Life and Culture (4 vols. in 2, 1926 and 1940)

Penna, A., *Isaia* (Turin and Rome, 1957)

Perdue, L.G., 'The making and destruction of the golden calf – a reply', *Biblica* 54 (1973), pp. 237–46

Pliny, *Natural History* (Loeb Classical Library, 10 vols., London, 1938–62)

Plutarch (See J.G. Griffiths)

Podechard, E., *Le Psautier* (2 vols. in 1, Lyon, 1949–54)

Pope, M.H., *El in the Ugaritic Texts* (*SVT* 2, 1955)

Job (3rd ed., New York, 1973)

Pope, M.H., and Röllig, W., 'Syrien. Die Mythologie der Ugariter und Phönizier', in H.W. Haussig (ed.), *Wörterbuch der Mythologie* 1 (Stuttgart, 1965), pp. 217–312

Porteous, N.W., *Daniel* (2nd ed., London, 1979)

Poythress, V., 'The Holy Ones of the Most High in Daniel VII', *VT* 26 (1976), pp. 208–13

Pritchard, J.B. (ed.), *Ancient Near Eastern Texts relating to the Old Testament* (3rd ed., with supplement, Princeton, N.J., 1969)

(ed.), *The Ancient Near East in Pictures* (2nd ed., with supplement, Princeton, N.J., 1969)

Procksch, O., 'Der Menschensohn als Gottessohn', *Christentum und Wissenschaft* 3 (1927), pp. 425–43, 473–81

Jesaia 1 (Leipzig, 1930)

Pseudo-Scylax, *Periplus* (See C. Müller)

Pusey, E.B., *The Minor Prophets with a Commentary. 2 Amos* (London, 1906)

Rabin, C., 'Bāriaḥ', *JTS* 47 (1946), pp. 38–41

Rad, G. von *Theologie des Alten Testaments* (2 vols., Munich, 1957–60). ET *Old Testament Theology* (2 vols., Edinburgh, 1962–5)

Der erste Buch Mose, Genesis (5th ed., Göttingen, 1958). ET *Genesis* (London, 1961)

Rahlfs, A., *Septuaginta, id est Vetus Testamentum Graece iuxta LXX interpres* (2 vols., Stuttgart, 1935)

Reif, S.C., 'A note on גער', *VT* 21 (1971), pp. 241–4

Rendtorff, R., 'Die theologische Stellung des Schöpfungsglaubens bei Deutero-jesaja', *ZThK* 5 (1954), pp. 3–13

'El, Ba'al und Jahwe', *ZAW* 78 (1966), pp. 277–92

Reymond, P., *L'eau, sa vie, et sa signification dans l'Ancien Testament* (*SVT* 6, 1958)

Rhodes, A.B., 'The Kingdoms of Men and the Kingdom of God: a study of Daniel 7:1–14', *Interpretation* 15 (1961), pp. 411–30

Richter, G., *Textstudien zum Buche Hiob* (Stuttgart, 1927)

Ridderbos, J., 'Jahwäh Malak', *VT* 4 (1954), pp. 87–9

Rimbach, J.A. 'Bears or bees? Sefire 1 A 31 and Daniel 7', *JBL* 97 (1978), pp. 565–6

Ringgren, H., 'Die Funktion des Schöpfungsmythus in Jes. 51', in K.-H. Bernhardt (ed.), *Schalom. Studien zu Glaube und Geschichte Israels* (*Festschrift A. Jepsen*) (Stuttgart, 1971), pp. 38–40

'Yahvé et Rahab-Léviatan', in A. Caquot and M. Delcor, *Mélanges Bibliques et Orientaux en l'honneur de M. Henri Cazelles* (*AOAT* 212, Neukirchen, 1981), pp. 387–93

Roberts, J.J.M., 'The Davidic origin of the Zion Tradition', *JBL* 92 (1973), pp. 329–44

'ṢĀPÔN in Job 26, 7', *Biblica* 56 (1975), pp. 554–7

Robertson, D.A., *Linguistic Evidence in Dating Early Hebrew Poetry* (Missoula, Mt., 1972)

Robinson, A., 'Zion and Ṣāphôn in Psalm XLVIII 3', *VT* 24 (1974), pp. 118–23

Rogers, R.W., *The Religion of Babylonia and Assyria* (New York, 1908)

Rogerson, J.W., *Myth in Old Testament Interpretation* (*BZAW* 134, 1974)

Rohland, J.P., *Der Erzengel Michael, Arzt und Feldherr: zwei Aspekte des vor- und frühbyzantischen Michaelskultes* (Leiden, 1977)

Röllig, W. (See H. Donner and W. Röllig)

Rost, L., 'Zur Deutung des Menschensohnes in Daniel 7', *Festgabe für Erich Fascher zum 60. Geburtstag* (Berlin, 1958), pp. 41–3. Reprinted in *Studien zum Alten Testament* (Stuttgart, 1974), pp. 72–5

Rowley, H.H., *Darius the Mede and the Four World Empires in the Book of Daniel* (2nd ed., Cardiff, 1959)

Job (London, 1970)

Rozelaar, M., 'The Song of the Sea (Exodus XV, 1b–18)', *VT* 2 (1952), pp. 221–8

Rudolph, K. (See H. Gese)

Rudolph, W., *Jesaja 24–27* (Stuttgart, 1933)

Jeremia (3rd ed., Tübingen, 1968)

Rummel, S. (ed.), *Ras Shamra Parallels* 3 (Rome, 1981)

Ruprecht, E., 'Das Nilpferd im Hiobbuch', *VT* 21 (1971), pp. 209–31

Saggs, H.W.F., *The Encounter with the Divine in Mesopotamia and Israel* (London, 1978)

Sahlin, H., 'Antiochus IV. Epiphanes und Judas Mackabäus', *Studia Theologica* 23 (1969), pp. 41–68

Sanmartín, J., 'Die ug. Basis NṢṢ und das "Nest" des B'l (KTU 1.3IV1f.)', *UF* 10 (1978), pp. 449–50 (See also M. Dietrich.)

Säve-Söderbergh, T., *On Egyptian Representations of Hippopotamus*

Hunting as a Religious Motive (Uppsala, 1953)
Sawyer, J.F.A., 'Joshua 10:12–14 and the solar eclipse of 30 September 1131 B.C.', *PEQ* 104 (1972), pp. 139–46
Sayce, A.H., 'The Astarte Papyrus and the legend of the Sea', *JEA* 19 (1933), pp. 56–9
Schaeffer, C.F.A. (See J. Nougayrol)
Schmid, H., 'Jahwe und die Kulttraditionen von Jerusalem', *ZAW* 67 (1956), pp. 168–97
'Daniel, der Menschensohn', *Judaica* 27 (1971), pp. 192–220
Schmidt, H., *Jona. Eine Untersuchung zur vergleichenden Religionsgeschichte* (Göttingen, 1907)
Schmidt, N., 'The "Son of Man" in the Book of Daniel', *JBL* 19 (1900), pp. 22–8
Schmidt, W.(H.), *Königtum Gottes in Ugarit und Israel* (*BZAW* 80, 1961; 2nd ed., 1966)
Die Schöpfungsgeschichte der Priesterschrift (Neukirchen, 1964)
Schoors, A., *Jesaja* (Roermond, 1972)
I am God your Saviour (*SVT* 24, 1973)
Schunck, K.-D., 'Jes 30 6–8 und die Deutung der Rahab im Alten Testament', *ZAW* 78 (1966), pp. 48–56
Scott, R.B.Y., 'Meteorological Phenomena and Terminology in the Old Testament', *ZAW* 62 (1952), pp. 11–25
Sellin, E., *Alttestamentliche Theologie auf religionsgeschichtlicher Grundlage* (2 vols., Leipzig, 1933)
van Selms, A., 'A systematic approach to CTA 5, I, 1–8', *UF* 7 (1975), pp. 477–82
van Seters, J., *Abraham in History and Tradition* (New Haven, Conn., and London, 1975)
Simons, J., *Jerusalem in the Old Testament* (Leiden, 1952)
Skehan, P.H., 'A fragment of the "Song of Moses" (Deut. 32) from Qumran', *BASOR* 136 (1954), pp. 12–15
Smart, J.D., 'Jonah', *The Interpreter's Bible* 6 (New York and Nashville, Tenn., 1956), pp. 869–94
Smend, R., 'Anmerkungen zu Jes. 24–27', *ZAW* 4 (1884), pp. 161–224
Snaith, N.H., *The Jewish New Year Festival. Its Origins and Development* (London, 1947)
von Soden, W., 'Die Unterweltsvision eines assyrischen Kronprinzen', *ZA* 43, n.F. 9 (1936), pp. 1–31
'Gibt es ein Zeugnis dafür, dass die Babylonier an die Wiederaufstehung Marduks geglaubt haben?', *ZA* 51, n.F. 17 (1955), pp. 130–66
Speiser, E.A., 'An angelic "curse": Exodus 14:20', *JAOS* 80 (1960), pp. 198–200
Genesis (New York, 1964)
Spinner, S., 'Die Verwendung der Synonymen im AT', *BZ* 23 (1935–6), pp. 147–9

Staub, U., 'Das Tier mit den Hörnern. Ein Beitrag zu Dan 7 7f.', *Freiburger Zeitschrift für Philosophie und Theologie* 25 (1978), pp. 351–97
Steffen, U., *Das Mysterium von Tod und Auferstehung. Formen und Wandlungen des Jona-Motives* (Göttingen, 1963)
Stephens, F.J., 'The Babylonian Dragon Myth in Habakkuk 3', *JBL* 43 (1924), pp. 290–3
Steve, M. (See L.H. Vincent)
Stolz, F., *Strukturen und Figuren im Kult von Jerusalem* (*BZAW* 118, 1970).
Strabo, *Geography* (Loeb Classical Library, 8 vols., London and New York, 1917–32)
Strauss, H., 'Zur Auslegung von Ps. 29 auf dem Hintergrund seiner kanaanäischen Bezüge', *ZAW* 82 (1970), pp. 91–102
Stuhlmueller, C., *Creative Redemption in Deutero-Isaiah* (Rome, 1970)
Swain, J.C., 'The theory of the four monarchies: opposition history under the Roman empire', *Classical Philology* 35 (1940), pp. 1–21
Sznycer, M. (See A. Caquot)
Thomas, D.W., 'A consideration of some unusual ways of expressing the superlative in Hebrew', *VT* 3 (1953), pp. 209–24
'בְּלִיַּעַל in the Old Testament', in J.N. Birdsall and R.W. Thomson, *Biblical and Patristic Studies in Memory of Robert Pierce Casey* (Freiburg, 1963), pp. 11–19
'Job XL 29*b*: text and translation', *VT* 14 (1964), pp. 114–16
'Some further remarks on unusual ways of expressing the superlative in Hebrew', *VT* 18 (1968), pp. 120–4
Thompson, H.O., *Mekal, the God of Beth-Shan* (Leiden, 1970)
Thompson, R. Campbell, *The Epic of Gilgamesh* (Oxford, 1930)
Tournay, R., 'Recherches sur la chronologie des Psaumes', *RB* 65 (1958), pp. 321–57
Review of A. Deissler and M. Delcor, *Les Petits Prophètes* 2, *RB* 72 (1965), pp. 427–9
Tur-Sinai, N.H. (H. Torczyner), ספר איוב עם פירוש חדש (Tel Aviv, 1954). ET *The Book of Job, a new commentary* (Jerusalem, 1957)
Ullendorff, E., 'Job III 8', *VT* 11 (1961), pp. 350–1
'Ugaritic Studies within their Semitic and Eastern Mediterranean setting', *BJRL* 46 (1963–4), pp. 236–49. Reprinted in *Is Biblical Hebrew a Language?* (Wiesbaden, 1977), pp. 139–52
Ulrichsen, J., 'Jhwh mālak', *VT* 27 (1977), pp. 361–74
de Vaux, R., 'Les combats singuliers dans l'Ancien Testament', *Biblica* 40 (1959), pp. 495–508. Reprinted in *Bible et Orient* (Paris, 1967), pp. 217–30. ET 'Single combat in the Old Testament', *The Bible and the Ancient Near East* (New York, 1967), pp. 122–35
Histoire ancienne d'Israël (2 vols., Paris, 1971–3). ET *The Early History of Israel* (2 vols., London, 1978)
'Jérusalem et les Prophètes', *RB* 73 (1966), pp. 481–509

Te Velde, H., *Seth, God of Confusion* (Leiden, 1977)

Vermeylen, J., *Du Prophète Isaïe à l'Apocalyptique* (2 vols., Paris, 1977–8)

Vincent, L.H. and Steve, M., *Jérusalem de l'Ancien Testament* (3 vols. in 2, Paris, 1954–6)

Virgulin, S., 'Il lauto convito sul Sion', *Bibbia e Oriente* 11 (1969), pp. 57–64

Virolleaud, C., *Le Palais Royal d'Ugarit* II (Paris, 1957) (See also J. Nougayrol)

Vlaardingerbroek, J., *Psalm 68* (Amsterdam, 1973)

Vollmer, J., *Geschichtliche Rückblicke und Motive in der Prophetie des Amos, Hosea und Jesaja* (*BZAW* 119, 1971)

Volz, P., *Das Neujahrsfest Jahwes* (Tübingen, 1912)

van der Voort, A., 'Genèse I, 1 à II, 4[a] et le Psaume 104', *RB* 58 (1951), pp. 321–47

Vosberg, L., *Studien zum Reden vom Schöpfer in den Psalmen* (Munich, 1975)

Wakeman, M.K., 'The Biblical Earth Monster in the Cosmogonic Combat Myth', *JBL* 88 (1969), pp. 313–20

God's Battle with the Monster (Leiden, 1973)

Wallace, H., 'Leviathan and the Beast in Revelation', *BA* 11 (1948), pp. 61–8. Reprinted in *BA Reader* (New York, 1961), pp. 290–8

Wanke, G., *Die Zionstheologie der Korachiten* (*BZAW* 97, 1966)

Watts, J.D.W., 'The Song of the Sea – Ex. XV', *VT* 6 (1956), pp. 371–80

Weinfeld, M., האל הבורא בבראשית א ובנבואת ישעיהו השני, *Tarbiz* 37 (1967–8), pp. 105–32

'"Rider of the Clouds" and "Gatherer of the Clouds"', *Journal of the Ancient Near Eastern Society of Columbia University* 5 (Gaster Festschrift, 1973), pp. 421–6

Weiser, A., *Das Buch Hiob* (2nd ed., Göttingen, 1956)

Einleitung in das Alte Testament (4th ed., Göttingen, 1957). ET *Introduction to the Old Testament* (London, 1961)

Die Psalmen (5th ed., Göttingen, 1959). ET *The Psalms* (London, 1962)

Wensinck, A.J., *The Ocean in the Literature of the Western Semites* (Amsterdam, 1918)

Westermann, C., *Der Aufbau des Buches Hiob* (Tübingen, 1956). ET *The Structure of the Book of Job* (Philadelphia, Pa., 1981)

Das Loben Gottes in den Psalmen (3rd ed., Göttingen, 1963). ET *The Praise of God in the Psalms* (London, 1966)

Das Buch Jesaia (Göttingen, 1966). ET *Isaiah 40–66* (London, 1969)

Genesis 1 (*Genesis 1–11*) (Neukirchen, 1974)

Wetzstein, J.G., *Das batanäische Giebelsgebirge* (Leipzig, 1884)

Wevers, J.W., *Ezekiel* (London, 1969)

Whitaker, R.E., *A Concordance of the Ugaritic Literature* (Cambridge, Mass., 1972)

Whitcomb, J.C., *Darius the Mede* (Grand Rapids, Mich., 1959)

Whybray, R.N., *The Heavenly Counsellor in Isaiah xl 13–14* (Cambridge, 1971)
Isaiah 40–66 (London, 1975)
Wifall, W., 'Son of Man – a pre-Davidic social class?', *CBQ* 37 (1975), pp. 331–40
Wildberger, H., *Jesaja Kapitel 1–12* (2nd ed., Neukirchen, 1980)
Jesaja Kapitel 13–27 (Neukirchen, 1978)
Willesen, F., 'The Cultic Situation of Psalm lxxiv', *VT* 2 (1952), pp. 289–306
Wilson, J.V. Kinnier, 'Hebrew and Akkadian philological notes', *JSS* 7 (1962), pp. 173–83
'A return to the problems of Behemoth and Leviathan', *VT* 25 (1975), pp. 1–14 (See also B. Landsberger)
Winter, P., 'Nochmals zu Deuteronomium 32 8', *ZAW* 75 (1963), pp. 218–23
Wiseman, D.J., 'The last days of Babylon', *Christianity Today* 2, no. 4 (25 Nov. 1957), p. 10
'Records of Assyria and Babylonia', D.W. Thomas (ed.), *Documents from Old Testament Times* (London, 1958), pp. 46–83
'Some historical problems in the Book of Daniel', D.J. Wiseman, T.C. Mitchell, R. Joyce, W.J. Martin and K.A. Kitchen, *Notes on some Problems in the Book of Daniel* (London, 1965), pp. 9–18
Wittstruck, T., 'The influence of Treaty Curse Imagery on the Beast Imagery of Daniel 7', *JBL* 97 (1978), pp. 100–2
Wolff, H.W., *Dodekapropheton 3 Obadja und Jona* (Neukirchen, 1977)
Wright, C.H.H., *Biblical Essays* (Edinburgh, 1886)
Wutz, F.X., *Die Psalmen, textkritisch untersucht* (Munich, 1925)
Zevit, Z., 'The Structure and Individual Elements of Daniel 7', *ZAW* 80 (1968), pp. 385–96
'The Exegetical Implications of Daniel viii 1, ix 21', *VT* 28 (1978), pp. 488–92
Ziegler, J., 'Die Hilfe Gottes "am Morgen"', *Alttestamentliche Studien* (F. Nötscher Festschrift), *Bonner biblische Beiträge 1* (Bonn, 1950), pp. 281–8
van Zijl, P.J., *Baal. A Study of Texts in Connexion with Baal in the Ugaritic Texts* (*AOAT* 10, Neukirchen, 1972)
Zimmerli, W., 'Ort und Grenze der Weisheit im Rahmen der alttestamentlichen Theologie', in *Les Sagesses du Proche-Orient Ancien* (Paris, 1963), pp. 121–37. ET 'The Place and Limit of Wisdom in the framework of the Old Testament Theology', *SJT* 17 (1964), pp. 146–58
Ezechiel (2 vols., Neukirchen, 1969). ET of vol. 1, *Ezekiel* 1 (Philadelphia, Pa., 1979)
Zimmerman, F., 'Bel and the Dragon', *VT* 8 (1958), pp. 438–40

INDEX OF PASSAGES CITED

A. OLD TESTAMENT

B. APOCRYPHA AND PSEUDEPIGRAPHA

C. NEW TESTAMENT

D. UGARITIC TEXTS

INDEX OF AUTHORS

GENERAL INDEX

UNIVERSITY OF CAMBRIDGE
ORIENTAL PUBLICATIONS PUBLISHED FOR THE
FACULTY OF ORIENTAL STUDIES

1 *Averroes' Commentary on Plato's Republic*, edited and translated by E.I.J. Rosenthal
2 *FitzGerald's 'Salámán and Absál'*, edited by A.J. Arberry
3 *Ihara Saikaku: The Japanese Family Storehouse*, translated and edited by G.W. Sargent
4 *The Avestan Hymn to Mithra*, edited and translated by Ilya Gershevitch
5 *The Fuṣūl al-Madani of al-Fārābi*, edited and translated by D.M. Dunlop (out of print)
6 *Dun Karm, Poet of Malta*, texts chosen and translated by A.J. Arberry; introduction, notes and glossary by P. Grech
7 *The Political Writings of Ogyú Sorai*, by J.R. McEwan
8 *Financial Administration under the T'ang Dynasty*, by D.C. Twitchett
9 *Neolithic Cattle-Keepers of South India: A Study of the Deccan Ashmounds*, by F.R. Allchin
10 *The Japanese Enlightenment: A Study of the Writings of Fukuzawa Yukichi*, by Carmen Blacker
11 *Records of Han Administration.* Vol. I *Historical Assessment*, by M. Loewe
12 *Records of Han Administration.* Vol. II *Documents*, by M. Loewe
13 *The Language of Indrafit of Orchā: A Study of Early Braj Bhāṣā Prose*, by R.S. McGregor
14 *Japan's First General Election, 1890*, by R.H.P. Mason
15 *A Collection of Tales from Uji: A Study and Translation of 'Uji Shūi Monogatari'*, by D.E. Mills
16 *Studia Semitica*, Vol. I *Jewish Themes*, by E.I.J. Rosenthal
17 *Studia Semitica*, Vol. II *Islamic Themes*, by E.I.J. Rosenthal
18 *A Nestorian Collection of Christological Texts*, Vol. I *Syriac Text*, by Luise Abramowski and Alan E. Goodman
19 *A Nestorian Collection of Christological Texts*, Vol. II *Introduction Translation, Indexes*, by Luise Abramowski and Alan E. Goodman
20 *The Syriac Version of the Pseudo-Nonnos Mythological Scholia*, by Sebastian Brock
21 *Water Rights and Irrigation Practices in Lahj*, by A.M.A. Maktari
22 *The Commentary of Rabbi David Kimhi on Psalms cxx-cl*, edited and translated by Joshua Baker and Ernest W. Nicholson
23 *Jalāl al-dīn al-Suyūṭī.* Vol. I *Biography and background*, by E.M. Sartain
24 *Jalāl al-dīn al-Suyūṭī.* Vol. II "*Al-Tahadduth biniʿmat allah*", Arabic text by E.M. Sartain
25 *Origen and the Jews: Studies in Jewish–Christian Relations in Third Century Palestine*, by N.R.M. de Lange
26 *The 'Visaladevarāsa': A restoration of the text*, by John D. Smith
27 *Shabbetha Sofer and His Prayer-book*, by Stefan C. Reif
28 *Mori Ogai and the Modernization of Japanese Culture*, by Richard John Bowring
29 *The Rebel Lands: An investigation into origins of early Mesopotamian mythology*, by J.V. Kinnier Wilson
30 *Saladin: The politics of the Holy War*, by Malcolm Cumston Lyons and David Jackson

31 *Khotanese Buddhist Texts*, revised edition, edited by H.W. Bailey
32 *Interpreting the Hebrew Bible: Essays in Honour of E.I.J. Rosenthal*, edited by J.A. Emerton and S.C. Reif
33 *The Traditional Interpretation of the Apocalypse of St John in the Ethiopian Orthodox Church*, by Roger W. Cowley
34 *South Asian Archaeology 1981: Proceedings of the Sixth International Conference of South Asian Archaeologists in Western Europe*, edited by Bridget Allchin (with assistance from Raymond Allchin and Miriam Sidell)